ALL IS MIND

ALL IS MIND

The Skolimowskian Philosophy of
the Participatory Mind

VIR SINGH

PARTRIDGE

A Penguin Random House Company

To order additional copies of this book, contact
Partridge India
000 800 10062 62
orders.india@partridgepublishing.com

www.partridgepublishing.com/india

Contents

PREFACE

Mind is the most fascinating faculty of the universe. – Henryk Skolimowski

Mind is the most fascinating aspect of human life. This universe, this world, and this life – all are, as they are, owing to Mind. Humankind, human cultures, and human faiths – all are what and how Mind conceives them, chisels them, shapes them, and reshapes them. All colours, all diversities, and all beauties are there because Mind is there.

All what has happened, all what is happening, and all due to happen is a firmament of Mind. Mind is the most interesting and yet an unfathomable riddle. Mind is the most complex and yet simply the most astonishing aspect of all human epochs.

Everything there is, is examined by Mind. Anything there may be, is imagined by Mind. Nothing can elude Mind. All phenomena of the universe pass through Mind. Mind itself is the most wonderful phenomenon of the universe. Indeed, a phenomenon of all universal phenomena! All cosmic drama is witnessed by Mind. Mind itself is the most interesting drama of the cosmos. Indeed, a drama of all universal dramas!

Illustrated ones in the past have said many interesting things about the Mind. Although sayings about the Mind are endless, I would like to quote a few:

The Mind is everything. What you think you become. – Buddha
It is all in the Mind. – George Harrison
Everything is created by the Mind alone. – Master Hua
The empires of the future are the empires of the Mind. – Winston Churchill

Henryk Skolimowski's philosophy of the Participatory Mind is unique in itself in the sense that it absorbs the whole evolution in it. He regards Mind as the most fascinating faculty of the universe. Mind in his philosophy, in essence, emerges as an *Epic of the Evolution* itself.

Story of the cosmos is the story of light, says Henryk Skolimowski. Therefore, Mind itself is the most fascinating story of the cosmic light. Skolimowski's theory of evolution transcends all previous theories: from Darwin to Bergson to Teilhard. He has dealt with evolution as if the evolution itself invited him to comprehend itself! Nothing is stationary, arid, hopeless, gloomy, repulsive, retrogressive, and dark in the Skolimowskian Philosophy. Everything in it – from amoeba to human being, from living planet to infinite cosmos – is dynamic, lively, full of hope, joyful, attractive, successional and transcending, and glittering with light.

From Skolimowski's evolutionary philosophy emerges a new delighting and intellect-blasting theory of knowledge and of the universe: THE PARTICIPATORY MIND. I call it the philosophy of the participatory Mind. This philosophy is the *crux* of the evolution. This philosophy is the *climax* of evolution. This philosophy is the absolute beauty of the evolution. This philosophy is the soul of evolution. This philosophy is the true spirit which evolution seems striving to instill into human beings for the perfection of their own evolution, and for the *deep and real purpose* of evolution itself. An exhaustive review of this philosophy is the main aim of the volume in your hands.

Henryk says that we are beautiful flowerings of evolution. In his philosophy humans fly with stupendous ideas. His philosophy helps us reach the stars. His philosophy attempts to cosmolize the human beings. Is Henryk himself a darling child of the evolution – born to unfold the designs and ecstasies of the evolution itself? A grasp of his philosophy of the Participatory Mind produces such *realization* in one's Mind. When I read his philosophy of *The Participatory Mind*, I realized one would have incomplete understanding and poor knowledge about our universe, if one does not find a chance (rather opportunity) to read and grasp this philosophy. So, I felt that a new avatar of this philosophy should come to descend on Earth (believing like Hindus). And that is why this volume.

The whole story of Skolimowski's participatory Mind has been published in his well acclaimed book *The Participatory Mind: A New Theory of Knowledge and of the Universe* (1994), Penguin-Arkana, 395pp. This book is a wonder in itself, from the point of view that it carries a potential of inventing the self by understanding the potencies of one's Mind. It guides to unleash the human capabilities by paving a path to new forms of creativity, for *enlarging* our cosmos infinitesimally through higher levels of understanding. It forms a new basis of new cosmology. It is impregnated with many promises for humankind.

A civilization embraces and nurtures a philosophy that determines its values-based karma and life-styles, that feeds on the past, keeps its people flourishing in the present times, and that guarantees a flourishing future. Henryk in his philosophy of the Participatory Mind attempts to encompass all the epochs of philosophy and beautifully elaborates all philosophies which illumine human Mind.

Outlining the participatory Mind, Skolimowski explains the centrality of Mind in life, elaborates the Minds ranging from an amoeba to Einstein, a sensitivities–consciousness–Mind relationship, a new concept of human, and introduces a model of Mind as reality – Noetic Monism.

Mind has probably been the most investigated and worked out aspect of life. Throughout the history of human civilizations, Mind has been a central idea of human thinking and discourse. Copious literature on Mind is available. However, none seems to be as complete, exhaustive, enlightening and compelling as the Skolimowski's Participatory Mind. Skolimowski explains empiricists' and rationalists' views of the Mind, pigeon methodology vs the co-creative Mind, Karl Popper's theory of partial liberation from positivism, and the three Western projects.

The Spiral of Understanding is a unique theory Skolimowski introduces. In this theory, he eloquently explains the circular relationship between ontology and epistemology, the walls of the cosmos and the spiral of the Mind, stability of the picture of the universe, and the peculiarity of the process of understanding.

Skolimowski devotes a complete chapter to the beauty and essential incompleteness of the Teilhard's story of complexity. Teilhard's legacy, gradualism, and the thesis of simplicity/ comprehension are the main components of the chapter.

The Western Mind has already undergone four great cycles, viz., i) Homeric heroes to lucidity of Plato, ii) Roman Empire Fall to the building of Chartres Cathedral, iii) Renaissance, and iv) Engines of Mechanos to run a new civilization. Now, the Mind is pulsating with new cycle and dawn of a new civilization seems around with emerging 'Evolutionary Telos' as new logos. Henryk Skolimowski fabulously examines, discusses and explains the evolutionary phases of the Western Mind and concludes with happy and optimistic notes: *We are opening up, the cosmos is opening up, evolution is unfolding...*

Looking into the serious pathogenesis accentuated by the objective Mind and deriving lessons from its chronic ills, Skolimowski proposes the methodology of participation as superseding the methodology of objectivity, and draws its consequences. He enriches his spectacular proposal by outlining participatory research programmes, participatory strategies, participatory thinking and sensitivity of matter.

Henryk Skolimowski's discourse on structures, symbols and evolution is undoubtedly a matter of deep research. His ecstatic discussion focuses on the structures and ascent of evolution, the origin of structures, symbols and their role in the ascent of man, dominant symbols in Buddhism, Hinduism and Christianity, scientific knowledge and its enigmatic symbols. In the end he reveals how the Mind is a creator of symbols.

The spiral of understanding works at individual level as well as at universal level. Henryk reveals its functioning at both the levels which helps us understand the indispensable and vital Mind–cosmos interrelationship. At individual level, he elaborates on the individuality–universality relationships, the pain of becoming, personal truth, the meaning of transformation, meditation, the fable of the brain's two hemispheres, a model of the integrated self, and the participatory Mind and space of grace.

Role of the universal spiral of understanding is more complex than that of the individual one. Skolimowski, in this context, enriches our knowledge about the spectacular diversity amongst different cultures, spirals and perspectives. He compares brains, Minds and computers, presents a historical record of interactionism and participatory Mind, makes a mention of some forerunners of the Participatory Mind, and also writes on dangers of subjectivism.

What is truth? This question has been baffling human Mind for ages. Skolimowskian Philosophy of Participatory Mind attempts to satiate the Mind by attempting to respond to the question about truth. Describing two theories of truth – the correspondence theory of truth, and the coherence theory of truth – he exquisitely explains the participatory truth. Participatory truth, he says, renders the search for the completeness of the universe. The answer to the question 'What is truth?' lies in his discourse on '*Truth is the consequence of the participatory context.*'

Furthering the Grand Theory in the participatory key, Henryk talks about the return of the grand theory. He exquisitely explains significant experiences, experiences and knowledge, new illuminations and new realities, the axis of reality and the axis of meditation, and knowledge as power and knowledge as liberation.

Participatory philosophy is a rich repository of promises. Henryk Skolimowski explains these promises in detail. Philosophy should be regarded, he says, as the pursuit of life-style of grace. He mentions about the journey of philosophy from perennial philosophy to scientific philosophy. He regards philosophy as courage: *Every new philosophy that breaks away from the cocoon of the established orthodoxy is an act of courage.* He attempts to illumine the Mind with participatory philosophy and with participatory ethics.

All the above aspects and values that the Skolimowskian Philosophy of Participatory Mind embraces have been intensively reviewed, complemented with some new ideas and theories and articulated in the *ALL IS MIND*.

"Those who exert the first influence upon the Mind, have the greatest power," says Horace Mann. Skolimowski's philosophy of the Participatory Mind, in essence, exerts the "First Influence" on human Mind to the highest possible degree – elevating the humans to the level of gods. If humans equate themselves with gods, they would cultivate right ethical values, articulate participatory philosophy and develop right karma. Thus, this new philosophy – by cultivating a right and real understanding – attempts to empower human persons to take up new role – of reconstructing our world, of fertilizing the universe, of preserving the beauty of our cosmos.

I am so much grateful to Prof. Henryk Skolimowski, the creator of the Philosophy of the Participatory Mind and the Father of Eco-philosophy. Prof. Skolimowski is also the Father of Lumenosophy, the Father of Lumenarchy, and the Father of Cosmocracy. He is a constant inspiration for me. His evolutionary philosophy is all-potent to do a new creation. My thanks are also due to Bish Petryka, Juanita Skolimowski and Dr. David Skrbina who are also a source of encouragement and inspiration to me in my attempt to articulate the enlightening Skolimowskian Philosophy. Communication with John Melhuish (The Seeker), a follower of the Skolimowskian Philosophy, is always stimulating.

My thanks are also due to Grazyna Cebo, a prominent Polish artist, poet and philosopher for giving stupendous ideas about designing cover and for herself taking up a project for creating the cover for the book. In her project, Grazyna has been assisted by Darek Chramienko. Some ideas for cover design were also given by Shreekant, a computer professional and page cover designer at the Communication Centre of the GB Pant University.

I am grateful to Rajny Krishnan who, on my request, has kindly provided two drawings of the Hamsa. She explains her drawings as follows: "The swan is a symbol of higher aspiration and the (swan's) soaring upwards indicates the direction the Mind should take; the figuration of the world with the aspiring and ascending bird silhouettes indicates a soul's flight to fulfilment – which could be translated as the aspiring Mind."

I feel proud of the love, support and encouragement I constantly receive from my beloved wife Gita, daughter Silvi and son Pravesh. My love and appreciation is also due to Constantine Tsokas who is so inquisitive about new ideas. My projects often accomplish in the creative environment my family builds up for me. A few chapters of the book were written when I was visiting my daughter and son in Toronto, from June to August in 2013.

It is my earnest hope that the intensive review of the Skolimowskian Philosophy of the Participatory Mind this book embodies will add to light of new evolutionary knowledge about the evolving Mind and the universe.

Vir Singh

Mind of the Universe and Universe of the Mind

All things were together; then came Mind and set them in order.[1] – Anaxagoras

We have been created by the Universe. How much and how well do we know about our creator, the Universe? We have been gifted by the universe with a unique and most evolved organ called Mind. How much and how well do we understand the Mind we have been gifted with. The Mind creates its own realities and a universe for itself. How much and how well do we know about the universe the Mind itself creates? The Mind universe has created and the Mind that creates its own universe always pose such questions. And through such questions the Mind generates knowledge and on the fertile ground of the knowledge it creates realities, unfolds the secretes of its own creator – the universe – and structures a universe it accommodates itself into and stays in continuous interaction with the real universe it goes on evolving.

The Mind, the knowledge and the universe speak together in full volume, sprinkling their aesthetic fragrance, in the Skolimowskian Philosophy. Not only speak in full volume sprinkling aesthetic fragrance, but they also help the evolution carry on further towards its destination. Evolution itself finds deep roots of its existence and offers us a *bonanza* of its unfolded mysteries in this philosophy.

The Skolimowskian theory of the Participatory Mind is the key to multifarious forms of new understanding. "The Participatory Mind, conceived as the herald of the universe, is offered in this theory as a form of liberation from the shackles of the prevailing mechanistic world-view," claims Henryk Skolimowski, the Creator of the New Theory of the Knowledge and of the Universe. "The same Mind also offers itself as a significant healer, since our world needs healing on a vast scale."

Philosophy excels, as it must do, other forms of human arts. However, the academic philosophy failed to revolutionize human vision. It should have proven to be the most important source of human inspiration, but it hasn't. Why? Because it is ridden with aridity and has no agenda worth appealing life; because it is not amusing, not intoxicating; because it is not life-enhancing; because it attempted to establish a vertical relationship with virtually all vistas of life; because, like Sanskrit in ancient India, it confined merely to some elites; because it was not evolutionary.

Somewhere deep in human conscience is the quest of new ideas. A young, inquisitive, enthusiastic, path breaking, enlightened, and extraordinarily genius philosopher, Prof. Henryk Skolimowski, created in 1974 an altogether distinctive philosophy – the Ecological Philosophy or Eco-philosophy. Henryk Skolimowski, the learned Father of Eco-philosophy, in 1970s was concerned with the state of our planet. His concern was deeper than some other people and organizations who were just concerned about the physical state of the environment. The environmental movements in 1970s were gradually and gradually embracing the masses, but they were far from a philosophical umbrella until Henryk Skolimowski's Eco-philosophy gave real, a deeper and a truthful meaning to the environmental movements by linking them with sanctity and human conscience.

Thus a new philosophy incarnated to cure the environmental ills by curing the ills of an ordinary Mind through the healing of this Mind. Healing of the Mind translates into ecological healing vital to save the living planet and humanity. Environmental pollution and ecological disruption are the consequences of polluted Mind. A philosophy not at all concerned with the sanctity of life and with the greatness of human Mind, the most evolved and the rarest organ of the universe, undermines the existence value of humankind, and such a philosophy does not endure for long. A philosophy that does not undertake the task of healing or inspire to heal the Mind cannot make a difference and comes to its doom sooner or later. "Our world needs mending and healing; so does our psyche, which has undergone an unprecedented battering in the twentieth century," suggests Henryk Skolimowski. "This fundamental healing cannot be accomplished through pop philosophies that provide a temporary psychological fix."

Henryk Skolimowski's philosophy unfolds the magical potencies of the Mind. This Mind mends and heals itself provided it is nurtured by a right philosophy. The Mind does not only mend and heal itself, the healed up Mind heals the tormented planet. The realities the Mind creates are set through the environment Mind passes through and is educated and trained in. And Henryk's philosophy builds up such environment to help the Mind pass through and work, understand, educate and train in. Henryk's philosophy fuses Logos with Eros. His Theory of the Participatory Mind interprets the Mind laden with evolutionary sensitivities. Skolimowski says, "The healing of the world (and of ourselves within it) and a new understanding of the universe are complementary aspects of the same process." Thus, the quality or virtues of the Mind are the qualities or virtues of the world we dwell in, and vice-versa.

There exists a wonderful unity and integrity in the cosmos. But we attempted to divide and disintegrate it. Environmental disruption leading to an environmental catastrophe is a stark example of rampantly going on division and disintegration of the cosmic structures. Our ordinary Mind is responsible for the division and disintegration. Yet the Mind could mould the universe and give it a new shape, new structure and fill it with beauty unlimited. The Mind which could give new and the real meaning to the universe is the most wonderful creation of the universe itself. It is the participatory Mind Henryk Skolimowski has sketched the portrait of. It is this Mind which can beautifully reunite and reintegrate the universe. It is this Mind which can restore the liveliness of our biosphere and which can pull our planet out of the going on disaster. "The key to our reconstruction of the universe is the Mind," says Henryk. "When we grasp the meaning and place of the Mind in the cosmos, we shall be astonished to discover that other things are falling into their places much more readily than we expected."

The Skolimowskian Philosophy of the Participatory Mind insists that Mind is more than the senses. "There is nothing in senses that has not been previously in the structure of our Mind." This contrasts the prevailing empiricism which, Skolimowski says, claims that there is nothing in the Mind that has not been previously in the senses. We need to get rid of outdating empiricism and metaphysical realism and, as Skolimowski suggests, we should need a new metaphysics and a new epistemology. The Participatory Philosophy of Henryk Skolimowski offers the both.

Skolimowskian Philosophy of the Participatory Mind rightly leads us to realize the central role of the Mind in designing new cosmologies, ontologies, and in determining social behaviour towards our nature, environment and the planet Earth as a whole. Mind is central to everything, every process, every phenomenon. Henryk recalls the Anaxagoras insight that all is *nous* – mind – and suggests that this luminous idea should be rediscovered and celebrated. "Mind not only beholds but shapes all," remarks Henryk. "From the Mind springs the multitude of things comprising all understanding." This world of ours is also a product of the Mind. Henryk cites Parmenides, "No Mind, no world." Mind shapes the world we live in and it can shape the world the way it likes.

Henryk's Philosophy of the Participatory Mind leads to a new understanding—"a new epistemology that engenders a new ontology." A human person embraces sensitivities without which a human cannot be a human. These sensitivities need to be continuously evolved and refined. Henryk puts it beautifully: "Life is a growing tree of sensitivities." The Participatory Mind contributes to develop a new concept about human beings through providing many dimensions of sensitivities. Thus the Participatory Mind creates a confluence of humanity and knowledge. The Humanity-Knowledge relationship when assumes new dimension of creativity which the Participatory Mind evolves, then new creation comes into being. The new epistemology opens windows towards a new world, towards a new cosmos. The flowing and the continuously evolving sensitivities help infuse and further cultivate new virtues amongst human beings—the virtues that contribute meaningfulness to everything. Henryk Skolimowski underlines the sensitivities that help mould our life and enrich human culture: "All human culture is nothing but a monument to our flowering sensitivities. The ascent of evolution is the ascent of sensitivities."

The Philosophy of the Participatory Mind transforms Martin Heidegger's idea of Being into Becoming. Heidegger's idea of Being has not been much illuminating in renewing philosophy in the 20th Century as he wished. Henryk's "new understanding of the nature of Becoming" emanating from his Participatory Mind Philosophy is a real concept to ignite renewal of philosophy in our times. "All universe is the flowering of Becoming," Henryk suggests. "The Mind itself may be seen as the evolution of cosmic dust into sparks of understanding, into visions that far exceed the horizons of the eye."

The latter half of the 20th Century, following the dawn of Henryk Skolimowski's Eco-philosophy (1974)[2] and The Participatory Mind (1994)[3], has been a period of transition. The old philosophies began crumbling and the new ones – the Skolimowskian Philosophy being one of them – began articulating slowly but steadily. The mechanistic image of the universe is still prevailing, but the universe is increasingly reverberating with lively ideas and is also increasingly assuming new dimensions of creativity, of evolution, of sensitivity. The mechanistic theories about the universe as well as secularism, in fact, grew in order to get rid of the life-eclipsing orthodoxies of religion during the 17th Century. However, the mechanistic theories and the secularism in today's context have themselves turned myopic, truth-distorting and life-eclipsing. In the 21st Century, seeds of the Skolimowskian Philosophy sown in the 20th Century are sprouting out, slowly and steadily turning into saplings and are set to assume the form of a complete tree with realities rooted into Earth and canopy reaching out for skies. It will dispel the darkness cast by religious orthodoxies and mechanistic viewpoint about our universe. The Participatory Mind, being central to new epistemology and new cosmology, is to be decisive in weaving new realities and helping out in Becoming.

Human beings tend to shift from the boring mode of living to the one which is more interesting and life-enhancing. People appear to slowly and slowly shying away from the religious style of living which often constricts human vision and confines freedom to a parrot cage. An intense will showing affinity to spirituality is growing, for this mode of living induces the integrity and enhancement of individual beings and of the society. Spirituality also takes us closer to nature and inspires us to be devoted to the healing of the self and of the nature. Now even science appears to embrace spirituality. Physics does not hesitate in incorporating religious elements into it. Medical sciences advocate yoga and meditation. Psychology now regards an individual human being more than a 'social animal'. Skolimowski's Eco-philosophy has already unified ecology and spirituality. It is eco-philosophy which has liberated ecology from its physical dimensions. It is eco-philosophy which has shot into more vital dimensions of ecology—dimension of healing the self, healing the world, saving the Earth, constructing a new world. Henryk Skolimowski extends the limits of ecology beyond planet Earth and links it with cosmology. The Participatory Mind emerges from the fertile ground of the Skolimowskian Eco-philosophy. The Participatory Mind evolves through the Skolimowskian Eco-philosophy and assumes cosmic dimensions.

Have our world views and lifestyles some connection? Yes, they have. They, Henryk says, are intimately connected. It is why, Henryk infers, the mechanistic conception of the world implies and necessitates in the long run a human universe that is cold, objective and uncaring. As a consequence, Henryk justifies, human meaning is reduced to quantity and consumption. He warns against the mess the human beings are in, by paraphrasing T.S. Eliot: A wrong conception of the universe implies somewhere a wrong conception of life and the result is inevitable doom.

It is an imperative of our times that we understand our universe in a new way. For this we need a new philosophy. Henryk Skolimowski offers this kind of philosophy and invites us to acquire a new understanding about our universe. For developing such an understanding about our universe, Henryk introduces a Mind which is different from ordinary mind, and which is an extraordinary Mind and yet the Mind a human being possesses. It is the Participatory Mind. The genuine philosophy to contribute to create a new universe, evolved through a new understanding reciprocally evolved through the Participatory Mind, must nurture humans to their complete and right evolution. Such a genuine philosophy, suggests Skolimowski, must address itself to the total person, his quests for understanding, for meaning, for consolation.

Skolimowski judiciously suggests, "We need philosophy connected with life and serving, philosophy that is not afraid of treading where angels fear to tread." The philosophy of Participatory Mind which he created in the closing decade of the 20ᵗʰ Century is a philosophy of human empowerment par excellence. The Universe has evolved this Mind as its own superb power—this is the power of the living universe. The Mind itself can create a new universe for the holistic human development. The Skolimowskian Philosophy serves as a culture to help the Mind becoming the Participatory Mind that is vital for transforming a human person into a human person the universal evolution distinctively meant to do, and it can help create a new world reverberating with fullness of life, and create a universe which is there in the fold of cosmic evolution.

Drawing by Rajny Krishnan

CHAPTER 1

Structure of the Participatory Mind

All things have a portion of everything, but Mind is infinite and self-ruled, and is mixed with nothing but is all alone by itself... And since the portions of the great and the small are equal in number, so too all things would be in everything. Nor is it possible that they should exist apart, but all things have a portion of everything.[1] – Anaxagoras quoted in Simplicius, *Commentary on Aristotle's Physics*

1. Mind in the Life and Life in the Mind

The story of life is the story of Mind; the story of Mind is the story of life. The real path of life is determined by the understanding of Mind. Which way the life goes is which way the Mind wants it to go. "The premise is that to understand life is to understand Mind; to understand Mind is to understand life," suggests Henryk Skolimowski. Mind attempts to understand everything including the cosmos, its own creator; and it also keeps understanding the self. Therefore, as Henryk puts it, "A deeper understanding of the Mind invariably means a deeper understanding of the self, and of the cosmos at large." A deeper understanding of the Mind (with the help of the Mind itself, which is the most interesting teacher of the universe), in fact, helps us understand the meaningfulness of life.

Modern medical sciences, biological sciences and modern philosophy all have reduced the Mind to brain. The whole body is also perceived as made up of individual organs and systems as if each one of them functions independently. The deeper knowledge goes up to tissues, cells and cell organelles. The body is an integrated whole and not part by part—this essence remains hidden and often undermined. Physiology of individual body organs and of systems (and neurophysiology of brain) makes the core of studies in biological and medical sciences. Modern philosophy separates Mind, brain, body and soul from each other. An understanding of the Mind and that of brain is virtually regarded as indistinguishable. This misunderstanding (or insignificant understanding) curtails meaningfulness of human life. Henryk says about this dilemma of our times: "We possess an abundance of knowledge of the brain and very little understanding of the deeper mysteries of the Mind." This turns human individuals into 'Bonsai' rather than a complete and fully developed tree of wisdom. While the brain is like a Bonsai, the Mind is like a fully developed banyan tree. Brain is accommodated into the skull while the Mind, through outreach tentacles, is connected with the whole cosmos. While the brain remains confined to the body, the Mind is all-pervading through its invisible tentacles and power of imagination.

"We have reached the limit of atomistic understanding and we no longer believe that more knowledge of the chemistry of the brain cells will resolve the riddle of the mind for us," remarks Henryk. Atomisation of the things for the sake of knowledge simply leads to atomization of our understanding, of our thinking, and erosion of our intellectual capabilities. Such knowledge itself is fragmented and full of lifelessness, not holistic and life-enhancing. When we analyse the living things at the level of electrons, we just attempt to approach lifeless objects and we feel life slipping from out grip. "The Mind is a mysterious phenomenon indeed," suggests Henryk Skolimowski. "To acknowledge this mystery is not to mystify the Mind but to express our recognition of the exquisite complexity of the knowledge."

A quest of understanding is inherent. Human quest of understanding, in fact, is an urge of the cosmos. "So great is this urge that sometimes we persuade ourselves that we understand when in fact we don't," Skolimowski argues. "This is not an act of hypocrisy, but a craving for security in this uncertain world of ours." Our intellectual strength and security go hand in hand. Skolimowski's opinion is that this drive for existential security via an intellectual understanding has been much more pronounced in the Western world than in other civilizations.

The evolution in its evolutionary journey evolved Mind and with it the reason. Mind and reason are the two powers which evolution has conferred on man. Mystery yet prevails. We feel imposition of some limits to unfold mysteries. "To accept our limits is right humility," Henryk suggests. "To try to transcend these limits is to help evolution in the process of becoming. Finally to accept and acknowledge mystery is part of the process of understanding in a deeper sense."

Henryk Skolimowski writes splendid things about the Mind and glorifies this fascinating organ of the universe and the most genius outcome of the evolution:

> Everything there is, is filtered by the Mind, chiselled by the Mind, sculptured by the Mind. When the universe wanted the human to co-create with it, it invented the Mind. And why would the universe do such a thing? Because we are part of the universe evolving itself. To contemplate itself, to see itself, the universe had to develop the eye and the Mind; and then the human eye and the human Mind. We are the eyes through which the universe contemplates itself. We are the Mind through which the universe thinks about its future and its destiny. This is not a form of anthropocentrism, but just the contrary: submitting the human to the overwhelming flow of cosmic evolution. We are not anthropocentrizing the cosmos. *We are cosmolizing the human.* Indeed, the cosmological and the anthropocentric are two aspects of each other. How could it be otherwise?

Nothing in the universe skips evolution. Nor anything can elude evolution. Everything keeps evolving. Continents evolve. Species evolve.

Human Mind and knowledge evolve. Our gods evolve. Henryk Skolimowski perceives everything as evolving. His interpretation of evolution is so pragmatic! He classifies the evolution of continents, species, human Mind and knowledge and of gods as geological evolution, biological evolution, epistemological evolution and theological evolution, respectively. This is such an intelligent way of looking at the things and phenomena evolving! While Charles Darwin confined his Theory of Evolution only to biological species, Skolimowski perceives evolution in everything, of everything, for everything.

Henryk regards evolution as a wonderful and divine agency. As it proceeds, he says, it brings more light, coherence and order to the original chaotic cosmos. Is the evolution God in itself? Henryk asks and answers himself that it is a difficult question to determine.

Science also keeps in evolution. Henryk writes: "Science unfolds all the time and sometimes brings such new light that it blinds our eyes and dazzles the human imagination. What happened during the first one-billionth of a second? Why did the Big Bang occur? What is the nature of those forces that created galaxies and then the human imagination? And finally the question we have contemplated so often: what is the nature of this strange, wonderful world around us?"

Evolution is not limited to biological species as Darwin put it before the world. It is all-pervading. Not only is the evolution has everything in its fold, it can be a source of inspiration for all of us and, if we are evolutionary ourselves and regard everything – even God – evolutionary, we would help transform ourselves and would perceive everything – even God – transforming. Skolimowski pens it beautifully, giving a gentle touch to our souls:

> If evolution is all-devouring and all-transforming, then
> *nothing* is out of reach of its wonderfully transformative
> flow. If all human knowledge is evolutionary (and none
> is absolute, fixed and unalterable), then our knowledge of

theology, of heaven, of God is *also* subject to evolution. If so, then not only our image of God, but the very nature of God is evolving.

If God and the evolution are indifferent, then is God not an evolutionary being? If we regard God as being evolutionary, we cannot return to our old anchors and dogmas. If we regard God an evolutionary being, we cannot cling to old images of religion and God. Henryk Skolimowski's concept of regarding God as evolutionary, in true sense, appears offering solution to one of the most critical socio-cultural problems of our contemporary world: fundamentalism. Religious fundamentalism fuels terrorism. Fundamentalism inevitably turns into terrorism. If we regard our God as evolutionary, we shall not develop intolerance in the name of religion, being evolutionary also makes you being rational, being a person of reason. Evolutionary thinking is higher thinking. Being evolutionary means living with realities. Being evolutionary means being futuristic. Being evolutionary means being a visionary. Being evolutionary means being in the quest of creativity, peace, solidarity and transcendence. Being evolutionary means being in line with truth—everything changes in tune with time.

"We now live in a new world," Henryk insists. "Thus, we must not cringe and sheepishly insist that God who is a perfect being cannot be conceived as evolving. He can! If God is perfect, we cannot deny to Him any attribute we think worthwhile." Evolutionary God will show us a right path, a real path. Evolutionary God will teach us to be perfect. Henryk says that *an evolving God is more perfect than a static one.* His suggestions are graspable, worth assimilating and articulating: "To understand this, we need to broaden our thinking and truly embrace the evolutionary perspective. We must start thinking evolutionarily, open our Minds to the wonderful flow of evolution." What will help us evolve an evolutionary perspective? Of course, our Mind. But not the ordinary Mind. Rather the Participatory Mind Henryk conceives and delightfully articulates. With this new Participatory

Mind is associated the new concept of the universe. Participatory Mind is to bring all the difference to life. Henryk writes:

> With the Participatory Mind in the background, we can see that we have unhinged ourselves from all past dogmas: cosmological, religious, scientific – and we are floating. The older dogmas were our anchors and our chains. We were very much tied to the ground and we were used to crawling. The floating universe is not for crawling. The expanding, all-open universe is not for obedience but for freedom.

What will be the difference if we are dwelling in a participatory universe? Henryk is very explicit: "we are creative and free." Creativity and freedom are complimentary to each other. If you are creative you crave for freedom. If you are free you crave for creativity. If you are creative you are a freedom lover. If you are free you are creativity lover. If you are creative you can acquire freedom for yourself. If you are free you will acquire zeal for creativity. Thus creativity and freedom go hand in hand. What will be a greater gift than creativity and freedom that we gain by living in a participatory universe? Can we love to live in an environment which is averse to our health and happiness? Will we be happy to be a part of a society that does not value our existence, our freedom and our creativity? Definitely not. To live in a life-enhancing and healthy environment, to be part of a loving and respecting society is our dream, our choice, our quest, our effort and our struggles. Let us think of living in and being a proud part of what is the biggest and the infinite—the universe. With the background of the Participatory Mind, we create a participatory universe for ourselves. Living in this participatory universe makes all the difference we crave for in life. Henryk Skolimowski attempts to create such a universe for us.

Our approaches to life must deal with the complex whole rather than with some piecemeal sort of things. Henryk aptly suggests: The piecemeal, atomistic, analytical approach, which so often goes in conjunction with the 'technological fix', does not work in relation to complex wholes such as the human being, society, the ecological habitat. He further adds that what is needed is a new conceptual framework, a new cosmology from which a broadened and more enlightened rationality would follow.

In the scientific arena there is always a talk of inadequate scientific-technological world view. Lack of scientific knowledge and technological knowhow are often thought to be the cause of our problems. Scientific-technological inadequacy is often linked with human and social inadequacy. Such dubious thoughts, in fact, lead to nothingness. They rather attempt to put the Human Mind in bondage. This is a serfdom science and technology fix the Mind into. Such a parochial world view is eclipse of reason leading to a distorted picture of the world in Mind. A wrong world view malnourishes the Mind and obstructs its balanced development. And a malnourished and undeveloped (or maldeveloped) Mind cannot evolve a life-enhancing world view. Such a Mind itself is an eclipse of life.

Life and Mind are indistinguishable. But the Mind adds to distinctiveness of life. Mind itself is the master, custodian and guardian of life. There is Mind in life that creates all the distinction in life. There is life in Mind which assumes the shape Mind likes it to assume. Existing and working of the Mind in ordinary form amounts to lead life ordinarily. In other words, ordinary life rears only an ordinary Mind. Existing and working of the Mind in an extraordinary mode transforms the life into an extraordinary mode. In other words, extraordinary life witnesses the Mind existing and working in an extraordinary manner.

Henryk's sacred words go on flowing: True and comprehensive rationality must help us to live, must connect life with knowledge, knowledge with wisdom, must illumine the paths of our individual destiny and connect us with the cosmos in a meaningful way. The philosopher, who has gifted the Participatory Mind to the humanity emphasizes on the understanding of the Mind and of human reason, which, he says, must bring about a deeper understanding of the self and of the cosmos at large. Henryk Skolimowski presents his Participatory Theory of Mind to this end.

2. Relationships among all Forms of Mind

Henryk Skolimowski aims at such a theory of Mind which could explain various forms of Mind, right from the Mind of an amoeba to that of Einstein. He gives examples of other forms of Mind, such as those of Buddha, Copernicus and Newton; as well as of Australian aborigines and the Mind of the Masai tribe of Kenya. He also beautifully attempts to explain relationships amongst various forms of Mind: These are related by the phenomenon of life.

What is the difference between the architecture of life and that of the Mind? Why is it necessary to be equipped with the understanding of various forms of the Mind? What theory of the Mind needs to be constructed? Henryk discusses fabulously:

> The architecture of life is the architecture of Mind. Understanding of various forms of life is ultimately understanding of various forms of Mind. Thus we need to construct a theory of Mind that is both comprehensive and at the same time discerning, so that it includes all forms of Mind and enables us to differentiate among them.

Albert Einstein has been one of the most genius scientists of the 20th Century. He had a unique Mind which is especially known for creating breakthroughs in physics. It is this great Mind that conceives the Theory of Relativity. But, Henryk says, it is not the whole of Einstein's Mind: it is only a slice of it. "Einstein's Mind was also the Mind of a mystic," he says quoting Einstein: "The most beautiful thing we can experience is the mysterious. It is the source of all true art and science. He to whom this emotion is a stranger, who can no longer pause to wonder and stand wrapped in awe, is as good as dead: his eyes are closed."

There exists a social tendency of binding a Mind in limits. The limit ranges up to some specific finding of the Mind, often the abstract computational finding. Physicists' vision does not go beyond Einstein's Theory of Relativity. Therefore, they measure Einstein's greatness against his Theory of Relativity, and he is categorized merely as a Physicist. His total Mind which is a wonderful philosophical Mind is seldom appreciated and he is seldom imitated as a philosopher.

Henryk asks to consider the Minds of Socrates, Plato, Aristotle; and of the Buddha and Jesus, and, pointing to those appreciating only the abstract computational Minds, he says, "If Mind is limited to that aspect of our intellectual activity which results in hard science, then these illustrious men would have to be considered mindless, which is absurd."

Henryk also gives an example of the Masai, said to be one of the most 'primitive' tribes that inhabit the planet and who are still roaming Kenya. Upon attaining an age of fourteen, a young man of the Masai tribe, after an appropriate ceremony, would be sent into the night to hunt a lion, with his knife and spear only. "To hunt a lion is not a joke", says Henryk. "It takes more than courage. It takes skill and dexterity and, indeed, a form of Mind that is so quick, subtle and cunning that we Westerners can only gasp in admiration." Such a uniqueness of Minds is worth celebrating. All the Minds are not alike. If all were alike, this world would have been so mindless! Sometimes a Mind's uniqueness is not recognized as distinct in its skilfulness, articulation and dexterity and just remains hidden in the mist of surprise and incredibility.

Appreciating the role of Australian aborigines in finding food and water in the most inhospitable deserts, Henryk refers to their Minds as subtle and sensitive Minds. In order to acknowledge the Minds of Masai, Australian aborigines and Einstein in a proper sense, Henryk starts to outline the Participatory Mind by distinguishing Mind I and Mind II:

> Mind I may be designated as that abstract coconut which
> revels in computation, abstraction and scientific calculation.
> This Mind roughly corresponds to the neo-cortex. Let us
> pause for a while and take in that our brain is not one

homogeneous entity. There are at least two brains built on top of each other. There is the 'old', reptilian brain; and there is the 'new' brain, known as the neo-cortex. Since we have no difficulty in recognizing two brains within each of our heads, we should have none in recognizing two or three Minds interlocked with each other within our splendid skulls only; they are distributed throughout our entire wondrous bodies... Mind II is an altogether different entity. It corresponds roughly to the 'old' brain, but only roughly. We can define Mind II as *the sum-total of all the sensitivities that evolution has developed in us.* By sensitivities we mean all the capacities through which we live our lives, thus sensing, seeing, intuition, instinct; the capacity to make love, to make poetry, to dance, to sing, to contemplate stars; as well as capacity for moral judgment, the aesthetic sense, the sense of empathy – the whole orchestra of different powers through which life is expressed, apprehended, and sculpted into recognizable shapes.

What constitute real 'content' that distinguishes Mind II from Mind I are the sensitivities. Mind II in its due course of development tends to assimilate all the sensitivities. These sensitivities make human Mind humane in real sense. Henryk provides beautiful expression to these sensitivities: Sensitivities are the artists which receive and transform, which nourish us aesthetically and inform us intellectually; they are the countless windows through which we commune with reality. This is what the Mind II is composed of.

Sensitivities which express themselves through Mind II mean everything in life. "Life always takes distinctive shapes and forms," Henryk Skolimowski peeps into various forms of art life expresses itself into and beautifies itself, which, indeed, are the marvels of sensitivities our Mind constantly nourishes with itself. "These forms are moulded not by cold intellect but by the variety of sensitivities – which are the sculptors, the transformers, the transmogrifiers of reality; the incredibly accurate registers of the changing seasons of nature and of the changing moods of human beings, of grief and sadness, of joy and ecstasy; the silent witnesses which can hear the stars singing as well as the cry of human hearts."

The Mind I and the Mind II are distinguishable but not separated from each other. They stay together inseparably; work in tandem with each other, process reasoning and intuition together. Skolimowski elaborates:

> Mind I and Mind II are not separated from each other; they are parts of each other. Mind I is situated within Mind II, and completely surrounded by it. Mind I can be considered as a form of crystallization of Mind II – just as the neo-cortex is an extension and a specific refinement of the 'old' brain... The two Minds constantly dialogue with each other, inform each other, even if at times they are at odds with each other; as happens in every family. The two Minds are of a family. If only we have enough patience to watch them in action, we shall be astonished to see what a supportive team they make together.

3. Mind through Sensitivities and Consciousness

Evolution has been enriching our universe with ever increasing and hierarchical orders of beings. The evolution infused higher degree of sensitivity and consciousness among more evolved organisms. In other words, more evolved the organisms are more sensitive and conscious they would be.

Sensitivities are the wonderful outcome of the evolution. Henryk Skolimowski so fabulously elicits sensitivities from the evolution: "Sensitivities are part of the legacy of evolution, an essential portion of evolution's endowment. As far as the evolutionary process is concerned, sensitivities are precisely those articulators through which evolution acquires new shapes and characteristics. Whenever the evolutionary process increases its scope and powers, it does so by generating new sensitivities. The meaning of sensitivities is intimately connected with the meaning of evolution."

Henryk regards sensitivities as articulators of the growing consciousness. Citing an important insight of Pierre Teilhard de Chardin (1881-1955), he says that evolution, as an ongoing process, can be best understood when we realize that it is the process of the augmentation of consciousness. His Theory of the Participatory Mind accepts many basic insights of Teilhard and Bergson, as well as evolutionary thinkers of our time such as Theodosius Dobzhansky and Gregory Bateson and builds on these insights.

"Our ideas of evolution have been indeed evolving," reiterates Henryk Skolimowski. He also suggests that Darwin should not be credited with the first step of the Theory of Evolution as Darwin's theory is only a rough approximation of what is going on in evolution. Henryk further suggests that the credit must go to Lyell who, in his epochal work *Principles of Geology* (1830-33), first conceived the idea of evolution by showing that continents have been evolving. That was the application of the idea of evolution to geology. Henryk says that Darwin went a step further and applied Lyell's idea to biology by showing that species have been evolving.

In the Skolimowskian Philosophy evolution is so lively everywhere! It speaks in its entirety and presents itself before you in all its creative dimensions, reflecting all its ecstasies. Skolimowski applies the idea of evolution further still by demonstrating that *evolution is continuously creative and that spiritual and cultural forms of human life are part of the flowering of evolution: as evolution unfolds, matter is becoming spirit.*

Narrating the story of the Teilhard de Chardin's elucidation of new idea of evolution, Skolimowski tells us that Teilhard builds on Bergson. "Henry Bergson was born in 1859, the year Darwin's *Origin of Species* was published." Skolimowski makes his narration pretty interesting: "By the time Bergson achieved maturity, the Darwinian story of evolution was not only absorbed, but could be creatively transcended. This is what Bergson did in *Creative Evolution*. Bergson does not deny the idea of evolution. He only gives it wings and a creative potency. For Darwin and Neo-Darwinians, evolution is an almost dreary process of chance and necessity. For Bergson evolution is an exquisitely creative process. This was the first step in liberating evolution from the dreariness of the semi-deterministic and at the same time semi-incomprehensible because it is impossible to explain the transition from lower to higher forms."

Teilhard showed that the creative evolution is all-pervading and leading from matter to spirit. He also regarded evolution not only creative but also spiritual in character. "Cosmogenesis is both a material (physical) and a spiritual process," Henryk adds. "Matter is transformed into matter, but matter is also transformed into spirit."

Skolimowski simplifies the great truth of evolution through a beautiful phrase: *evolution means continuous transcendence.* This inference of the great philosopher itself reveals the all-creative power of the all-pervading evolution. In reading, defining, expressing and revealing the creativity of the all-pervading evolution Bergson transcends Darwin. Teilhard transcends Bergson. Skolimowski transcends both. He searches all the missing dimensions of evolution. Evolution itself intensively blossoms in the philosophy of Henryk Skolimowski. The evolution is seen at work in the Skolimowskian philosophy in a variety of ways: in redefining everything on Earth and in the cosmos, reinventing the self, expressing human conditions, setting principles and ethos for human species, reconstructing the world, designing cosmocracy, creating new knowledge, and in human imagination extending into the whole sphere. The transcended evolution in the Skolimowskian Philosophy reverberates in everything, in every process, in every phenomenon. Skolimowskian Philosophy does not see evolution only as it is, but it lives evolution; and it celebrates evolution. If evolution finds anywhere a status of supreme celebrity, it is the Skolimowskian Philosophy. The all-pervading and the all-creative evolution seems to have been squeezed into Skolimowskian Philosophy – as if all oceans have been squeezed into a jug!

There is an Indian proverb: *Jahan na pahunche ravi, vahan pahunche kavi* (where even sun cannot reach, there reaches a poet). Skolimowski reaches where no scientist or philosopher has ever reached. He has reached even the deepest core of the evolution. Not only reached, he has even tenderly touched it. Not only touched, he has even felt it. Not only felt, he has even understood it. Not even understood, he has even unfolded its designs. Not even unfolded its designs, he has even understood its evolutionary *agenda* of the future.

Henryk has plucked the beautiful flowers of the evolution blossoming all over, on Earth, and across all planets – throughout the cosmos; and his philosophy is full of the aesthetic fragrance of these flowers. Whatever is there in us Henryk has perceived to be there in the cosmic evolution; or how could it be there in us. As if the evolution itself created Henryk Skolimowski to unfold its own designs of creativity! We ourselves are, as Henryk says, beautiful flowerings of the evolution.

Henryk gives new meaning to evolution. He is the philosopher with a Third Eye. The Third Eye sees what the two eyes miss. He sees sensitivities coiled with evolution. "The meaning of sensitivities is intimately connected with the meaning of evolution," says Henryk. He examines how the evolutionary process has operated through the acquisition of new sensitivities: "When the first amoebas emerged from the primordial organic soup, they were victorious because they acquired a new sensitivity enabling them to react to the environment in a semi-conscious manner, which was the beginning of all learning. For learning is above all a capacity, a sensitivity, to react to environmental conditions. The glory of evolution starts when organisms begin to use their capacities, thus their sensitivities, in a conscious and deliberate manner to further their well-being."

Henryk goes on elaborating: From the organic soup via the amoeba to the fish; from the fish via reptiles to primates; from primates via the chimpanzee to man – this has been a continuous and enthralling story of the acquisition and refinement of ever-new sensitivities.

Transcending the all-pervading and transforming evolution, Henryk Skolimowski attempts to reach the deepest layers of it:

> When matter started to sense and then evolved the eye (as the organ of new sensitivity), this was an occasion of momentous importance, for reality now could be seen, could be articulated according to the power of the seeing eye. *No eye to see – no reality to be seen. It is the eye that brought to reality its visual aspect.* The existence of the eye and the existence of visual reality are aspects of each other. One cannot exist without the other. For what is the seeing eye that has nothing to see? And what is the visual reality that has never been seen?

Was there eye since beginning of the evolution's journey of living creativity? It is unbelievable that there was no eye at a point of evolution. Skolimowski seems to be seeing the reality through his Third Eye. An example of how he weaves the story of eyes into our eyes is excerpted from his work on *The Participatory Mind*:

> The story of the evolution of the eye is pregnant with meaning and points to some truly amazing possibilities. We have not only evolved eye to see, but also to apprehend reality aesthetically. For the eye is the receptacle of beauty… What if one day some new 'eye' is opened to allow us to apprehend some of the new aspects of reality which so far are beyond our comprehensions? Are not some of the extrasensory powers possessed by some persons an indication that some 'new eye' is in the process of being opened?

All the sensitivities evolution has developed in humans are sensitized by seeing. As the evolution is furthering its journey of creativity by implanting more sensitivities, it would be an evolutionary imperative to develop what in India is called the 'Third Eye' – the hidden extra eye, the unseen (hidden) eye that sees what the two eyes cannot. The deeper the visual power of the eyes the greater the intensity of the sensitivity and closer we find ourselves to the reality. "The seeing of the eye is a form of sensitivity through which we articulate reality around us," insists Henryk Skolimowski. "Sensitivities are articulators of reality. The emergence of every new form of sensitivity is a new window on the world."

"With new sensitivities we articulate the world in new ways; we elicit new aspects from the world," Skolimowski further clarifies. "The power of sensitivities is the power of co-creation." He searches deeper layers and destinations of evolution:

> *The power of creation is the power of articulation.* This is the simplest expression of how evolution unfolds – by endlessly articulating. Such is the story within the human universe. By acquiring new sensitivities we acquire new powers of creation. Sensitivity, therefore, holds the key, not only to our understanding of evolution, but to the understanding of ourselves.

Evolution writes the story of ever evolutionary consciousness and with it the ever higher degree of sensitivities and with them the ever increasing organism-environment interaction. Thus, there is wonderful evolution-consciousness-sensitivities triangle that determines organism-environment interaction (as well as organisms' ethology). Henryk Skolimowski beautifully elucidates: *As their sensitivities multiply, organisms elicit more and more from the environment. They draw upon reality in proportion to their ability to receive it and transform it.*

Our evolutionary enrichment keeps on adding to our consciousness and new dimensions of sensitivities. And this phenomenon keeps on strengthening our quest and power of knowing, of understanding, of reflecting, of discovering, of inventing, of interacting, of constructing reality. The more sensitive we become the more intensive becomes our quest to know, to understand, to reflect, to discover, to invent and to construct and reach the reality.

"There is no such thing as reality as it is, which the Mind visits and on which it works," Skolimowski makes the reality clearer. *Reality is always given together with the Mind that comprehends it.*" It is not that Mind constructs reality in first hand. It itself lives in a reality. It articulates reality and weaves around it a reality in which its lives and to which it comprehends. Living in, articulating and constructing reality, and constantly comprehending it determines our overall ethology in this world. Our actions are oriented in accordance with the reality the Mind articulates, creates and lives amidst.

Henryk reveals many contentions of his Theory of the Participatory Mind, relating the Mind with the reality amidst which it works and prospers:

> Mind is the part of the real. It is a fragment of evolution unfolding itself. But rather a special fragment: once it has emerged, it acts as a refracting instrument. It 'bends' reality according to its peculiar laws, propensities and faculties. Mind is that particular part of reality which is both a part of reality and also apart from reality... Any situating of it in reality is really situating reality within it. Hence the participatory Mind is at the same time an interactive Mind, a co-creative Mind. Reality and Mind constantly interact with each other. There is no other way of grasping reality but through the Mind... There is no reality given to us except together with the Mind... The more versatile and subtle the Mind, the more versatile the reality, and richer the experience of it. *The organism receives from reality as much as it puts into it...* The wonder and mystery of the Mind in evolution is its capacity to enlarge reality as it grows and transforms itself. The vision and the seeing cannot be

separated from the eye. What the eye is to the act of seeing, the Mind is to act of comprehending reality."

4. Human Beings Beyond Biological Evolution

At his best, man is the noblest of all animals; separated from law and justice he is the worst.² – Aristotle

Conventional perspective of the human beings is built around what the past philosophers have conceived the human. For Aristotle, a man is a *rational animal*. This Aristotelian definition of human species is still widely held in the West. The word *Rational* in this context is equated with intelligent. Thus, if we recognize the Aristotelian definition of a human being we shall simply regard ourselves *intelligent animals*. We shall be proud of being *intelligent*, but we shall also feel disgusted being equated with *animals*. Of course, an animal is not an abuse in itself, and there is no reason why we should feel ashamed of being equated with animals. Animals too are the products of the universal evolution. But, there is certainly the basis of reason why we need to be distinguishable from the animals. There is varying degree of consciousness conferred on animals by the evolution. But human species is a distinct and, undoubtedly, the most distinctive creation of the universal evolution. If by the definition we are called rational or intelligent animals, we would be either intelligent or only animals. If we were referred to as animals, being 'intelligent' would look bit uncomfortable and inconvenient. If we were referred to as intelligent, we would not feel to be equal to animals.

Thus, the Aristotelian definition of a man itself is not something we could be proud of our own species. It attempts to create in us a hesitation to celebrate ourselves as an outstanding creation of the universal evolution. So popular has it (Aristotle's definition of man) been, says Henryk Skolimowski, that we have come to deify reason and the rational faculties of the species.

Rationality, according to Aristotelian inference of human beings, is the only indicator of human superiority. The greater the degree of rationality (if it is at all measurable), the higher the status of a human being. Intelligence Quotient (IQ) has been devised to measure the status of 'superiority' of a human being, which often appears to be ridiculous. There are examples whose IQ is recorded high but the persons concerned have turned criminals. Henryk emphasizes the need of Compassion Aptitude Test. "A moment's reflection must make it clear that anyone who is completely void of compassion and empathy hardly deserves the name of 'human being'," he reiterates.

Rationality or reasoning is important but not everything to proclaim a man. "Cold reason often wreaks havoc with impunity because it knows that we have chosen to enshrine it as the most essential characteristic of the human species – for man is a rational being," Henryk infers. "A lopsided definition of man leads to innumerable consequences, some of which – later – surprise us with their savage outcomes."

There are specific circumstances for every definition and conception. These are especially tied with the times in which the definition of a thing or phenomenon comes to the fore. In the same way, as Henryk tells us, Aristotle's definition emerged at the time when reason crystallized as a distinctive faculty, of which the Greeks were immensely proud. In specific circumstances, certain words, phrases, or sayings find more importance than they would otherwise do. We can also recall the phrase "sustainable development" coined and defined by Mrs. Gro Harlem Brundtland in the Brundtland Commission Report *Our Common Future* (1987). In the last decade the word "sustainable" deluged our vision and the word became a prefix in so many concepts; e.g., sustainable development, sustainable agriculture, sustainable village, sustainable society, sustainable world, and so on. Sustainability, in fact, became a mantra of our times when ecological or environmental issues got precipitated out of the scenarios of ecological ruins and environmental catastrophe.

The other example is "ecology"—the term coined by German biologist Ernst Haeckel in 1866. The term had to wait for about 100 years to become popular. Ecology began becoming popular since 1960s when natural disasters began to emerge as a great human concern. Henryk Skolimowski in 1974 coined the term "Eco-philosophy" which revolutionized human conscience and awakened our consciousness towards intensifying ecological disasters. In his eco-philosophical discourse, Skolimowski also coined several phrases like ecological justice, ecological consciousness, ecological thinking, ecological healing, ecological lifestyles, ecological dance, ecological ethics, ecological mind, ecological age, ecological man, ecological dharma, and the likes. Now, ecological economics, ecological agriculture, ecological development, ecological perspective, ecological security, etc. are the frequently used terms in education, research, development discourses, and in everyday life. Ecological development is the sustainable development, in real sense. I have attempted to develop the concept of ecological integrity. Ecological integrity is the essence of sustainability. In this way, emphasis on ecology has borne out of the current circumstances.

Let us now look into another definition of man. The other definition too has come out of the (changed) circumstances—in tune with the Industrial Age. In the Industrial Age, tools and machines dominated human environment. "Man began to be defined as *Homo faber*, or tool-making and tool-using animal," writes Henryk Skolimowski. "The conception emerged when the Industrial Revolution was in its full swing and we had become intoxicated by our immense capabilities for making tools and using them." This definition, however, could not make roads into human hearts. "Small children up to the age of five cannot make tools and are often unable to use them; yet they are human," Skolimowski argues. "Chimpanzees can use many tools dexterously and even make some tools, yet they are not human."

Language is one of the greatest attributes human beings have been gifted with by the evolution. Thus, Henryk cites examples of some workers, like Piaget and Chomsky, who conceived the language in defining man: *man is a language animal.* But, this definition of man too is wingless. "It does not enable us to enlarge ourselves," Henryk derives conclusion. "It does not invite us to reflect more deeply on the meaning of human destiny."

Henryk laments that twentieth-century Western philosophy has been deficient in generating new concepts of man which would help us to live. He says that most vocal and influential among philosophical schools have produced pitifully small visions of man. Rightly unsatisfied, rather disgusted, with such incomplete definitions of man, Henryk writes:

> The pseudo-scientific and half-baked philosophical venture known as 'behaviourism' has shamelessly attempted to reduce the human being to simplistic behavioural schemata, the kind of schemata that do not even do justice to the behaviour of pigeons. That we have tolerated this philosophical farce for a number of years as a 'new vision of man' is a wonder which must make us ask: how rational we are? That we still tolerate some of the lingering shadows of behaviourism in social science and in social interaction is another wonder which must make us reflect how gullible we are and how stupid in trying to explain very complex and subtle matters through very crude schemata.

Another absurdity relating to the conception of man Henryk looks into is existentialism, which he finds as the fruit of shrunken vision of human being. "We are the lonely monads doomed to existential anguish and cosmic despair, so existentialism tells us," he concludes and condemns it remarking that "to celebrate existentialism as a universal philosophy of man is profoundly to short-change ourselves."

Marxism has been the predominant philosophy of humanity during the 20th Century. There was a time when Marxism ruled over the world and it fought in a bid to bring the whole world under its umbrella. It was until the end of the ninth decade of the 20th Century. By the early years of the 10th decade the rule of Marxism was uprooted from most of the world. "In the best of all possible scenarios, we march towards Communism and when we reach it, we have arrived at Utopia. What kind of utopia? Alas, a consumerist utopia," Henryk Skolimowski says dismissing the philosophy of Marxism. "The Marxist vision is predominantly a materialistic one, without any sense of transcendence at a deeper level and without spiritual dimensions."

Dismissing behaviourism, Marxism and existentialism, Henryk Skolimowski emphasizes on a philosophy of hope. "The phenomenon of man is made of many subtle fibres. One of them is hope," he says. He elaborates the philosophy of hope in soul-soothing words:

> Hope is part of our ontological structure. Hope is a mode of our very being. To be alive is to live in the state of hope. Hope is a precondition of our mental health. Hope is the scaffolding of our existence… Hope is a reassertion of our belief in the meaning of human life; and in the sense of the universe. Hope is the precondition of all meaning, of all strivings, of all actions. To embrace hope is a form of wisdom; to abandon it is a form of foolishness… The logic of hope is the logic of affirmation. The logic of hope is the logic of solidarity. The logic of hope is the logic of responsibility. All these attributes: affirmation, solidarity, responsibility, compassion, courage, are the very stuff of which life is made; that is life, which is alive, life which leads to peace, harmony and wholeness.

Skolimowski attempts a new concept of man: Man should be conceived as par excellence a self-sensitizing animal, for he is literally made of the vibrant fields of sensitivities through which he maintains his relationships with the world and by which he is uniquely defined as a multifarious being. What is most important about man is that he is a self-sensitizing, that is, self-transcending and self-perfecting being.

Refining his concept of man, Skolimowski writes, "New sensitivities are new windows which enlarge the horizons of our world; they are also the vehicles by which we carry on the evolutionary journey, and through which we make ourselves into more human and more spiritual beings." Describing the relationship between sensitivities and evolution, Skolimowski writes:

> Through sensitivities evolution is articulated. Through sensitivities the mind of the human being is created. Through sensitivities the scope of our humanity is delimited. Through sensitivities matter is transformed into spirit.

Henryk relates thinking with sensitivity: *Thinking is a form of sensitivity*. He further unfolds thinking: *Thinking is one of the many threads with which the tapestry of our sensitivities is woven*, it is only one aspect of our evolutionary endowment. He also relates intuition, moral sense, aesthetic sense, and the capacity of formal deductive thinking with sensitivity. "All thinking is light that we shed on the objects of our understanding," Henryk goes on evolving thinking into its higher dimensions. "This light, when it illumines life, becomes reverence. Reverence for life is a form of human sensitivity towards it, and at the same time is a form of thinking about it. Thinking so conceived can be seen throughout our traditional cultures. Plato's fusion of truth, goodness and beauty is a manifestation of it."

Skolimowski makes attempt to define man on the firm ground of sensitivity. Defining man as a sensitive being, in fact, amounts to appreciate evolution. For the evolution of the sensitivity itself is a great gift of the evolution. Evolution in its fold has special favour, special care, special affection, and everything special for human species. Evolution is so caressing for human beings! It is revealed through the sensitivity imbibing within humans. Defining man as a sensitive being amounts to sing the glory of the evolution. It also means, as Skolimowski says, making sense of man's future while making sense of his past. Thus, a concept of man as a sensitive being links us with all the times—the past, the present and the future— broadening our perspective, intensifying our existence, and making us sensitive to all things happening and to happen across times and ages and to every phenomenon associated with everything else and with the whole universe.

Our sensitivities are all-vital in elevating us to be participatory in the universal phenomena. "Participatory concept is all-inclusive and maintains that man is a rational animal, *Homo faber*, *Homo ludens*, and *Homo religiosus*, and *Homo aestheticus*," says Henryk Skolimowski. "These attributes are all combined and orchestrated in one dynamic structure which is *the structure of our sensitivities*."

Sensitivities in amoebas and humans are different. Therefore they outline different forms of life. The higher degree of sensitivities in a human person makes him or her quite distinctive. With participatory concept of man Henryk throws light on the phenomenon of Einstein, which is homage to this great man of the twentieth century:

> The participatory concept of man sheds a new light on the phenomenon of Einstein. And not only Einstein-the-physicist, but also Einstein-the-mystic. Playing the fiddle and wearing two socks of different colours (out of sheer absent-mindedness) does not make Einstein less rational as a scientist but more exquisite as a human being. In the phenomenon of Einstein we witness human life in its completeness: sensitivities flowering abundantly; a mathematical genius and a vulnerable, endearing, slightly crazy little man with his fiddle. We salute him for he did not sacrifice one aspect of his life for the sake of another.

Is evolution evolving us into perfection? Sensitivities are helping us advance towards perfection, but still evolution has some 'slips'. Skolimowski quotes Koestler who insisted that evolution has made a mistake by developing our intellectual capacities so much and our moral sense so little. "He (Arthur Koestler) thought that this would be the cause of our doom," writes Skolimowski. "He was in despair over this 'slip' of evolution."

Skolimowski, however, is optimistic and deeply understands the pulse of the evolution. He writes, "We need not be in despair. For it is very likely that the next stage of our evolutionary unfolding will consist precisely in developing this range of sensitivities which will bring about the acquisition of a deeper moral sense, deeper compassion, a deeper understanding of all there is, including human being."

The participatory concept of man around which we need to weave a perfect definition of a man amounts to obey evolution for its outstanding creation in the form of human being. This concept has many attributes. Skolimowski suggests:

> …The participatory concept of man unifies man with the cosmos, as well as the human world with all forms of life. They are all bundles of quivering sensitivities; and so are we. The participatory concept paves the way to holistic understanding of all that exists. It inspires us to celebrate our uniqueness without giving us a license to arrogance or superiority… Among all creatures it is we, human beings that can understand fully and completely the meaning of compassion and can act on it; can take the responsibility for all; can defend the rights of species different from our own. Compassion and responsibility for all life are forms of sensitivities acquired late in our evolutionary saga. Their possession makes us proud to be human. The use of these sensitivities lies at the heart of the evolutionary process.

What emanates from the basic ecological studies is that man is the most dangerous species on Earth who is responsible for all the ills the planet faces. But, would the human species like to sacrifice itself for the sake of the living planet? No, not at all. The question cannot even be debated. Every species, every life form on Earth is a part and parcel of the whole life and laden with the existence value of life. Life tends to be in the state of enhancement and, naturally, every species is wholly devoted to live in its fullness. Fullness of life in every species, however, cannot be equated with its perfection. Man has not attained perfection—it is true. Perhaps evolution has not given this opportunity to man so far. Had our species been perfect or near perfect, we might not have stepped into a state of ecological disaster advancing towards ecological doom exacerbated by none other than our own species.

The Skolimowskian eco-philosophy has attempted to correct the concept of the conventional ecology: that we are a cancerous species on Earth. Skolimowskian concept of participatory Mind further attempts to sensitize human nature and attempts to free human Mind from the analytical ecological bondage:

> The participatory concept of man objects strongly to the idea promoted by some trends of ecological thought that we are the cancer among species. We are not perfect. No species is. Not even evolution itself. But we are aware of our imperfections. Awareness is the first step to improvement. We can develop and perfect ourselves. This is now our imperative. Other species are innocent – but stuck in their niches and their unawareness. The eternal dilemma as outlined by John Stuart Mill is: What is better – to be an unhappy Socrates or a happy cabbage?

Ecology is regarded to be a subject which could be a reprieve for the planet. But the ecology, as it is, cannot play a role in saving our planet. For the conventional ecology is analytical ecology. Through analytical means it describes well the state of our environment, ecosystems, species and genotypes with the proximate conclusion that *ecological disruption is inevitable at the hands of human species*. It, however, avoids giving solution to the gravest problem of the planet, or if it does, the solutions are superficial, which are hardly achievable. Skolimowskian Eco-philosophy and the concept of the Participatory Mind unfold the potencies of revival of ecological phenomena emanating from the phenomenon of man. Analytical ecology proves man responsible for disaster. Eco-philosophy and the concept of the Participatory Mind help the man become responsible for restoring ecological affluence of planet Earth.

5. Noetic Monism: Mind for Reality

Noetic Monism is a concept of reality Henryk Skolimowski has devised drawing upon the ontological consequences entailed in the concept of sensitivities. "Our in-depth understanding of sensitivities not only affects our concept of man but also radically reshapes our basic notion of reality," Henryk reasons. We have experienced various forms of monism in history. Henryk distinguishes four kinds of monism in the history of philosophy, namely:

(1) Materialist Monism (Marx), the doctrine which claims that all is matter; or that whatever exists (in the real sense of existence) is a body;

(2) Idealist (or Spiritual) Monism (Plato), the doctrine which claims that what exist in the primary sense are forms (ideas, spirit);

(3) Mentalism (Bishop Berkeley), the doctrine which claims that what exist in the primary sense are our perceptions (*esse percipi*: it exists because it is perceived);

(4) Naturalist Monism (Spinoza), the doctrine which claims that God is nature, and that nature is God. This doctrine is sometimes called Pantheism.

Noetic Monism is a different kind of monism; quite different from outlined above. Skolimowski explains it as follows:

It (Noetic Monism) claims that both bodies and ideas (spirit) exist. But their existence takes different forms.

What unifies these different forms of existence is *the evolutionary matrix*, which explains both the unity of all existence – hence monism – and also the difference within the underlying unity. All forms of being come from the same evolutionary barrel. Yet they represent different stages of the transformation of evolution. *The different stages of the evolutionary becoming are responsible for different forms of existence.*

Noetic Monism maintains that things *become* what our consciousness makes out of them through the active participation of Mind. Henryk's Noetic Monism is akin to, and perhaps an improved version of, the Hindu *Arya Samaj* Philosophy of *Advaita*. Therefore, Henryk also calls it 'Advaitism' or 'New Advaita'. Henryk explains Advaita as follows: Advaita asserts a seamless unity of things which, however, can be organized in different compartments, and then named with different levels such as material, mental, spiritual.

The quest of understanding the nature of reality is found in all philosophies. According to Henryk Skolimowski, Taoism is quite close to Noetic Monism. Henryk finds Advaita of Hindu philosophy and the Buddhist doctrine of Mind Only worthy precursors of Noetic Monism.

"The history of the Western metaphysics, by and large, has been the metaphysics of *being*," says Henryk Skolimowski. "From Pythagoras via Plato and Aristotle, the mainstream of Western philosophical thinking about the cosmos was rooted in the idea of structure and of being – fixed and permanent whether these were Plato's Forms or Democritus's atoms. This tradition of the metaphysics of being was powerfully reinforced by Christianity – that is, after Aristotle's metaphysics became the backbone of Christian metaphysics through the reconstruction accomplished by Thomas Aquinas."

Emergence of science as one of the dominating thinking of human world also witnessed continuance of the metaphysics of being. Science,

Henryk says, continued the metaphysics of being in another idiom: for science is par excellence a metaphysics of being; that is to say, classical Newtonian science. He points out that Western perception, thinking and language, therefore, have been thoroughly biased toward the metaphysics of being.

Henryk says that we tend to think of reality as 'that object out there.' Hence, he maintains, we have enormous difficulties in conceiving of reality differently; for instance, as a continuous flux. For this reason, he continues, we have great difficulty in coming to terms with the findings of quantum physics.

In the context of participatory universe and participatory Mind metaphysics of becoming comes to the picture. "The metaphysics of becoming, although pushed to the margin for centuries, has never died out," reminds Henryk. "It started with Heraclitus, for whom to understand the world is to understand the process of its change."

Henryk Skolimowski tells us about interesting time connections of the tradition of metaphysics of becoming: "The Heraclitean tradition of metaphysics of becoming was continued during the Middle Ages, mainly through the writings of various mystics, such as Meister Eckhart. . . In the nineteenth century this tradition was powerfully reintroduced by Hegel; and then in the different idiom by Karl Marx. . . In the twentieth century the metaphysics of becoming has been magnificently restarted by Whitehead for whom PROCESS is the crucial ontological and epistemological category. Quite independently, Teilhard de Chardin outlined his metaphysics of becoming within which evolution, as the motor of cosmogenesis, takes the centre of the stage."

Linking Noetic Monism, metaphysics of becoming, consciousness, and reality with each other, Skolimowski writes:

> We are at the mercy of reality. But reality is, in a subtle way, at our own mercy; at the mercy of our Minds. Whenever you make sense of reality, you make sense of it by filtering

it through your Mind. Let us note: 'reality' that you never make sense of is as good as non-existence. *Whenever there is a notion of reality there is a substratum of consciousness within which this reality is grounded.* No consciousness, no reality. To say it once more, within the participatory Mind, reality is not given to us on a silver platter; simply it is not given to us at all. Even if it were given to us, we should not know how to make it. If and when we begin to take it, we do not take it as it is, but invariably and inexorably through our human filters, by processing and transforming it.

"Instead of 'exploring reality' we should be talking about reality-making," suggests Henryk. "Each journey into 'reality' is always a journey into our Mind." Henryk unfolds:

> Reality-making is the new term for describing this process of interaction of the Mind with the participatory Universe as the result of which we obtain first this configuration of the cosmos, then that configuration of the cosmos, according to the powers and patterns of our articulation. In each of these configurations there is the signature of the artist who has co-created it. This artist is our co-creative Participatory Mind. No Mind, no consciousness; and thus no reality to behold.

Reality as an output depends on the amount of input. Henryk says that the organism receives from reality as much as it puts into it. He establishes lovely relationship between beholding, articulation and co-creation emanating from the source of reality created by Mind: *In beholding we are articulating. In articulating we are co-creating. In the act of articulation Mind and reality merge; reality becomes an aspect of Mind.*

One of the best aspects, rather attributes, of the Skolimowskian Philosophy is that it regards Mind not simply an organ of the human body, as the proponents of biological and medical sciences would do, but as a whole *sphere* – like biosphere, and explores its relationships with the whole universe, as well as with the all-creative factors of the universe. Mind is extended beyond body. Through its outreach tentacles the Mind connects itself to a very vast sphere. I would like to call the Mind as *Nousphere*— to compare and relate it with photosphere, biosphere, and all creative spheres of the universe. The notion of Nousphere to describe the sphere of Mind, intellect or thought sounds better than *Noosphere* introduced earlier by Teilhard de Chardin (1881-1955). For the term Nousphere seems denoting *Nous*, the Mind or intellect, more appropriately than Noosphere. (Both terms are to be pronounced similarly.) Skolimowskian exploration of the role of Mind as *coexisting with reality* would support the notion of Nousphere. Such a vital, wonderful and evolution-complementary role of Mind elevates Mind to the level of a sphere, a sphere complementary to biosphere and photosphere or lumenosphere in its roles, functions, creativity, and destinations.

Biosphere has limits. Photosphere (the universe) is limitless. Nousphere overlaps biosphere and extends into photosphere. Nouspehre's extension into photosphere denotes the limits of understanding. The Mind is active in creativity, and through its continuously evolving understanding it attempts to enlarge its sphere and penetrate deeper into photosphere. The spiral of understanding (to be described in chapter 3) is decisive of the limits of Nousphere.

The nousphere itself has three spheres. These spheres have been named and extensively elaborated by Skolimowski:

> Mind I is Mind in the narrow sense, the abstract Mind. Mind II is the sum-total of all the sensitivities residing within the human species. Mind III is 'reality' – that is,

the sum-total of the interactions of our sensitivities with the stuff outside, as delineated and articulated by Mind I and Mind II.

Skolimowski represents each of these Minds by a concentric sphere which is merging with the next. "In fact, these spheres are aspects of each other," says Skolimowski. However, he also distinguishes Mind I from Mind II on the basis of different states they exhibit and their different modes of articulation of evolution, despite the fact that they are aspects of each other. "Mind I has provided the material for the making of Mind III; while Mind II makes human sense of Mind I," Skolimowski explains. "Noetic Monism does not insist on sameness of things as Materialistic Monism, for instance, does. It insists only on the *noetic unity*, on the unity of comprehension, as based on sensitivities."

Henryk Skolimowski addresses the role of the Mind in the universe of becoming. "The becoming of the universe is inseparable from the becoming of the Mind," he infers. The old ideas and schemes are unable to solve the new problems – the problems of our times. Henryk says that Noetic Monism offers itself as a new solution. "Within Noetic Monism we do not negate the versatility and beauty of the cosmos, including the 'reality' of subatomic particles. Yet we maintain that this beauty and all the 'realities' indelibly bear the imprint of their co-creator – the Mind."

Henryk's attachment to our universe is overwhelming and touching. He trusts universe like the truest being of it: "Ours is the universe of becoming— the universe of emergent qualities, the universe of new forms of understanding, which, although they first appear as conceptual shocks, after a time resolve themselves as new illuminating insights into the nature of things."

As Henryk says, there is an intimate unity between the concept of reality, the concept of knowledge and the concept of the Mind. "The three are bound together in a triangular co-defining relationship."

Henryk tells us that within the empiricist tradition the Mind is conceived as a *tabula rasa* – a clean sheet of paper on which experience does all the work. "There is a congruence between the static (dead) universe that empiricism postulates and its concept of static, entirely passive Mind. With the rediscovery of the universe of becoming, which the New Physics supports in a variety of ways, the role of the Mind must of necessity be redefined," he suggests.

The Participatory Theory of Mind Henryk Skolimowski proposed seeks to transcend to take possession of the new freedom in which, unanchored from the shores of determinism, we shall be floating through the new unfolding universe. Aided by new imagination, Henryk maintains, we shall be discovering new forms of understanding of which philosophers and scientists have never dreamt in their narrowly conceived rational ivory towers of academia.

The Skolimowskian Philosophy puts forth the mysterious, all-empowered, imaginative and unfolding Mind. An understanding of this Mind is a must to understand the self, to understand the world we live in and to unfold the cosmos. Skolimowski makes us be one with this wonderful Mind:

> The emergence of the Mind is one of the lasting mysteries. To conceive of Mind as a mystery is less mysterious and less mystifying than to take the Mind to be a mere brain working according to physiological, mechanistic laws alone; for it is to admit that mystery is part of the natural order of things. Mind and imagination are bound together. The nature of imagination gives us a far better clue to the understanding of the Mind than a 100 neurophysiological studies. The nature of imagination is wonderfully mysterious. And wonderfully mysterious is the quality of the universe that Mind/ imagination render to us. The unfolding universe is at the mercy of our Mind/ imagination, for it is our Mind/ imagination.

Summary

Professor Henryk Skolimowski outlines the Participatory Mind. In our approach to unfold the cosmos, the key lies with the Mind. A deeper understanding of the Mind is of absolute importance for a deeper understanding of the cosmos. In his Mind-enhancing, Mind-stimulating, Mind-boggling, Mind-nourishing, Mind-empowering, and Mind-unfolding discussion Skolimowski underlines Mind and life, compares the Minds of Amoebas and the Mind of Einstein, establishes the sensitivities–consciousness–Mind relationship, presents a new concept of the human, and proposes a model of Mind as reality: Noetic Monism. He summarizes his outlining of the Participatory Mind as follows:

> There is no objective reality in the absolute sense, as there is no such thing as objectivity independent of our cognitive faculties. We do not photograph this (purportedly objective) reality in our scientific theories. What is out there is brought about by the alchemy of our Mind – which is an inherent part of the real. The nature of our Mind is the nature of our knowledge is the nature of our reality. (Try to be an amoeba and 'think' what your 'knowledge' and 'reality' would be like then.)… Different forms of knowledge, different epistemologies, different cosmologies are different ways of articulating the cosmos, different ways of processing and transforming 'what is there'. What is there can never be separated from the way we obtain it. Extrasensory perception is one form of processing, mathematical equations of quantum physics are another. They are all united by the Mind that participates in each of them. No Mind, no articulation of knowledge – no quantum physics, no cosmology, no quarks. They are all creative products of the genius of the Mind. The participatory Mind is one of

the chief actors on the stage of the participatory universe... Through rapid advances in knowledge we have split the cosmos open and are now reassembling it *de novo*. Noetic Monism outlines the matrix of evolutionary unity. In this matrix the Mind is not only the mapper but an inherent part of the matrix itself. We always map reality on the map made with the coordinates of the Mind. The idiom is again incorrect: map-making and territory are one. As our capacity for map making increases, our territory becomes larger and richer. Process, becoming, evolutionary change, transformation are the basic modes of our reality-making. For every act of reality-making is an act of change, part of the process of transformation. Structure and being are to be considered special cases of the process of becoming... The mystery of the Mind is the key to unlocking the mystery of the cosmos. But in deciphering the cosmos we only look deeper into the mystery of our Mind.

CHAPTER 2

Mind in Retrospect

Plato spoke of the great and the small, the Italians of the finite, Empedocles of fire, water, and air, Anaxagoras of the infinity of homogeneous things.[1] – Aristotle

1. Mind from the View Point of Empiricists and Rationalists

Mind has been in the Minds of people throughout the history of civilizations. Theories of the Mind and that of reality have been running parallel. In most of the cases, rather almost invariably, the Mind and reality have been kept separated from each other. There are numerous theories about the Mind and the reality in Western philosophy too. However, as Henryk Skolimowski lets us know in depth, with some singular exceptions, Mind and reality are separated from each other and viewed independently of each other. Some pre-Socratic philosophers understood Mind-reality in a better way. Henryk gives an example of Parmenides who said: 'No Mind, no world.' "In these four words a whole magnificent insight is contained," Henryk astonishes, but laments at the same time. "In earlier centuries and millennia we had insufficient knowledge, and perhaps also insufficient courage, to translate this insight into a complete model of Mind/ Reality."

Knowledge has a lot to give to a civilization. But a wrong understanding happens to be ghastly for the civilization. It is owing to a wrong understanding of the things that we are compelled to live in a split and atomized world. Henryk Skolimowski in his writings often brings to the fore certain cases showing how such a split and atomization of the world is caused. In the context of 'Mind in History' he traces yet another example: "Existential and social traumas have often been caused for Western man by the way in which we have split and atomized the world around us. Cartesian dualism, which radically separates the Mind from the body and Mind from nature, has been at the root of many of our misconceptions and quite a few of our dilemmas." He expresses an urge to overcome this dualism suggesting that we must create a unified theory within which Mind and reality can be treated as aspects of each other. Henryk's theory of Noetic Monism precisely contributes to unify the Mind and reality.

Henryk makes a close look at some of the theories of Mind that have been most influential in the West and that still hold sway.

EMPIRICISM

"Empiricism is both a theory of knowledge and theory of Mind," Henryk Skolimowski explains. "It holds that there is nothing in the intellect that there has not previously been in the senses. Mind is conceived here essentially as a *tabula rasa*, white sheet on which experience writes its designs. The active role of the Mind is that it allows experience to write on it." However, how transformations of raw experience and of impression occur has never been satisfactorily explained by empiricism.

Empiricism in no way contributes to make human Mind content with its unlimited capabilities and only seems to maintain a bonsai out of it. Skolimowski says that empiricism goes under many names nowadays, such as positivism, operationalism, methodology of science or simply scientific method is still prevalent in our world. Skolimowskian views on and interpretation of the theory of empiricism brings to the fore interesting and noteworthy facts:

- Empiricism, as a theory of Mind, is a gross caricature of what is going on in the human Mind, and what we know about the marvels of human comprehension.

- The main reason for the acceptance of this clearly defective theory, in my opinion, has been ideological.

- Empiricism maintains that everything is acquired from the physical universe via the senses, thus instructs us that no authority of any sort needs to be obeyed.

- In the long run, the physical universe becomes the only reality, which we not only explore but also *worship*. All other gods are dethroned.

- Empiricism claims that there is nothing beyond the physical and beyond the senses.

- Empiricism is devoid of any spiritual dimension.

- Empiricism claims to be objective and value-free but supports view of the world in which the physical is elevated and the spiritual suppressed; in which the values of objectivity, rationality and efficiency are constantly upheld, whilst the values of compassion, empathy and altruism are ignored or suppressed.

"We are living in a period of nihilism and cynicism," Henryk reminds us. "In this setting students, who naturally look for some moral guidance, get disoriented, confused, frustrated and often angry – without apparent reason. But the reason is there. In their deeper selves they are dissatisfied with nihilism, which eats at the core of their being."

RATIONALIST THEORIES OF MIND

Mind is not a clean slate or *tabula rasa* in rationalist theories. The Mind has an active role to play. These theories contrast the empiricist theories which, in fact, happen to be an eclipse for the former. Both the theories, according to Henryk Skolimowski, run parallel to each other. "Many of the rationalist theories claim that Mind is endowed with capacities and propensities that are inborn, therefore a priori," says Henryk. He mentions about three of the rationalist theories, viz., Plato's, Berkeley's and Kant's.

Pondering over Plato's theory of the Mind, Henryk writes: "Plato envisaged Mind as active but only in so far as it recognizes ('remembers, recollects') Forms, those ideal, incorruptible, unchangeable blueprints to which all objects of our knowledge and all objects of existence must comply. Objects are what they are *because* ideal Forms, predating their existence, are embodied in them."

Skolimowskian views on Plato's theory are as follows: "Plato's doctrine seems very dry and abstract. But actually it is much more than that. For Plato wove around it a marvellous conception of man, of human life as a passage from darkness to enlightenment. The human body, in the biological form, is bondage, which the soul must overcome. In overcoming it – its coarseness, limitations and distortions – the total soul clears its vision and approaches the Form, which is often identified with Godhead. In this context, the rules of conduct that underlie human behaviour are exactly the ones that enable us to make the transition from darkness to enlightenment, from amorphousness to the beauty of the Form. Plato's theory of Mind and reality is far from an abstract theoretical construct; it is ladder to heaven. In ascending it we build the good life and pursue meaning worthy of human beings."

Skolimowski explains Berkeley's conception of Mind as Follows: "Berkeley's conception of Mind is active in the extreme. Bishop Berkeley (1685-1753) maintained: '*esse percipi*': things exist only insofar as they are perceived. All existence is, in a sense, a figment of our imagination. Things are 'brought' into existence through acts of our perception, and exist only insofar as we perceive them. The consequence is subjective idealism: there is no reality independent of our perception. An ingenious and startling doctrine, particularly when defended by a scintillating Mind, but making nonsense of all that we know; and also making nonsense of evolution itself, especially evolution as striving towards greater and greater complexity, attainment, perfection."

Skolimowski finds the rationalist theory of Mind provided by Immanuel Kant (1724-1804) closest to the participatory conception of Mind. He writes about this theory of the Mind as follows: "Kant reversed the whole process envisaged by empiricists. Instead of objects impressing themselves on the Mind, Kant claimed that it is the other way round – it is the Mind, its specific structure and its specific categories, that is imposed on objects outside, which are shaped according to the categories of the Mind. There is conformity between objects and the Mind, but this comes about *as the Mind imposes its order on things*. We perceive a certain order in the outside world. We structure things with a certain inevitability – because we cannot do otherwise. The structure of our Mind continuously impresses itself on the order of reality. The order of reality is really the order of the Mind."

Skolimowski finds the whole conception of reality as opaque in Kant. There is no room for evolution in the Kantian system, which, according to him, is the major reason for the collapse of Kantian philosophy. "With the growth of science in the nineteenth century, with the discovery of non-Euclidian geometries and non-Newtonian physics and the acceptance of the idea that time is not absolute (as both Newton and Kant imagined), the 'unalterable' structure of the Mind was undetermined; according to some, invalidated," says Skolimowski. "Kant's major shortcoming was to envisage the Mind's categories and Mind's structure as fixed and absolute. But in postulating an active role for the Mind, and in claiming that the world is shaped and determined by the categories of our knowledge, he achieved great and lasting influence."

Skolimowski maintains that Kant's heritage has been continued (though in a changed idiom) throughout the nineteenth and twentieth centuries. He mentions that what Kant attributed to the Mind – the shaping and determining of reality – various other thinkers subsequently attributed to language. "First came Henri Poincaré with his ingenious conception of conventionalism," he names many other. "Then came Kazimierz Adjukiewicz, Benjamin Lee Whorf and W.V. Quine, who radicalized Poincaré's conventionalism. More recently, Noam Chomsky has crusaded for the recognition of man as a language animal. Each of them has recognized *language as a co-definer of knowledge and of reality*. Each was close to seeing that reality and Mind co-define each other."

From the two theories of the Mind – the empiricist and the rationalist theories – Henryk Skolimowski attempts to distinguish the evolutionary and transcendental theory of Mind, which is the Participatory conception of Mind. "This Participatory Mind is much closer to rationalist theories than to empiricist ones," Henryk clarifies. "The hallmark of the participatory theory is that it recognizes Mind not only as active, but as co-creative, as a shaper of all reality around us. Because the Mind is woven into the whole fabric we call reality, any adequate theory of it must also be a rendering of reality itself. The participatory theory is ecumenical. It can accommodate most of the existing theories of Mind. They are all partial renderings of the prowess and versatility of Mind. Each has attempted to elucidate one particular aspect of Mind, and each is a tribute to the Mind reflecting upon itself."

Henryk narrates about the interesting and understandable account of the Greek Minds: "The Participatory theory of Mind is a restatement of Parmenide's seminal insight 'No Mind, no world.' One explanation how it is that these Greek Minds could conceive ideas of such depth and beauty is that they lent their Minds to the daemon of imagination. And 'daemon' was not a bad word in the Greek vocabulary, but one sublime in tone and denoting extraordinary powers. Yet it has taken twenty-five centuries of reflection and articulation to understand some of these ideas in depth."

In the light of the Greeks' Minds, Henryk suggests that in particular, we needed to invent and refine the theory of evolution in order to perceive the Mind as one of the great vocabulary forces, which articulates evolution and at the same time articulates itself. His discourse on the Mind in history is stimulating and helps our Minds to elucidate unique feelings about the Mind. An example follows:

> That there have been so many theories of Mind in history
> is astonishing. That none of them has proved lastingly
> 'true' is not astonishing at all. Rather, it is a demonstration
> that Mind's agenda is forever open, that insofar as Mind is

creative, unfolding and reflecting upon itself, it is bound to transcend whatever structure we impose on it, including that of the Participatory Mind.

2. Mind in the Throes of Pigeon Methodology

Knowledge makes a man unfit to be a slave.[2] – Frederick Douglass

With pigeon methodology applications in life, life is bound to shrink. Haplessly the twentieth-century philosophy is not free from such methodology. "Twentieth-century philosophy has mummified our understanding of the Mind," says Henryk cursing such philosophy. "Instead of exploring the creative and extraordinary aspects of Mind, it has continually attempted to reduce Mind to the scope of activities characteristic of pigeons." Henryk candidly cautions – "If you use pigeon methodology, you are bound to arrive at pigeon-like understanding."

Henryk tries to trace the historical circumstances that led to the elevation of the pigeon methodology as the tool of universal understanding. He tells that there is a great tension within the framework of twentieth-century scientific understanding (by the twentieth-century philosophy Henryk Skolimowski means 'the empiricist-bound, analytically-oriented philosophy of the Anglo-Saxon persuasion that dominates our present universities and has exerted a considerable influence on our thinking all over the globe in the second part of the twentieth century'). "On the one hand there is a tendency to impose the ethos of science, its language and formulations, on all the phenomena of life," Henryk argues. "This ethos is pursued by some with such an exemplary zeal that human behaviour is reduced to conditioning-response schemata, which are hardly adequate for the study of even the more intricate problem of pigeons. On the other hand there is an opposite tendency: at its cutting edge, physics has been systematically deserting the positions of Newtonian science for the last eighty years. The general public is more victim of the dogmatic image of past science than beneficiary of the new exciting vistas of physics at the cutting edge."

Skolimowski says that with the discovery of non-Euclidean geometries, space in the Newtonian sense started to totter. After the foundations of Newtonian physics started cracking, it was realized that many different geometries are possible within which we can describe the physical cosmos. Out of this realization conventionalism was born, which was 'an ingenious doctrine developed in the first decade of the twentieth century by Henry Poincaré and Pierre Duhem, who claimed that a system of knowledge does not necessarily describe reality faithfully, in a one-to-one way, but rather that it much depends on the system of axioms accepted at the outset of its development.' "We have much liberty as to which system of axioms to choose, for instance, in developing geometry," Henryk suggests. "This was an ingenious way of resolving the problem of non-Euclidean geometries."

"Conventionalism solved many problems, but it opened up a Pandora's Box of many other problems," Henryk makes it clear. "In particular, it profoundly undermined the very notion of truth as expressed through science... The problem of truth is central to science and all learning. We feel that we must have some notion of truth, otherwise how can we assess the validity of our cognitive claims, particularly in science? To put it more emphatically: since conventionalism emerged over a century ago we have not come to terms – faithfully, adequately, unequivocally – with the notion of truth, and with the notion of reality that science purportedly describes."

As Henryk tells us, big problems began to emerge in science in the nineteenth century. He maintains: When radioactivity was discovered, the phenomenon was clearly beyond the framework of Newtonian physics. To deal with radioactivity, and a host of other problems, new theories were invented—Einstein's theory of relativity, Bohr's quantum theory, Heisenberg's principle of uncertainty.

Describing the big problems that began in the twentieth century, Henryk Skolimowski talks about Karl Popper's distinctive philosophy of science drawn from Einstein (the over thrower of Newtonian physics) and revisits the quantum theory. He writes: The quantum theory represents a wonderfully fluid universe which has been called 'the eternal dance of Shiva.' A most startling aspect of this fluid universe is that observer and observed are so intimately connected that they are inseparable from each other.

Henryk cites another example — of Ernst Mach — with whom we observe the shift from the correspondence theory of truth to the coherence theory of truth. "Since science could not claim to be the guardian of truth, understood as a faithful description of reality out there, scientists and philosophers decided that perhaps we should consider statements and theories as true insofar as they are coherent with the rest of accepted knowledge. However, within the coherence theory of truth we have difficulties in distinguishing fact from fiction, particularly when fiction is coherent (*Alice in Wonderland*)." Henryk's following views open a new window of our Mind towards a science related reality:

> We are living in an exciting era when science marches from one triumph to another. Yet concealed underneath lie much uncertainty and confusion which even the best Minds cannot dispel or come to grips with. To cover up the obvious conceptual shortcomings of our theories, we invent all kinds of ad hoc theories and 'isms'. Some of 'isms' are no more than hypotheses to save previous conceptions, that is to say, to perpetuate the impression that all is well in the kingdom of science and that science is coping well.

Henryk then mentions about the doctrine of operationalism conceived by Perry Bridgeman. "Meaning is to be sought in operations," wrote Bridgeman in 1934. Henryk says that a more liberal definition was provided in 1938: Operations are a necessary, but not a sufficient condition for the determination of meanings. However, the formulation was still weakened in 1952: The operational aspect is not by any means the only aspect of meaning. "These semantic strategies were taken at face value and gave rise to a host of new theories, including the theory of Mind," writes Henryk. "*The Concept of Mind* by Gilbert Ryle (1949) is a crowning achievement of the whole epoch *bent on attempting to find salvation through semantics.*"

About behaviourism formulated first by J.B. Watson and then in its more 'sophisticated' version by B.F. Skinner, Henryk tells us that behaviourism was actually a doctrine quite different from operationalism and logical empiricism. "But it had the same purpose: to eliminate everything complex, subtle and human and reduce it to the stuff of pigeons," writes Skolimowski. The purpose of all the new 'isms' Skolimowski describes – logical empiricism, operationalism, behaviourism, and other forms of positivism – was the same: to reduce all layers and aspects of human existence to those of inanimate matter. Skolimowski expresses his deep concern about humanity:

> A conspiracy has been created against *human beings* – to crucify us on the procrustean bed of one-dimensional philosophies which reduce us in stature, deny us larger horizons, and suffocate our souls. That those philosophies turn us off intellectually and excite our Minds not at all is one thing. However, these philosophies have become institutionalized. They are predominant orthodoxies in our schools and academia. When a learned professor tells us that whatever cannot be counted does not count; when our chemistry instructors tell us that all the mystery of life is contained in chemical interactions, this first creates a climate of opinion, and after a while a social reality of a certain kind. We are coerced to follow the 'authorities'. We are each vulnerable to the manipulations of culture, and each culture has a tendency, indeed an urge, to compel and hypnotize us.

Disapproving B.F. Skinner's views – freedom is an illusion and dignity is illusion – as laid down in his 1971 book *Beyond Freedom and Dignity*, Skolimowski suggests that they are not illusions and we do need them.

Henryk holds Ryle's *The Concept of Mind* (1949) as a magnificent book but also says that it is but an offering on the altar of the reductionist ethos. "The whole venture is simply reductionist: the idea is not to understand MIND as it is, and as it works, but to reduce it to its observable by-products," opines Henryk. "Ryle's is a materialist theory of Mind. It is also a behaviourist and operationalist theory, as it tries to avoid the problem of Mind by studying its outwardly observable behaviour. Thus in Ryle we see a synthesis of materialism, operationalism, logical empiricism and behaviourism. The result is virtuosity in applying the pigeon methodology, which fundamentally obscures a real understanding of the Mind."

Further 'operationalizing' the Ryle's theory, Henryk maintains that he (Ryle) marks a pivotal point of the materialist-reductionist-operationalist tradition and that his works set the tone for the next decades of endless epicycles on the theme of the semantic-materialist theory. "The tradition here outlined was born of the crisis in the foundations of Western knowledge which is still with us," explains Henryk. "This tradition, perhaps inadvertently, has created a monumental body of distinctions and semantic refinements which contribute little to our understanding of the world at large. Now if a body of knowledge which obscures rather than illuminates the purposes of our understanding can be called scholasticism, then the semantic empiricist tradition of the twentieth century deserves the name of the New Scholasticism."

3. Karl Popper and His Philosophy of Partial Liberation from Positivism

The twentieth century has witnessed enormous intellectualization as well as tremors and revolutions almost of all sorts. In this process the human world has been pervaded by many philosophies. Many of the theories have been eliminated, some have been partially rectified, and yet some new theories put forth by illustrious philosophers have illuminated human

Mind. Skolimowski, whose eco-philosophy arose like a morning sun, brings to the fore some interesting revolutionary events:

> One of these (twentieth century) revolutions was the creation of a no-nonsense philosophy called logical empiricism, by a group of thinkers in Vienna in the late 1920s and early 1930s, led by Moritz Schlick. They called themselves the Vienna Circle, and for this reason their philosophy has sometimes been called the Vienna Circle philosophy. This was a positivism with a vengeance. Whatever limitations of empiricism and positivism were revealed in the eighteenth and nineteenth centuries (and indeed Kant demonstrated how shallow empiricism was), the thinkers of the Vienna Circle decided to forget them and build another empiricist edifice, this time on the foundations of modern formal logic. The edifice was impressive. But *as a philosophy it was a disaster*. Its fall-out has affected our thinking and our mentality to the degree that we have often behaved like positivist morons. Reviewing the decisions made by our policy-makers and all those who are leading us into the new electronic era, and realizing that these decisions are not enlightened by any deeper values or any larger philosophy and yet are hailed as 'rationally justified' – and proclaimed with pride – we cannot escape the conclusion that *the fall-out from positivist thinking has incapacitated us on countless levels*.

Reviewing some of the historical happenings, Henryk Skolimowski narrates that Kant was astute indeed in postulating that the structure of our knowledge (and thus of our world) conforms to the categories of our Mind, and not conversely, as classical empiricism had assumed. But, according to Henryk, Kant's great insight was marred by one misconception: He made the structure of the Mind too rigid and too dogmatic. "There is a paradox here, and an epistemological tragedy," Henryk maintains. "Kant set out to liberate Newtonian Physics from the straight-jacket of empiricism, and this he did. Yet in the process of the intended liberation, he imprisoned himself in the rigidity of the conceptual universe of Newtonian mechanics."

"The genius of Kant consisted in inventing the structure of the Mind from which Newtonian physics follows," concludes Skolimowski. "But this genius also played a part in the Kant's undoing." The specific structures and categories that Kant presented as attributes to Mind were grossly undermined. Skolimowski makes us understand categorically: Kant meant to finish empiricism once and for all. Yet, in spite of Kant's marvellous insight into the nature of human Mind, we witness the return to empiricism, wave after wave, as if Kant had never existed.

Skolimowski reiterates that through fastidious and exact systems of semantics, logical empiricists (and then analytical philosophers) have hoped to reconstruct traditional philosophy so that it would be on a par with precise systems of exact science. "Surely an impossible dream, as science itself is becoming more and more elusive," he says. "But philosophy is full of impossible dreams; indeed, thrives on them."

Henryk Skolimowski regards positivism as a tortured philosophy. "Seldom in the history of philosophy has such an enormous and sophisticated labour produced so little understanding," he says. He finds Karl Popper's *Logic of Scientific Discovery* (1934, 1959) as epoch making and says that Popper showed the importance of the creative agency of the Mind.

Skolimowski regards Popper as a source of revolution in philosophy. "With Popper we witness another revolution in philosophy," he reiterates. The main problem of Popper is to understand *how knowledge grows.* Skolimowski states some of the premises of Popper's philosophy:

> To understand the world is to understand the nature of our
> knowledge. To understand our knowledge is to understand
> its growth and vicissitudes. Human knowledge does not

grow like a pyramid, made of the same kinds of stones (physical facts). The shape of the pyramid is continually reconstructed as some parts of it are destroyed or at least significantly changed. The material of which the pyramid is made is also varied – all kinds of things are built into it.

"For logical empiricists the chief inspiration was Russell and the *Principia*," Henryk Skolimowski mentions. "Popper's chief inspiration was Einstein and his theory of relativity. Einstein's theory has shown, according to Popper, that no knowledge is absolute… The conclusion that follows is that all knowledge is tentative and conjectural. The best we can do is to play imaginatively with new conjectures (tentative theories), and then submit them to relentless scrutiny."

Skolimowski unquestionably regards Popper as one of the intellectual giants of the twentieth century, "a man who has helped us liberate ourselves from the strait-jacket of logical empiricism." However, Skolimowski adds, with the passage of time Popper too has become a new orthodoxy as his followers are seeking to monopolize truth and behave as if they had key to all right solutions.

There is a lot to be admired in Popper's philosophy. Pluralism which Popper attempted to augment is one of the distinctive attributes of Popper. Skolimowski writes:

What was especially liberating in Popper was his pluralism as he led us away from the one-track approach of logical structuralists. Popper has promoted pluralistic epistemology and open-ended rationality. It was the open-endedness of Popper's philosophy that was so refreshing and promising for the future. To try to make Popper's opus a closed and untouchable system is to do violence to the very nature of his enterprise, according to which *everything* is open to questioning and criticism. It follows therefore that – as our perspectives and problems change – so do our approaches and solutions. And our perspectives and problems *have* changed.

Why have Einstein's theories no longer been at the centre of controversy, either in physics or epistemology? While discussing Popper's philosophy of pluralism, Skolimowski gives an example of Albert Einstein: "Quantum theory or, to use a more general term, the New Physics has been posing the most fascinating and most mind-boggling problems both for physicists and for epistemologists."

In the context of the Popper's philosophy, Skolimowski suggests the following to be admitted: in contradiction to logical empiricism, Popper acknowledges the active role of the Mind. The Mind is constantly active, either in generating new conjectures or in ingeniously thinking up new tests of existing theories.

Logical empiricism overshadowed Popper's philosophy for some time. However, in the meantime, Popper was immensely supported by Thomas Kuhn in his *Structure of Scientific Revolutions* (1963), which is Popperian in its approach through and through. Paul Feyerabend and Imre Lakatos later on added much popularity to Popper. "The process of the historical reconstruction of science, within Popperian epistemology, has led to the undermining of *every* creed and contention that was ever held about science," says Henryk.

Recalling Paul Feyerabend's announcement that *anything goes*, Henryk Skolimowski writes: "The enterprise of science, when examined penetratingly, according to Feyerabend, appears to be incoherent and amorphous, and full of question-begging. Feyerabend ultimately argues in his article 'A Plea for the Hedonist', that a world without science would be more pleasant to live in."

"In the panorama of twentieth-century thought Popper once appeared a bright light," writes Skolimowski. "Now this light appears dimmer and dimmer as Popper holds rigidly to his old concepts while new visions, vistas and insights, particularly of New Physics, open up new horizons." The new light of holistic understanding is drawing on us – in this light, Skolimowski suggests a new philosophy in tune with our times:

> …Logical positivism was the philosophy for the first half of the twentieth century. Popper's was the philosophy for the second half of the twentieth century – the period of transition. Now we need a philosophy for the twenty first century, a philosophy cognizant of all the developments of the last quarter of the century, and capable of integrating them.

4. Shadows of The Three Western Projects

Mind has been observed, analyzed and interpreted in different ways by different scholars. Mind's astonishing capacity has been comprehended in numerous ways. Many intelligent persons in the philosophical history of the world have not been able to perceive the Mind in its perfection. "When we consider such Minds as Descartes', Locke's or La Mettrie's, we are puzzled as to why, with so much brilliance, they could not *see* any better," asks Henryk Skolimowski with surprise, and then answers himself that they did not choose to. He further elaborates: "They deliberately wanted to view phenomena in a certain way and then employed their formidable intellects to 'prove' what they chose to see. Why would they embark on such strange paths? For a variety of complex ideological and cultural reasons."

Different epochs have been marked with different problematics. For example, almost each philosopher in the Middle Ages was 'busily constructing his proofs of the existence of God.' Henryk poses questions: Were they all so interested in the problem? Each one of them? Or was the problem imposed on them by the spirit of the time? The philosophers of our times, however, are not engaged in accumulating "proofs" of the existence of God? "Because we are interested in different problems," explains Henryk further posing a question. "Why? Because different problems have come to the fore. Why?" And then he gives the gist of the problem: "We might say that we are interested in certain kinds of problems because others around us are interested in those problems. That is an easy answer and a superficial one. Besides, it reduces us to merely aping what others are doing. To explore a new realm of thought and come up with new, deep insight within it requires a devotion to the subject and fascination with it."

Francis Bacon and René Descartes showed the light of seeing at the things in a new way. Things needed to be liberated from old vistas and visions and from the dogmas and teachings of the church. Henryk tells us that an entirely new 'project' is under way today. "The project is a trans-rational entity," Henryk takes us deeper into the nature of a project. "It is a matter of a vision and deep beliefs. After people invest their beliefs in it, they try to justify it rationally."

The project inspired by Descartes and Bacon, then by Newton and La Place, then Locke and La Mettrie, then Bertrand Russell, B.F. Skinner, Percy Bridgman, Rudolf Carnap et al., was not the first major project of Western culture; nor is it the last— Henryk clarifies and proposes to distinguish the three main Western projects:

> The first was the Greek project, or the Promethean Project, continued from Antiquity roughly to the sixteenth century. In the seventeenth century a new project started to take shape, the secular project, or the Faustian one. The third, the Evolutionary Project, is emerging under our very eyes. It is a holistic and integrative project.

THE GREEK: THE FIRST PROJECT

The whole legacy of the great Greek philosopher Plato encompasses the First Western Project. Henryk says that knowledge for Plato was sacred as well as an extraordinary instrument of self-enlightenment. Henryk puts Plato's perspective in our terms and reminds us the human project emanating from Plato's rich legacy of philosophy: *to reach enlightenment and unity with the Godhead.*

Underlining clear parallelism of the legacy of Plato and ancient Greek philosophers, Skolimowski writes: "In both the Eastern and Western traditions (of the time) we see an enormous importance attached to the Mind. In Buddhism, especially, the role of the Mind, of right thinking and of right assumptions is particularly emphasized. But this element is also luminously clear in Hindu tradition, especially in the Upanishads."

For St Augustine (354–430), one of the chief architects of Christian world-view, knowledge is very important as well, reiterates Henryk: To possess right knowledge is to be in the right state of being. Put otherwise, one's being is determined by the nature and quality of the knowledge one beholds. For one's knowledge is a form of prayer that leads us to God.

"It is important to realize that for Augustine knowledge is intimately connected with life," elaborates Henryk on the Greek Project. "Right knowledge means right life (or right livelihood, as the Buddhists would say). This is of course a version of the Platonic position... The conviction is still held that to possess a superior knowledge leads us to a superior life."

Dutch philosopher Boruch Spinoza (1632–77) still upholds the conviction. "He himself insists that virtue is its own reward and that the right cultivation of the intellect is a precondition of the good life," Henryk elaborates Spinoza. "Wise life is good life. Ignorance and stupidity are the causes of calamities, of misery and human suffering."

Knowledge appears to be at stake. It is diminishing. It is witnessing its own erosion. It is contrary to our expectations that knowledge must evolve continuously. Henry is also worried about how the knowledge itself is diminishing and losing its own light. One interesting paragraph extracted from *The Participatory Mind*:

> . . .the tide of time is moving from the idea of knowledge
> as enlightenment. Spinoza is an exception. The dominant
> cast of the Western Mind has changed. The Western Project
> has changed. It is best exemplified by Francis Bacon (1561–
> 1626) and his new conception of knowledge, according to

which *knowledge is power*: power to extricate secrets from nature, power to subdue nature to our wishes, demands and whims, power to make nature serve the ends of humankind.

THE SECOND PROJECT

For most of the past 2000 years, (Western) civilization has been dominated by two overreaching worldviews: the Christian outlook, and the mechanistic view of the world as a machine. In both cases, 'spirit' and Mind are largely restricted to mankind. But this places humanity in an unusual and awkward position – as the 'great exception' to the natural order, as a kind of freak of nature.[3] – David Skrbina

Henryk Skolimowski characterizes the Second Western Project: *To put the universe on a plate and cut it with an analytical knife; then to manipulate it to our advantage.* "The analytical knowledge acquired in this manner becomes a tool to harness and exploit nature," says the philosopher. "This is the first or intellectual aspect of this Second Western Project."

Secularism and no salvation, according to Skolimowski, are the major ideological aspects of this Project. The idea of fulfillment here on Earth inherent with the Project becomes a new form of salvation, he says. The following are the other peculiar characteristics of the Second Western Project Skolimowski attempts to put forth:

- Fulfillment and happiness on Earth through our own efforts,
- Creating paradise on Earth,
- Paradise on Earth becoming a new theology, a new religion,
- Challenge to the traditional idea of God,
- Secularism's assuming that we are as powerful as God,
- Elevation of human knowledge and human reason to extraordinary heights,
- Radical separation from the major spiritual traditions of Buddhism, Hinduism, Taoism and Zen,

- Emphasis on the importance of the exploration of the physical world,
- Emphasis on the pragmatic aspect of knowledge, namely that knowledge is generated for the sake of the manipulation of the external world.

"In earlier times cosmology (usually inspired by religion) defined the nature of knowledge," laments Skolimowski. "Now cosmology is defined by science and is indeed a branch of it, with all the corresponding limitations." He underlines the following basic assumptions of the Second Project:

(1) We can know the world. It is ours for the taking.
(2) There are no mysteries. Science will explain all.
(3) Western rationality or scientific rationality is universal. Other cultures must submit to it.
(4) Human progress can be universal if all mankind applies to the tools of Western science and technology and the canons of Western rationality.

Within the Second Western Project, Skolimowski claims, knowledge and science have attained the status of a religion. Western education based on the foundation of this Project being operationalized in the West has arrogantly taken virtually the entire world in its fold. "In consequence, they perpetuate the ideology of science and of the Western Project in their own countries," Skolimowski exposes the truth associated with the Second Western Project. "We can see how insidious and subtle are the workings of a powerful Project, how it mesmerizes and compels men's Minds, and produces types such as Skinner, Carnap and other guardians of the status quo."

Skolimowski looks into the inner layers of the Second Western Project. He categorically says that the most vital aspects of the Project are not rational but trans-rational, that basic secular beliefs are not rationally justified, and that salvation through consumption was not a rational proposition. However, says Skolimowski, secularism has had a universal appeal because of the impact of Western education system which has led non-Western people succumb to the Western form of salvation.

Skolimowski finds the Hindu Mind more resilient than the Minds of the people of other cultures. "It seems the tradition of the Upanishads and the great learning of the Vedas have inspired and guided the Hindu Mind and enabled it to see through the limitations of Western assumptions," he says underlining the Hindu Mind to be different. Has the triumphant secularism come to an end? Let it reflect from Skolimowski's perspective:

> After three centuries of pursuing the scientific-secular project, the Western Mind is now reassessing its entire strategy and the ends that have motivated it. The assumptions so dear to the Western mentality, under closure scrutiny, do not appear so universal and indubitably valid as was once surmised. In fact, they appear to us now to be Western dogmas – dazzling but limited, powerful but dangerous. Moreover, the Second Western Project, instead of bringing fulfillment to all people of the Earth, has created a nightmarish pseudo-rational reality, with environmental degradation, famines, violence in full abundance.

In conclusion, Skolimowski says that the present Western Mind is confused and that *the confused Mind is a dangerous one.*

THE THIRD PROJECT

Henryk Skolimowski finds the Western Mind now in search for wholeness, for integration, for values that sustain life, and for God-within. "The realizations occur within the context of an intense, though often concealed, search for spiritual values, for the meaning of life which goes beyond material gratification," Henryk looks deeply into current stream of time. "The

Western Mind is now prepared to eat humble pie (though still reluctantly) and learn from others and not only *teach* others."

The Third Project is not clearly defined. However, Henryk presumes it to be three dimensional one:

> Holistic project emphasizing the unity of all things;
> Spiritually inclined project; and
> Ecologically oriented project

I have tried the Skolimowski's concept of the three-dimensional Third Project in the mandala (figure 1). Henryk calls the Third Western Project as evolutionary because: "We are finally aware of the nature of evolution." There can be three attributes of the new project Skolimowski, himself a son of the West, conceives as the Third Western Project:

i)   being aware of it, we are responsible for it;
ii) in full consciousness we are designing our destiny; and
iii) in full consciousness we shape the destiny of our Minds, which will be destiny of our world.

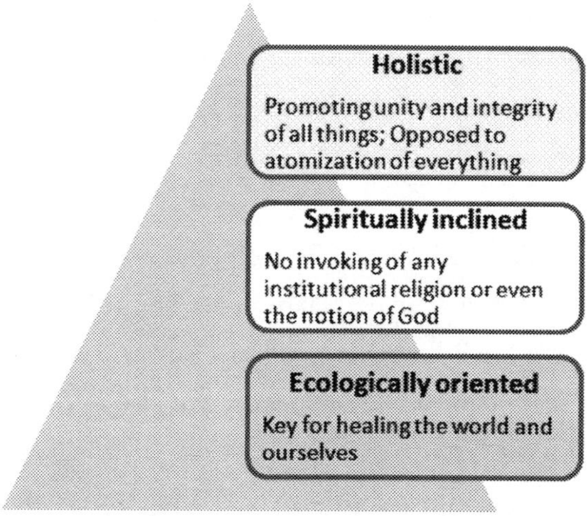

Holistic
Promoting unity and integrity of all things; Opposed to atomization of everything

Spiritually inclined
No invoking of any institutional religion or even the notion of God

Ecologically oriented
Key for healing the world and ourselves

Figure 1: Skolimowskian concept of the *Evolutionary Project*:
The Three-dimensional Third Project

Potential attributes of the new project are those which the East still follows. Through this new project, Henryk seeks reconciliation between East and West, or the synthesis between East and West.

If the new project – the Third Western Project – is accomplished, which is a very tedious process, then, says Skolimowski, we shall be able to show that:

(1) The Buddha Mind and the objective Mind are aspects of the same universal/ human/ cosmic Mind.

(2) The objective Mind is one extreme articulation of the Buddha Mind, and the Buddha Mind can also be seen as objective – that is, when we grant the context (and the assumptions) within which the Buddha Mind can manifest itself.

(3) The split between the East and the West represents different propensities of the same human Mind which can articulate itself, and the world around itself – first in this way, then in that – and each articulation is part of the unfolding of the evolutionary process.

(4) With the rise of the New Physics – when its metaphysical and ethical consequences are clearly spelt out – we have at least the rudiments of the matrix for reconciliation of the West and the East, on a deeper conceptual level, and beyond superficial borrowings. The matrix of the New Physics informs us unequivocally that:

(a) Objective evidence as such does not exist, for in every bit of the 'objective' evidence a part of our psyche is built.

(b) We are allowed to see ourselves as part of the cosmos not merely in the physical sense but also as Atman participating in the Brahman.

(c) We are allowed to see the entire cosmos as interconnected; moreover, as one magic dance of Shiva.

(5) When all these new metaphysical insights are absorbed and
digested, we shall live in a different universe because we shall have
created a new universe.

This Project Design, however, is not an imposition on all other
cultures as the Second Western Project did. Skolimowski clarifies it: "The
'ecumenicalism' of the Third Western Project is not born out of our desire
to submit others to our will but out of will to include the perspectives and
vistas of others while we seek a universal philosophy capable of sustaining us
all." The Third Western Project is perfectly transcendental and evolutionary
in nature, as Henryk makes it clear and graspable:

> In a sense the Western world has travelled the whole circle:
> from early holistic unity of the pre-Socratic and Plato
> via the period of fragmentation and atomization of the
> empiricist era, to a new wholeness based on evolutionary
> unity, which is reminiscent of early Greek philosophy but
> which nevertheless is not a return to the original point.
> We have not travelled in a simple circle, but rather in a
> spiral. Although we have come to re-embrace many points
> that have been kept as constant stars in firmament of
> Eastern thought, we do not dissolve ourselves in Eastern
> philosophies. Rather, we bring them to our level, give them
> a new sense of coherence and meaning. The East and the
> West are merging by one absorbing the other, but by each
> transcending its previous positions.

Thus, the Skolimowskian designs of the Third Western Project are
so exciting, so interesting, so inspiring, and so much intoxicating, that the
participatory Mind would love to articulate all aspects in the process of
reconstruction. If all the human Minds of the world are exposed to this
cosmic design of living on Earth, I am sure, there would be left no reason

why the Minds would not like to participate in this New Project. After all, human Mind keeps evolving and always stays in the quest of occupying higher and more evolved states of living.

Summary

No history in its complexity and beauty is parallel to the history of Mind. All history, in a sense, is the history of the role of the Mind. For the Mind is central to all activities. For the Mind is the supreme commander of all activities. History is the basis of evaluation of everything. Henryk Skolimowski attempts to go for the valuation of the Mind by opening windows towards history. A historical understanding of the Mind is necessary to understand its role in making and moulding realities along the passage of time, and also to understand how the Mind has undergone its own evolution and how it has so far performed its role in the service (and disservice) of the world and of the cosmos. The passage of time through which Mind has been working and evolving itself has not been linear, smooth and easy to comprehend the realities. It is so difficult and challenging for a philosopher and a cosmologist to evaluate the Mind on the ground of history. Henryk Skolimowski, however, did it beautifully, fabulously, and filling in it all the content every Mind will be interested in. He captures all rhythms, all dimensions, all quests, all creativities, all potencies, and all beauties of the Mind across ages and also sketches a state-of-the-art Project for the Mind to work upon for the future.

The historical (as well as futuristic) portrait of the Mind Henryk Skolimowski brings to the fore is a unique one offering to solve human, social and global problems and comprehend the right cosmology. Let me quote Skolimowski summarizing the Mind in history:

> Mind in history is the maker of realities. Understanding this
> Mind is understanding how cosmologies and world-views
> were formed, and how they have conditioned individual

human beings. Individual Minds serve the Minds of the epoch because they are moulded and conditioned by it. People of various epochs may entertain, with deep convictions, very strange notions. This simply demonstrates that the human Mind can articulate reality and culture of a given epoch in a great variety of ways, and sometimes odd ways. This also shows that there is no one prescribed way of articulation. The Mind is an artist. And artists are sometimes singularly odd in their creation. As Mind is evolving, it will evolve beyond the moulds of its present articulations. But we need to help Mind to evolve. Without changing the direction and structure of our present mechanistic Mind, we shall be stuck in our present predicaments. In changing the propensities of the present Mind (which is actually the Mind of a past epoch), we shall only be following the historical and evolutionary imperative.

CHAPTER 3

Understanding the Spiral of Understanding

To know that we know what we know, and that we do not know what we do not know, that is true knowledge.[1] – Confucius

1. A circular Relationship between Ontology and Epistemology

Ontology and epistemology exist in circular relationship. None of them is the first; none of them is the second. Sometimes it is ontology serving as a source for epistemology; sometimes it is the other way round. Sometimes they both exist almost independently without much commonality.

Henryk Skolimowski compares prominent philosophers and tells us which the primary inspiring source in their philosophies was: ontology or the epistemology, or vice versa. "In Plato's system ontology is primary," explains Henryk. "The Forms, as conceived by Plato, delineate the basic modes of being. The existence of these Forms necessitates certain cognitive faculties which we must possess in order to apprehend the Forms. The theory of recollection is the epistemological doctrine that follows from the ontology based on the existence of the Forms. Plato's theory of enlightenment, as stripping away the distorting influences of the body which prevent the soul from seeing, is another consequence of Plato's theory of being."

In Kant's system, however, epistemology is primary, while his ontological doctrines are secondary. "From the conception of Mind as imposing itself inexorably on the nature of reality, there follows clearly the ontological doctrine that reality (mode of being) is at the disposal of the

Mind, shaped and moulded by it," explains Henryk. "The categories of the Mind shape only the phenomenal world, the world accessible to the senses. Beyond it there lies the noumenal world, the world of 'things in themselves', independent for their existence on the working of our Minds. We do not know anything about this noumenal world." It is science or the scientific world-view that takes ontology and epistemology independent from each other. Henryk puts the truth before us:

> Although science and the scientific world-view seem to consider ontology (the structure of the real world) and epistemology (the right ways of exploring it) as independent of each other, the two are dexterously tied together, feed on each other, and *elicit from each other what they assume in each other*. They are mirror images of each other. Epistemology brings about and illumines what ontology assumes.

How various cultures understand the cosmos—this question emanates from the intricate ontology-epistemology relationship. Henryk finds the reason of slicing the universe in so many ways, epistemological as well as anthropological one. He suggests that instead of languages and non-verbal portion of knowledge we must identify the role of the Mind in making the cosmos appear to us as it does.

2. The Spiral of the Mind in the Walls of the Cosmos

"The walls of the cosmos and the spiral of the mind" is a critical and interesting part of Henryk Skolimowski's theory of the Participatory Mind. He says: *The universe is never given to us as such. The universe is always given to us with our Mind contained in it.* The universe is boundless and infinite; it has no walls, no boundaries, no limits. However, because of the limitations of our understanding, it is always limited or bound. On this premise, Skolimowski presents the boundaries of our universe as a cone opening upward.

"Only what is within the cone is the known and the knowable universe," explains Skolimowski. "The walls of the cone delineate the walls of our cosmos. They contain our understanding, the sum-total of all knowledge. Our universe must be supported by our knowledge; otherwise it would be an empty universe. The best way to conceive how knowledge fills the cone is to imagine that the cone is wired inside by a spiral. This spiral is what I call *the spiral of understanding.*"

Henryk considers using spiral of understanding as our epistemology, the accepted ways of knowing the world; or what we assume to be the case 'out there'. He states some of its consequences:

> The spiral of understanding exactly fits the walls of the cosmos. But we can look at the situation the other way around. The walls of cosmos conform exactly to the spiral of understanding. There is wonderful fit between the two of them. And this is in all cultures. This is the first conclusion. Another conclusion is that although the walls of the cosmos on the one hand, and the spiral of understanding on the other, can be analyzed out as independent entities, they are not independent of each other. They cannot exist apart from each other. They are always given together. In any cosmology, the universe or reality is given together with the knowledge and through the knowledge of this reality. Thus we can say that *the outer walls of the cosmos are the inner walls of the Mind.* This insight is of crucial importance.

Some other interest-blasting conclusions emerging from Skolimowski's theory of the Spiral of Understanding are:

- The dimensions of the universe correspond to the spiral of our understanding.

- To claim that the universe is as it is, independently of us, is to deny the vital truth that any conception of the cosmos is always given with the spiral of understanding that corresponds to this cosmos, expresses and articulates it. *The unarticulated cosmos is the universe before the day of creation.*

- From the crucial dependence of the walls of the cosmos on the spiral of understanding it follows that there is no world given to us outside the categories of understanding that the spiral of understanding delineates for us.

- *To know is to constitute the world.* To apprehend, grasp, behold, seize the world is to embrace it in the tentacles of our knowledge, in the spiral of our understanding. Beyond the tentacles of our knowledge, the world is a buzzing confusion.

- To speak of the world is to commit it to the tentacles of our knowledge, to commit it to the dimensions of our spiral of understanding. To speak of the world is to sentence it to the categories of our knowledge, to embrace it by the spiral of our understanding.

- As knowledge unfolds so the *universe enlarges* (for extremely rigid cultures and close societies the universe does not unfold itself).

- In open societies, as knowledge grows so does the spiral of understanding; so do the walls of the cosmos.

- *The universe reveals nothing to the unprepared Mind.* When the Mind is prepared, through its strange magic, it co-creates with the universe. The story of co-creation is one of the marvels of human existence and one of the mysteries of the human Mind.

3. A Picture of the Stable Universe

Nothing happens until something moves.[2] – Albert Einstein

Do we really live in a dynamic world, in ever evolving and ever changing universe? Or do we live in a permanent world and in a stable universe? It depends on the culture we belong to and nurtured by and the state of the Mind (and mentality) of a culture is determined by the state of knowledge. Virtually each culture has somewhat a permanent picture of the world and of the universe. Henryk Skolimowski, in the context of his theory of the spiral of understanding, puts it in a very interesting and meaningful way: "Every culture assumes that its universe is stable and permanent. Each culture is a guardian of the status quo – it inculcates in us the belief that we live in a permanent world, and that therefore the walls of the cosmos are permanent and static."

It is not that cultures do not change. They change. It is not that knowledge stays where it is. It grows. It is not that the universe does not enlarge. It continually enlarges. But these changes are not realized without a Mind to realize. It requires some pain to see and experience the things always changing, growing, enlarging. We can realize this happening with, as Henryk suggests, some tribulations and considerable resistance.

"Almost every system of knowledge historically known behaves as if it were final." Henryk puts this face of truth before us. When an open society or an evolving culture cultivates new insights to the continuous growth of knowledge, the old walls of the cosmos which were accommodating the earlier spiral of understanding exist no more. They further expand to further enlargement of the universe. But this is not so simple. Why? Let us know from Henryk's perspective:

> The process is usually traumatic. At first the existing walls refuse to budge. That is to say, the guardians of the status quo, who are numerous and powerful in every society, refuse to recognize the new insights. Their argument is, whether stated or unstated: 'We know what is what, and what the world is about. Nobody can tell us that there are things beyond the limits of the world. If there is such a person, he must be demented.'... Thus the rule is that whenever a radically new insight appears, it is put

down. The culture knows best. Its guardians, with due righteousness and support of the culture, act swiftly and unequivocally in holding back potential geniuses, madmen and trouble-makers. The manner of the guardians may be subtle or crude: crude in authoritarian regimes, subtle but nevertheless effective in democratic societies.

Boundaries of the cosmos of a given society are defended as a holy ritual also; for a good reason too, as Henryk says: To *question the boundaries of the cosmos of a given culture is to question the identity of the people of that culture. Let us remember that human identity is formed by and anchored in the underlying cosmology.* Henryk Skolimowski presents such a scenario in front of our eyes which we have never seen, not will ever see:

In the mental climate, some individuals with wonderful new insights are intimidated at the outset, and their insights are never revealed to the world. We shall never know what wealth of knowledge we have lost in the process. Other individuals, more stubborn and tenacious, refuse to give up. The establishment is invariably hard on people with 'mad ideas'. The lives of gifted and original individuals have been wasted as a result of the establishment's relentless attacks on new insights which are called heresies. Innovative thinkers have ended their lives seized by madness, or have died prematurely. We shall never know how many geniuses have rotted to their death in lunatic asylums because their ideas were derided and destroyed. This is a dark and unwritten chapter in the history of human knowledge.

However, some people, despite all the odds they face, leave their everlasting impact. Henryk implants hope amidst dismal scenario. "Yet some people with new insights persist," he says. "They evade all the traps laid for them by the guardians of the status quo. Through their persistence and luck they hammer out their messages until, gradually, they begin to be heard by reluctant ears. It is acknowledged that new ideas are not mad, after all, and may even be right. The new knowledge contained in them indicates that the boundaries of the cosmos must be expanded, the walls of the cosmos must be changed, usually enlarged, to fit the enlarged spiral of understanding… The astonishing thing is that after such an operation is completed, *the guardians of the status quo behave as if nothing has happened*, as if the walls of the cosmos were as permanent as a rock, and established forever… Another astonishing thing is that *the process of enlarging the spiral of understanding is going on all the time."*

Thus, glancing through the historical perspective, we find that *ontology is always conservative; epistemology is always revolutionary,* Henryk concludes. Some very stimulating notions Henryk coins for us in this regard are: *In the long run evolution spells out continuous revolution.* In order to be alive we must unfold. The imperative of life is to unfold, to change, to transcend.

4. Understanding the Peculiarity of the Process of Understanding

If you can't explain it simply, you don't understand it well enough.[3] – Albert Einstein

Knowledge and understanding go hand in hand. In Skolimowski's words, the more knowledge we possess the better for our understanding. However, beyond a certain limit this relationship is proportional. "For understanding is an elusive entity and it has laws of its own which defy the crude process of just amassing knowledge," clarifies Skolimowski.

Henryk says that the process of understanding is dialectical, leading from the simple to the complex and then back to the simple. He narrates in an interesting manner the astonishing things that begin to happen:

- After we have amassed a lot of knowledge of a given phenomenon or a given branch of knowledge, we are less certain about our understanding. We are confronted with some puzzling, unexplained phenomena that do not fit... They are the result of our relentless acquisition of knowledge. It is at this level that a curious dialectic occurs.

- After we have accumulated considerable amount of knowledge, our picture – of whatever we investigate – grows more and more complex. More and more things bother us. What we gradually obtain is not growing clarity but growing obfuscation.

- The more relentless we are in amassing relevant information on a subject, the more surely shall we come to a juncture at which our picture becomes so complex that we are simply lost in it. Understanding we receive no more. Our Mind is too perplexed and bewildered, and it cries for help. But it cannot receive any help but from itself.

- At the points of unimaginable complexity and obfuscation, the Mind decides on radical surgery: it cuts across the bewildering complexity and establishes new patterns of simplicity.

- From the point of establishing the pattern of simplicity a new journey begins... until the complexity again grows to the point that it is unimaginable.

Henryk gives two convincing examples to further explain his view points: one of a cell, and one of an atom: The cell is simple when we consider it as a building block of an organ (or of a body). If we look into the cell itself, it is amazingly complex; it mirrors the whole universe. The atoms are simple when regarded as building blocks of molecular structures. But when we look into the structures of the atom itself, it is again amazingly complex. And the more we know about it, the more complex it becomes.

Elaborating upon the peculiarity of the process of understanding, Henryk Skolimowski elucidates interesting inferences:

- *To comprehend is to simplify.*
- Things do not become either simple or complex – whether they are atoms, cells or galaxies – by themselves. *It is our knowledge that makes them so. It is our Mind that makes them so.*

-   When we unfold the universe we invariably unfold the Mind. If we allow our creative wings to open up, we can bring about new dimensions to the universe and to ourselves.
-   Simplification is the *modus operandi* of the human Mind. Expressed in other terms: *simplicity is the methodology of the Mind.*

Skolimowski also brings to the fore three paradoxes of knowledge. These are:

(1) It is incomprehensible that we comprehend anything; how we comprehend is a big mystery.
(2) The more deeply we explore any subject-matter the more surely we are going to arrive at unexplained phenomena which challenge the entire framework of our quest for knowledge.
(3) The pursuit of knowledge is the pursuit from comprehension to incomprehension. We always start with something we know fairly well and end up with big puzzles.

Summary

Henryk Skolimowski's theory of the Spiral of Understanding is outstanding in understanding the knowledge-universe relationships. Ontology and epistemology exist in a circular relationship. Some philosophers have the ontology as primary and some epistemology as primary source in their systems. Science and scientific world-view consider ontology and epistemology independent of each other, but, in fact, they are not and ingeniously feed on each other. As understanding of a society or a culture enhances, the old walls of the cosmos are further stretched. Expansion and revelations of the cosmos are directly proportional to the capacities of the Mind.

Each culture is a guardian of the status quo, always resisting new ideas, knowledge and understanding and, thus, further expansion of their universe. Many genius Minds have been prematurely destroyed by the guardians of these cultures but some Minds sparkling with new ideas and philosophies survived and became a vehicle to trigger desirable understanding leading to enhance the limits of the unlimited universe. The process of understanding is very peculiar in itself. Mind attempts to simplify the things and processes to comprehend the universe. In other words, simplification is the *modus operandi* of the human Mind. Henryk Skolimowski summarizes his theory of the Spiral of Understanding as under:

> The outer walls of the cosmos are the inner walls of the Mind. The dimensions of the universe correspond to the spiral of our understanding. To speak of the world is to sentence it to the categories of our understanding, to embrace it by the spiral of understanding.
>
> The recognition of the creative nature of man necessitates the universe that is open and mysterious. The mystery of the universe and man's essential creativity can be now seen as parts of the fundamental structure of the universe. Unless the universe is open and undetermined, we cannot hope for new articulations, new knowledge, the growth of the spiral of understanding. But since the spiral of understanding has grown, we can safely deduce that the universe is open and undetermined.
>
> Simplicity and complexity are attributes of human Mind and not of objective reality; and so are all cognitive orders we find in the universe. The spiral of understanding is the key to the comprehension of our knowledge and to the metamorphosis of reality through our knowledge, as well as the key to understanding the mystery and beauty of individual human existence. Cultivate the right spiral and you will dwell in the right universe and will embrace the right mode of life.
>
> 'What is impenetrable to us really exists manifesting itself as the highest wisdom' (Albert Einstein). The human

agent is one part of the triangle of which the other two parts are the participatory Mind and the participatory universe. The presence of the participatory Mind immediately implies the existence of the human agent, which is essentially creative, and vice versa. Our creativity is inherent in the structure of the participatory universe.

CHAPTER 4

Complexity and Beauty of the Teilhard's Story

The universe as we know it is a product of the observer and observed.[1]
– Pierre Teilhard de Chardin

1. Teilhard's Rich Legacy

Pierre Teilhard de Chardin (1881 – 1955) distinguished himself from his contemporaries. He did not allow his philosophy to be infested by the philosophy of his times. "His protean Mind shone in an age dominated by tedious atomization," says Henryk Skolimowski about Teilhard. "He had the power of exquisite synthesis in an age of shrunken vision. We have all learned from Teilhard the courage to be comprehensive and visionary, the capacity to weave together large cosmic tapestries, the wisdom of including science and religion into our ultimate designs."

A distinctive characteristic of the human being, as Henryk identifies, is of the being, essentially a holistic being, who lives in integrated totalities. "When the human being is forced to lead a fragmented life, he/ she shrinks, is frustrated, diminished and dwarfed," says Henryk. Teilhard's philosophy attempted restoration of the right values. "Teilhard's synthesis restored for us the right evolutionary context in which we acknowledge ourselves to be physically small but spiritually significant," Henryk continues. "Above all, it restored our confidence to live integrally and wholly in an age in which even atoms are split and disintegrate into a myriad of sub-elements whose variety bewilders our comprehension." Teilhard's philosophical attributes are delighting. Let us know from Henryk Skolimowski:

> Perhaps Teilhard's greatest achievement is his compelling reconstruction of the story of evolution. In Teilhard's rendering, evolution is an epic of unsurpassed grandeur and glory. While following this epic one is humbled and at the same time elevated by it... Teilhard's genius lay partly in capacity to weave one huge homogeneous tapestry in which the prehistory of life, life and the phenomenon of man are parts of one unbroken stupendous flow – all unified by the ascent of evolution. Evolution is not only unifying. It is also creative... Teilhard introduced the idea of *noosphere*, the sphere of the Mind or the sphere of thought, as a natural envelope of life at large. He also showed that all life has been groping to articulate itself in the shape of the noosphere. By broadening the conception of evolution, Teilhard also broadened our vision of ourselves in it. This led to the idea that *we are evolution conscious of itself.*

We are not just ordinary creatures. "Our deepest intuition informs us that we are a form of life that incorporates all previous forms of life," Henryk explores deepest layers of human life's secretes. "We resonate with other forms of life. We emphasize with earlier forms of life because we have incorporated them into our structures. We are aware of the genius of life because we feel it in our bones, blood and flesh; in our deepest intuitions."

Comparing with the neo-Darwinian rendering of evolution, Henryk infers that Teilhard's rendering of evolution is much closer to the truth. No discussion on evolution can be complete without Teilhard's deep insights into creative nature of it. Henryk's own discourses on evolution unfold the truth in true sense of the word. Arguing Teilhard's rendering of evolution, Henryk adds: "By its inner imperative, the origin of which we do not know, evolution has consistently been trying to make something first of matter, then of life, then of the intelligence it has created. For we live in an intelligent universe."

Questioning neo-Darwinism, Henryk writes, "Neo-Darwinism can be justly called a theory of evolution if and when it explains satisfactorily the phenomenon of man, the phenomenon of culture, the phenomenon of religion, the phenomenon of spirituality, the phenomenon of matter becoming spirit – without explaining these phenomena away; otherwise it is only a limited theory of mutation within *some* evolutionary cycles."

In the post-Teilhard era, Skolimowskian Philosophy has assimilated all dimensions and all expansions and creativities of the evolution and, without a dispute, this philosophy is all vibrant with evolution, and is genuinely the richest source of knowledge on evolution. As evolution itself is an epic of the universe, the Skolimowskian Philosophy is an epic of the evolution itself.

2. What is this Gradualism?

Henryk Skolimowski questions: What about the gradualist-punctualist controversy? Has evolution been proceeding smoothly by small imperceptible tiny steps? Or has its development been marked by discontinuities and leaps?

Henryk has explored deepest possible aspects of evolution. Not only explored, the evolution itself seems to be reverberating in his heart. So, he tries to clarify everything the evolution has been dealt with by different workers, including biologists, physicists and philosophers.

In the context of the gradualism, Skolimowski says that since every event that occurs in evolution takes such a long time, each can be considered gradualist in nature. "The argument is logically right," he goes on. "But it is a barren argument, and a question-begging one: gradualism assumes from the start that everything that happens in evolution happens by small, imperceptible, incremental steps."

Henryk denounces gradualism or punctualism modes of evolution: "Who cares whether the main modus of evolution is gradualism or punctualism as long as it delivers its wondrous works?" He notices that gradualism vs punctualism is not a scientific but epistemological problem. "Neo-Darwinism cannot claim that it has established scientific basis," argues Henryk. "For gradualism as an idea is outside science; it is an epistemological category as it pertains to the order of knowledge." Henryk again questions: How should we look at those changes in evolution which represent the process of *transcendence*, at the end of which some new quality, some new sensitivity, some new form of life is created. He answers himself: These are the non-trivial changes through which the miracle of life is manifested.

Two Nobel Laureates, Albert Szent-Gyorgyi and Ilya Prigogine, were also unimpressed by the gradualist theory of evolution. Discussing their views, Henryk concludes:

> Teilhard, Szent-Gyorgyi and Prigogine may still be in a numerical minority in our age dominated by the metaphysics of Newtonian science. But the tradition they represent is ancient and noble. This is the tradition of Heraclitus, the tradition of *becoming*, the tradition which was pushed to the margin by Plato's metaphysics of being, but one which was never eliminated from Western thought. This is incidentally the tradition of the Dancing Shiva – of the cosmos conceived in a perpetual state of *significant* change... Discontinuous changes are in the nature of the evolving universe. Take the beginning of the universe and the Big Bang itself. This was not a gradualist change! I hope we all agree that at the outset of our universe there was a monstrous convulsive change. The universe started with a magnificent explosion, not through small tinkering changes.

"Deep down in their souls the neo-Darwinians think that gradualism is more scientific than punctualism because it bars the divine intervention from the realm of evolution and the universe at large," Henryk exposes the reality. "So at bottom the debate is ideological and religious rather than scientific."

Henryk, through yet another example, cites an interesting story: "When Darwin published *The Origin of Species*, Karl Marx hailed it as an extension of the materialist view of the world. In his enthusiasm for Darwin, Marx wanted to dedicate *Das Kapital* to him. Darwin politely declined. But there was no question in the Minds of materialists and atheists that Darwinism was the water on their mill."

Evolution is evolution. Evolution is writing story of all there is in the universe. Evolution is writing script of the future of the universe. Evolution is not at the whims of Darwin and Marx. Evolution, as Skolimowski says, is both *natural and divine.* Let us appreciate, enjoy and sing the extraordinary complexity, rhythm, beauty, divinity, and mystery of evolution.

3. Simplicity and Comprehension

We are not human beings having a spiritual experience. We are spiritual beings having a human experience.[2] – Pierre Teilhard de Chardin

Henryk Skolimowski says that the specific focus of Teilhard's theory of evolution and one of the most original insights in his thesis is his idea of complexity/ consciousness. He adds: As evolution unfolds the complexity of organisms grows. As complexity increases so also *consciousness increases.*

"The more complex the system, the more performance it is capable of, and therefore the more potential it contains," Henryk fabulously elucidates. "Thus *complexity emerges as the crucial concept of evolution* – the hidden spring that guides the process of growth; as well as the overall concept that enables us to understand the unfolding of evolution." Relating this to the Teilhard's story of evolution, Henryk reveals that Teilhard's thesis is the metamorphosis from the simple to the more complex, and the more complex still… that this story is beautiful and compelling, but it is essentially incomplete. How?

"Teilhard's reconstruction assumes that there is only one process: that of building up ontological complexity, the complexity of the world out there," Henryk further makes it clear. "Only the ontological dimension is present in Teilhard's idea of complexity. The epistemological dimension (how the Mind receives and comprehends this complexity) is missing."

Henryk Skolimowski fills the void left by Teilhard. His epistemological dimension with human Mind's role in unfolding the complexities and ecstasies of evolution is astonishing. In the Skolimowskian Philosophy evolution stunningly unfolds itself. Whether Mind is in evolution or evolution in Mind, it becomes challenging to distinguish in Skolimowski's theory. Some instances:

> ...whatever complexity we attribute to 'the real world', it is complexity as received and conceived by our Mind. Complexity is an attribute of our understanding. What is complex and what is simple is a very intricate question. *Nothing is complex by itself but only through the intervention of our Mind...* If the story of evolution were an uninterrupted growth of complexity in the ontological sense, sooner or later this complexity would grow to such a degree that it would be beyond the comprehension of Mind, and the world would appear to us as utter chaos... Yet this does not happen. We have the capacity to command immense complexities through simple patterns of our understanding. Why? Because the Mind imposes its epistemological order on those otherwise unruly complexities. The Mind intervenes and subdues these complexities to the imperatives of its understanding... Now the Mind is not a set of patterns imposed from the outside on the sea of complexities. The sea and the sailor are one. Whatever complexities or simplicities we perceive out there, the order of the Mind is built into them.

Skolimowski in his theory of the Participatory Mind beautifully completes the incompleteness of the Teilhard's story of evolution. Without the essential epistemological dimension in Teilhard's theory, the evolution appears to be lame. Skolimowski gives this evolution a Mind, which happens to be our own Mind. With an ecstatic, vibrant and creative Mind, the Skolimowskian theory of evolution assumes a vital and significant order in constant cosmic creativity.

"The ontological complexity is not independent of Mind," explains Henryk. "In actuality we witness two parallel orders: the ontological order (the order of reality) and the epistemological order (the order of the Mind). Complexity on the ontological level and simplicity on the level of our understanding (on the level of Mind) are inseparable companions. We always simplify, in order to understand. Understanding *is* simplifying. Human knowledge represents the patterns of simplicity through which the extraordinary richness of the universe is digested by the human Mind."

Our Mind tends to comprehend at the level of larger patterns. It does not like to conceive reality in bits. These large patterns, as Skolimowski tells us, are cultures, systems of philosophy, systems of beliefs, or the architecture of the individual Mind. Through these patterns reality is rendered in specific ways. Skolimowski calls this rendering as *realitying*: transforming reality while comprehending it.

Skolimowski brings to our knowledge various glimpses which are created with respect to the walls of the cosmos and spiral of understanding. Our Mind satiates with the knowledge the Skolimowskian Philosophy of the Participatory Minds pours into, and is further filled up with renewed energy, enthusiasm and inquisitiveness:

❖ When a radically new insight appears, then the walls of the cosmos are ruffled… In some periods of history the new insights are so numerous and so profound in their implications that the entire walls of the cosmos tremble, sometimes they fall down; the paradigm is shattered. At such periods a civilization or a culture collapses and has to be reconstructed.

❖ The spiral of understanding is continually changing. Most of the time it is changing gradually – by accommodating new insights into its existing structure. Sometimes it changes fundamentally, and at such times a new vision of the cosmos emerges. Simultaneously, new ways of looking at it and thinking about it manifest themselves.

❖ In Western industrial civilization at least a partial collapse of its spiral of understanding can be witnessed – some would contend a total collapse – and the corresponding collapse of the walls of its collapse.

The following suggestions elicited from Skolimowski's discussion on the Teilhard's thesis of simplicity and comprehension are of vital implications for reconstructing new realities for reconstructing new patterns of understanding and for further expanding our cosmos to its infinity, and for our own reconstruction and for the reconstruction of the whole:

❖ We are at a seminal juncture of history at which we attempt to create a new reality. We strive to construct a new spiral of understanding for the whole culture so that our *reality*-making can become compassionate, gentle, cooperative, creative and based on the ideals of solidarity with all living creatures.

❖ Our reality is at the mercy of our Mind. Our Mind is directed and guided by our will and our higher aspirations. Mind in the universe of becoming simply means that we must transcend whatever station we have attained, whatever goal we have reached, whatever spiritual level we have elevated ourselves to. Only then do we do justice to our evolutionary potential, to our cosmic potential, to our divine potential.

❖ We are guided and conditioned by our respective spirals of understanding which grow and evolve. And conversely, when our spiral of understanding grows and evolves, we grow and evolve.

❖ The spiral of individual understanding should not be limited to our intellectual capacities, nor to our abstract knowledge. This spiral includes all the sensitivities we incorporate into the structure of our being, all our spiritual heritage. The spiral is the essence of our being.

❖ Our individual spiral is sometimes inspired by wonderful new insights. However, sometimes we are weary of new insights for the more radical and beautiful the insight, the deeper inner reconstruction it requires. These reconstructions may be joyous – when we are ascending to new spiritual heights.

❖ Our entire life needs to be reconstructed, which is never easy, sometimes impossible (nevertheless full of possibilities).

Summary

The most outstanding aspect of the Skolimowskian Philosophy is that it reverberates with evolution. Evolution expresses itself in its completeness in this philosophy. It seems that Henryk Skolimowski writes with his finger on the pulse of the evolution. Evolution pulsates with all its rhythms in his philosophy. As if the evolution in its cosmic journey passes through Henryk's Mind! As if Henryk's philosophy is written in conciliation with the cosmic evolution! This is the beauty, grandeur and power of the Skolimowskian Philosophy.

Many philosophers have let evolution bypass their philosophy, including even the distinctive philosopher like Pierre Teilhard de Chardin. Spelling out the rich legacy of Teilhard, Henryk Skolimowski attempts to complete the Teilhard's theory of evolution, which suffers from the lacuna of incompleteness. Henryk dismisses the concept of gradualism in the theories of evolution which neo-Darwinism adopts and which the scientific world-view upholds. He presents the thesis of simplicity and comprehension elaborating how the Mind can comprehend all cosmic complexities. Let us glance though the summary of Teilhard's Story of Complexity – its Beauty and its Essential Incompleteness as written by Henryk Skolimowski himself:

> With the emergence of the self-conscious Mind, which creates knowledge as the vehicle of its understanding, the story of complexity/ consciousness is punctuated by the stages of simplicity/ comprehension. The thesis of simplicity/ comprehension is the missing dimension of Teilhard's story of complexity. The human Mind cannot cope with too many complexities, especially with infinite complexity. If the cosmos is infinitely complex, and there is no reason to assume that it isn't, the Mind does not have the capacity to deal with that complexity. Thus it must simplify – in order to comprehend. Understanding is simplifying.
>
> Every act of understanding is an act of simplification. Specific systems of knowledge are specific patterns of simplification – according to the prevailing views of a given culture and in congruence with the level of articulation a given culture has attained.
>
> All knowledge is species-specific. All knowledge is culture-bound. It was a mistake, and a great presumption, on the part of science to assume that it represents universal knowledge for all cultures and for all times.
>
> In actual encounter with the cosmos, we are not just its passive observers. The cosmos is continually transforming itself, and so are we. The power of the creative Mind signifies the act of logos imposing itself on the cosmos, and the combination of the two results in what we call human knowledge of the world. The role of logos in controlling unruly cosmos is of significance second to none. Without logos, cosmos would be of incoherent mass of confusion – if it existed at all. 'No Mind, no world' (Parmenides).

Mind in the universe of becoming means that we must transcend whatever level we have attained. Only then do we do justice to our evolutionary potential, to our cosmic potential, to our divine potential.

Our deepest intuition informs us that we are a form of life that incorporates all previous forms of life. This intuition informs us that Teilhard's rendering of evolution is much closer to the truth than the neo-Darwinian of evolution which can only conceive of its magnificent panorama through the stupid metaphor of the blind watchmaker.

Gradualism as a theory of evolution may be more an expression of an ideological (or even a theological) position than a scientific one. Gradualism is an ingenious way of using evolution to safeguard the old-fashioned mechanistic-secular-aesthetic world-view. To pit science against religion at the present time is deeply to misunderstand the essence of both science and religion.

CHAPTER 5

The Western Mind and its Four Great Cycles

In many other countries of the world, reflection on the nature of existence is a luxury of life. The serious moments are given to action, while the pursuit of philosophy comes up as a parenthesis. In the West, even the heyday of its youth, as in the times of Plato and Aristotle, it learned for support on some other study as politics or ethics... In India, philosophy stood on its own legs, and all other studies looked to it for inspiration and support.[1] – S. Radhakrishnan

1. A Recap of the Story Thus Far

The theory of the participatory Mind Henryk Skolimowski has developed thus far has five distinctive but interconnected components, namely:

(1) The theory of sensitivities

(2) The theory of the three Minds

(3) Noetic Monism

(4) The theory of the spiral of understanding as filling the walls of the cosmos, and

(5) The thesis of simplicity and comprehension

(1) The Theory of Sensitivities

Reality is not something like a static picture hanging in front of our eyes. Reality is a dynamic phenomenon of our Mind. It is such a powerful phenomenon of the Mind that it contributes to reshape the things, reshape the society and the world we live in and reshape the image of our cosmos. Sensitivities play powerful role in receiving and creating reality. The striking elements of Skolimowski's theory of sensitivities are as follows:

- All creation is articulation.
- The shape of the world is acquired through a distinctive articulation.
- Sensitivities acquire the status of epistemological entities.
- The fluidity of sensitivities is a fact of life.
- Sensitivities prestructure our perception and reception of reality.
- Whatever our sensitivities elicit is processed through language and through accepted categories of knowledge.
- Each system of knowledge is only a specific form of articulation.
- All sensitivities are forms of cognition.
- Articulation and sensitivities are key concepts of epistemology of becoming and of the participatory Mind.
- As evolution evolves, it moves on the spiral of articulation via the vehicle called 'sensitivities'.

Thus, Skolimowski's theory of sensitivities prepares a fertile ground for the growth and evolution of the participatory Mind.

(2) The Theory of the Three Minds

Human Mind is one. Nevertheless it can be categorized into three forms based on the sensitivities it is exposed to and it accumulates. Henryk Skolimowski's conception of the Mind – which is a participatory Mind, not the ordinary Mind – is unique. He discovers three Minds: Mind I, Mind II and Mind III.

In the theory of the three Minds, Skolimowski defines the Minds as follows: Mind I and Mind II are in a continuous dialogue with each other; they are one continuous Mind. The combined Mind I and Mind II dialogue with Mind III. The result of this dialogue is *reality-making* – receiving reality as a continuous process of transformation.

In this way Henryk connects the concept of sensitivities with reality via the three Minds. "The three Minds' structure is one that elucidates the meaning of sensitivities and the meaning of reality," Henryk opines. "Thus presented the three Minds appear to be a structure in between the sensitivities and reality – the bridge connecting the two (logos). Conceptually we can *think* of the three Minds in this way. In reality all is connected."

(3) Noetic Monism

The theories of sensitivities and of the three minds, combined together, result into Noetic Monism. What a beautiful Skolimowskian synthesis! Our eyes can see but they are always programmed; they see what they are programmed to see. Our vision is always 'contaminated'. The retina of our eyes is wired with all kinds of theories.

Skolimowski goes on spelling through his magical words the ecstasies of Noetic Monism, or New *Advaita*. An excerpt from his discourse in *The Participatory Mind*:

> Noetic Monism states in ontological terms what the theories of sensitivities and of the three Minds assert in epistemological terms. There is one unitary reality. Bodies exist and ideas (spirit) exist. But their respective existences take different forms. What unifies these different forms is the evolutionary matrix: the different stages of evolutionary becoming are responsible for different forms of existence... What finally makes an existence, and all existence, comprehensible is Mind – *nous*. All existence is formed by the Mind and through the Mind. Mind gives its imprimatur to all existence. What exists is only that which is comprehensible to the Mind, that is, prestructured by

the Mind. *Pure existence is a meaningless term.* 'Being that encompasses all' is beyond words. Whenever we decide to utter the term 'being' or 'Being', in whatever form, we have resigned ourselves to the recognition of Mind as shaper and maker of being. Mind shapes all. Mind unites all. *Noetic Monism is the recognition of the quintessentially Noetic nature of all knowledge and of all reality.*

(4) The Spiral of Understanding

Reality manifests itself in a variety of ways. Different cultures, organizations and cosmologies receive and project reality in different ways. Henryk explains this reality through his theory of the spiral of understanding. "The spiral of understanding is a specific articulation of a given cosmos," he makes it explicit. "The spiral is not objective in the strict scientific of positivistic sense. It is culture-specific. Within a culture it is intersubjective... The participatory universe is trans-subjective. But it is not objective, let alone absolute. All acts of participation are culture-bound and species-specific."

Both the spirals of understanding and that of the culture, according to Skolimowski, are historical entities, not whimsical ones. He fabulously explains the spiral of culture: "The spiral of culture is inculcated into us. For this reason, within a given culture, we receive reality intersubjectively (we process reality in a very similar way). We are *realitying* in a very similar way. Yet the species changes. And cultures change. Evolution goes on. The spirals of understanding undergo change. Thus the rendering of reality and the shapes of reality change."

(5) The Thesis of Simplicity/ Comprehension

Skolimowski's thesis of simplicity/ comprehension simply reasserts that there are parallel orders running together: complexity/ simplicity, cosmos/ comprehension, ontology/ epistemology, reality/ Mind.

"The mystery of the Mind is the mastery of the Mind in riding on the crests of extraordinary complexities, the mastery of the Mind in simplifying and yet not losing depth, the mastery of the Mind in moving across various levels of recalcitrant reality without losing the Ariadne's thread of human meaning," enlightens Skolimowski on his theory.

Based on the above five components Skolimowski has developed a new model of the universe, which is a systematic evolutionary model; and a transformative-systematic-evolutionary model; and a transformative-transcendence-systematic-evolutionary model. "The participatory Mind is model of the universe," envisions Skolimowski. "It not only offers a new conception of the cosmos and of the human person in it. It also redefines the meaning of life and the meaning of cultures; and the meaning of history and the meaning of the future."

2. From Homer to Plato

ION: A great difference there, Socrates! It is much finer to be considered divine!
SOCRATES: Then that finer thing is yours, Ion, in our belief; you are divine, and not an artist, when you eulogize Homer.[2] – Great Dialogues of Plato

Skolimowski's spiral of understanding is all-pervading. A culture tends to be in the state of transition, and spiral of understanding works in tune with this cultural transition. Skolimowski traces the ancestry of the Western culture back to the Greek Mind. The Greeks formed our logos, says Skolimowski, and we in turn have perpetuated their cosmos, with some notable departures, of course. He aptly suggests reconstructing the enthralling story of the emergence of Western Mind and its consecutive manifestations; which is also the story of the spiral of understanding of Western civilization at large.

"The translucent Greek Mind did not spring forth as a *deus ex machina*," Skolimowski argues. "It is a continuation of the Homeric tradition. Though a continuation, it is also a radical departure, and what a wonderful departure it is!"

Skolimowski stupendously attempts to answer pertinent questions which he himself raises by using the model of the participatory Mind, and in particular, by analysing the change in the spiral of understanding of the various cultures: How did this transformation of the Homeric culture into the Socratic culture occur? How do transformations occur from one culture to another? How does a new cosmology emerge? Is there a rational way of studying the vicissitudes of the ever-changing cosmologies?

On the basis of the main thesis Skolimowski surmises that *as the logos of a given culture changes so does its cosmos.* He deems new organizing logos as the new spiral of understanding the reality of any people is woven around. "The spiral provides the foundation, the matrix that defines the reality for us, determines what phenomena are there and how we should perceive them; and also how we should justify them rationally," Skolimowski maintains adding that the ways looking at reality and of justifying it constitute what we call the rationality of a given cosmology. He discovers that there are probably as many different rationalities as there are different cosmologies. He lays two important aspects of the situation: What we perceive is part and parcel of what we assume to be there; and every culture develops ways of perceiving phenomena which are invisible to the naked eye.

Henryk's account of the events is so exciting, so touching and so digestible! Let us discover some landmark values out of his description of the following sequences of events:

> ➤ The ancient Greeks of the Homeric period saw in the stories of their lives the visible presence of gods, intervening into their lives from Mount Olympus. The great Greek tragedies and Greek heroes' exposure to the inexplicable blows of an outrageous fortune are seen as a result of negative karma, which came back to haunt people whose ancestors transgressed in a fundamental way. Rationality of the Homeric heroes was distinctively shaped by their cosmology.

> ➤ The Greeks recognized the fact that we can be masters of our own destiny only up to a point. Beyond this point the world is inscrutable and our lives mysterious. To account for this inscrutable and mysterious human condition, the Greeks invented the intervention of gods – which was a rational act. The gods were responsible for what was otherwise inexplicable and incomprehensible.

> ➤ There was another scheme at work behind the interventions of gods. This scheme was related to the law of karma. The Greeks recognized that as you sow, so shall you reap. We gather the fruits of our early doings, even if these occurred in a previous incarnation.

> ➤ The underlying form of reasoning of the Homeric people was one based on myths. We shall call this form of reasoning *Mythos*. For a number of centuries the form of rationale based on mythos – and its corresponding cosmology – worked well. Then at the transition from the sixth to the fifth century BC something happened: the Greek *logos* were born. A new luminous light started to be shed from the human Mind. New dimensions of reason were discovered. New lucidity was acquired.

In the transition from mythos to logos, says Henryk, we witness the emergence of a radically new form of understanding. As a consequence, he deduces, extraordinary flowering in art, philosophy, and science, and in social and political institutions.

"These new forms of logos exploded on the scene of human history like a supernova," Henryk maintains. "Never in the history of human Mind has the transition from one form of reason to another been more significant and far-reaching. Never before and never since has human thought been capable of exploding with achievements of such staggering dimensions and lasting beauty."

Furthering his conclusions, Henryk states that as a result of this transition from mythos to logos, a new sense of reality was created: The lucid logos of Greeks, of the classical era, created a new cosmology within which things were explained by the natural powers of reason, and without the intervention of gods from Olympus. Henryk maintains:

> At a certain point, the Greeks assumed that the whole world around them was pervaded with *nous*, a coherent and harmonious order of the universe… Logos meant both: understanding the rational structure of nous and acting it out in life through creating ever-new forms expressing the underlying harmony… A new spiral of understanding created new walls of cosmos. The two, logos and cosmos, go hand in hand, co-define each other… The lucid logos of classical Greece produced memorable and lasting achievements. It was the light shining through everything the Greek Mind touched. Yet around the fifth century AD we witness the exhaustion of the Greek-Roman cycle. The whole civilization collapsed – and with it the Greek form of reason and its distinctive cosmology.

3. From the Roman Empire Fall to the Chartres Cathedral Build-ups

Out of the ruins of the Roman Empire a new civilization arose. Henryk continues the story of the second great cycle of the Western Mind. The new logos required about four centuries to consolidate itself, he tell us. It did so in small monasteries scattered throughout Western Europe, the bearers of new light, of the new purpose and determination. Henryk makes special mention of the monasteries in Ireland, particularly as far as the ninth and tenth centuries are concerned: When most of Western Europe was still steeped in darkness, Ireland was already beginning to shine. The Irish

Renaissance is still inadequately appreciated for its role in revival of Western Europe culture.

"From the eleventh century the light was spreading across Western Europe," Henryk continues his story of the second great cycle of the Western Mind. "The haunting sense of doom that was to come with the expectation of the second coming of Christ in the year 1000 released in people an extraordinary amount of energy which has been following ever since. The new form of reason, which emerged out of the ruins of Graeco-Roman logos, I shall call *Theos* – the reason inspired and guided by the monotheistic Judaeo-Christian God."

The cosmology that is woven around it, Henryk tells us, emphasizes the transient nature of physical reality and of earthly existence. He observes that the medieval troubadours were the heralds of individuality, but this individuality was very timid. For, as Henryk makes it clear, it never tried to change or challenge the existing order; it expressed the longings of the heart, not the yearnings for freedom of the Mind and soul.

This great cycle of the Western Mind had several crucial attributes and implications. Henryk Skolimowski artistically digs them out:

> Under the inspiration of the medieval world-view, with God constantly viewing the vicissitudes of the human lot, great new achievements are accomplished. God-inspired energy drives people onward and upward: from the Gregorian chant to Chartres Cathedral, from the poetry of the medieval troubadours to the subtlety of scholastic arguments of the fourteenth-century philosophers, we witness the flowing of a new form of logos, medieval Theos... To consider the Mind of medieval man is to realize at once what a colossal change has occurred within the spiral of understanding... We witness a different reality, a different conception of man, a different idea of knowledge... Medieval man did not consider his way of approaching the world to be irrational.

On the contrary, he thought of himself as a pre-eminently rational being... His world had an exuberance and variety that we often forget. Medieval communities managed to build magnificent cathedrals. Medieval cities and towns competed to build the most magnificent cathedral, and each was a project mobilizing the entire community. It was a celestial competition. To erect a new house of God, and to adorn it with lavish art, the best that was available at that time, were the highest aspirations. People considered themselves the children of God... All was woven into a tight hierarchical structure with God at the top, the church and the bishops on the ladder, and lowly peasants at the bottom of it. But it was a celestial ladder... The medieval world was completely coherent and it responded to every need of man on every level of human existence. It was almost inconceivable for medieval man to think that things could be otherwise. *This psychological comfort, of knowing that things were right in heaven and on earth, was a great solace to medieval man.*

However, phenomenal growth of the power of church led to disintegration of the centre. The Roman Catholic Church emerged into an empire. With the accumulation of more and more power, the Church became more and more corrupt and the Western Mind found itself in a sort of messy situation.

"Every culture is entitled to be judged by its greatest accomplishments," says Henryk judging the medieval culture in toto with Chartres Cathedral as a great achievement not only with reference to medieval culture, but to all human cultures. "It contains a symbolic summation of all that medieval man stood for, longed for and aspired to; it displays the medieval logos superbly articulated. The cathedral is the vertical expression of the mystical longings of medieval man: its outside shapes reach upward to heaven to embrace God, while its exquisite internal geometry leads us back to the Pythagorean mysteries of Forms which cannot be fully comprehended by the rational Mind."

4. The Renaissance

The Renaissance has been one of the most significant movements in the history of the West. "The Renaissance is an intriguing and fascinating period in the history of the West, one of an extraordinary outburst and exuberance, a period of liberation which was, however, incomplete – it did not lead to a new path, a new civilization," argues Henryk Skolimowski. "For all its novelty, courage and exuberance, the Renaissance was an ephemeral flower."

The Renaissance did not create a new blue print, a new logos around which a new cosmos could be woven, a new civilization developed, Skolimowski says, adding that it did what it meant to do – it opened up new vistas on the physical world, and on the nature of man. He finds that the Renaissance was a profound awakening. Let us learn significant attributes of the Renaissance from Skolimowski himself:

> It was, first, the awakening of senses. With Giotto we begin to *see* the world differently. Painters, and then ordinary people, rediscovered the lushness, beauty and exuberance of nature. Giotto was a revolutionary... After Giotto came Botticeli and Leonardo da Vinci. The period of the rediscovery of nature was intoxicating indeed. In an almost somnambulistic trance, Renaissance artists rendered nature in such compelling forms that these forms delight us five centuries later... Clearly, a new spiral of understanding is guiding the new perception. This new spiral is no longer God-centred, Theo-dominated. It is a man-centred spiral; often sense-centred, but not in a narrow, hedonistic way. The senses are the windows on the glory of nature and the

world at large. Thus Leonardo da Vinci on 'learning from the objects of nature'... Leonardo and other Renaissance painters did not *just* discover nature and render it as it was. They *impregnated* nature with their dreams and visions. They brought sanctity to nature... The Renaissance was a period of transition, belonging to three different periods... The *ethos* of the Renaissance was not continued into the next century... In summary, the Renaissance did not produce its corresponding form of logos which could have given birth to a new civilizational cycle.

Skolimowski raises many intriguing questions: "Why did the Renaissance fail to produce a new civilizational cycle? Because it concentrated its energies entirely on the perfection of individual, discrete achievements? Or because its conception of 'man as the measure of all things' was too narrow? Or because it did not have one unified vision, one over-arching metaphor (like the mechanistic metaphor of the seventeenth century), which would have allowed for a new, cumulative development?... Were Renaissance philosophers not good enough, deep enough, original enough to weave their own cosmological tapestries? Or was it too early for them to do so?"

Skolimowski attempts to summarise answers to all the fascinating questions he raises, as follows: "Perhaps the significant point lies in the nature of Renaissance man as we now see him: his main energies were spent elsewhere – on building magnificent palaces, chiselling sculptures of unsurpassed perfection and power, and simply living and enjoying realization that man is the measure of all things..."

5. A New Civilization on the Wheels of Mechanos

We are living in *Kaliyuga*, which, in Hinduism, means the Age of Machines (*kal* = machine, *yuga* = age; though there are different interpretations too of the word *Kaliyuga*). The entire civilization is on the wheels of machines.

What is the direction? What is the fate? Where will it end up? Our world, trying to fly with the wings of *mechanized* consciousness, is unable to answer whats, whys, whos, wheres, hows, whens etc. of the life. Henryk Skolimowski, whose philosophy comes as a distinctive aesthetic flavour to our world, looks deeper into the far-reaching consequences of the 'engines of Mechanos beginning to run a new civilization' and presents enlightening solutions of all the problems emerging from the environment of the new civilization.

A new form of logos Henryk Skolimowski calls *Mechanos* are dominating the contemporary civilization. "Mechanos is a distinctively new way of organizing reality, a distinctively new way of understanding," Skolimowski explains. "The basic metaphor is that of a clock-like mechanism. The universe is considered a sort of mechanical clock, moving according to well-defined deterministic laws. To know these laws is to understand nature, and to have the capacity to control it."

The system, despite its simplicity, worked well and powerfully for so long, to Skolimowski's amazement. Skolimowski unveils the reason behind its success and terrifying power posing twin questions: Is it because of its bloody-minded simplicity that the scheme has become so powerful? Or is Mechanos a malevolent god who gave us power as part of the Faustian bargain? – we enjoy it beyond our capacity to control it and the end will be an inevitable doom?

However, a philosopher creating a life-enhancing and life-glorifying philosophy does not contemplate images of doom. Therefore, Skolimowski denies to foresee a doom saying that the more we engage in imagining pictures of doom, the more surely (in a subtle and not quite explicable way) we bring about that doom – such is the power of Mind. He adds: What you most contemplate becomes real.

Skolimowski makes mention of the workers who have left a critical impression on the Mechano, in the development of mechanistic cosmology. They are Francis Bacon, Galileo, Descartes and Newton. Their concepts are different but have similar tone when we interpret them from the view point of generating Mechano-feeding realities.

Skolimowski narrates in short the novel work of Francis Bacon (1561–1626), claimed as one of the founders of the modern world-view, a Renaissance man as well as a maker of the seventeenth century. His (Bacon's) view of knowledge, Skolimowski tells, was refreshingly novel; he called for knowledge that can generate. *The conception of knowledge as power was Bacon's distinctive contribution to our new picture of the cosmos.* He emphasized, Skolimowski further tells, that the knowledge of the ancients was the knowledge of childhood, it can speak but it cannot generate and it is full of words but barren of works.

Skolimowski then tells about the legacy of Galileo (1564–1642), the great scientist, the great philosopher and a great genius known to one and all. Galileo wrote, as Skolimowski tells, that the book of nature is written in the language of mathematics without which it is virtually impossible to understand a single word of it.

"This compelling vision (of Galileo) came to dominate the Western Mind in times to come, and to such a degree that we finally desired to express everything mathematically, even the nature of love," Skolimowski continues expressing his views. "It is not appreciated what a strange desire it was to be persuaded that the book of nature is written in the language of mathematics, and what we must try to express everything in mathematical terms. The single-minded attempt to express everything in the universe and in human life in mathematical terms was a fantasy bordering on phantasmagoria, if not an obsession."

Skolimowski lets us know that the combined visions of Bacon and Galileo – knowledge is power and it should be expressed in mathematical terms – became the kernel of our new understanding, adding that the pursuit of this vision brought about an immense amount of power which in the end has terrified our wakeful hours.

The third example Skolimowski puts forth is that of the scheme of the new understanding of René Descartes (1599–1649), which, he says, should not be forgotten. "He was one of the chief architects of the Western Mind," Skolimowski writes about Descartes. "His *cogito ergo sum*, his separation of the body from the Mind, and above all his invention of the reductionist method, are hallmarks of a new understanding. Descartes' *Discourse on Method*, a seemingly simple and innocuous little essay, has been immensely important in shaping our analytical and reductionist strategies; it laid the foundation for our atomistic-analytical approach to knowledge and the world. 'Divide and rule' was Descartes' motto: divide every problem into smaller problems, and smaller problems still. And then seek the solution to the big problem by the arithmetic addition of the solution to the small problems. And *hope* that the meaning and scope of the big problem can be entirely exhausted by subdividing it into smaller problems." Dismissing the reductionist-analytical strategy, Skolimowski says that one cannot understand the nature of the cosmos by analysing cosmic dust; nor can analysis of the chemical structure of human bones reveal the nature of human beings."

Skolimowski also throws some light on Newton's *Philosophiae naturalis principia mathematica* (The Mathematical Principles of Natural Philosophy) of 1687 which, he says, was the epitome of the new designs of the universe. "During the last three centuries we have been sitting at Newton's feet and licking his boots," Skolimowski states categorically. "What Aristotle did for formal logic in the fourth century BC Newton did for our understanding of the physical universe… It (Newton's mechanical conception) virtually imprisoned us in a deterministic straitjacket."

A fabulous suggestion can be drawn from the following excerpt from the Skolimowskian discourse on *The Engines of Mechanos* which is so vital for our contemporary times: "We are all aware that the mechanistic cosmology, via science and technology, has brought about enormous material benefits. But we are also aware of the dark side of the mechanistic cosmology – ecological devastation, human and social fragmentation, spiritual impoverishment."

6. New Logos of the Evolutionary Philosophy

What a glorious universe, in that it is personal and progressive, not merely mechanical or even passively perfect! – The Urantia Book (75:8.7)

When philosophers and their philosophies search new horizons of creativity a dawn of a new epoch begins. When philosophers and their philosophies work for constant enlargement of the spiral of understanding and expansion of the limits of our universe new realities come into being and a new Mind begins to hatch out. When philosophers and their philosophies imaginatively tap the creative potentialities of the Mind and lead to transcendence of Mind into a participatory Mind, new logos begin to emerge and a new civilization begins to see its own dawn. When philosophers and their life-enhancing and logos-synthesizing philosophies work to spiritualize, empower, revolutionize, and cosmologize people, new cosmologies and new civilization begin evolving.

The Skolimowskian Philosophy has reached such a horizon at which we can discover a new sunrise to the life on Earth, and at which we can help the universe becoming more fertile for life and becoming livelier. Henryk Skolimowski helps us get rid of hopelessness and infuses infinite hope and spirit in human Mind. "Beyond despair and hope there is the inexorable rhythm of history," Henryk says with all optimism. "Human logos is unfolding, taking up new shapes as it encounters new problems and unprecedented dilemmas… We should not look at our present situation as one of chaos and confusion, although partly it is. We should, rather, look at our present time from the depth of our spiral of understanding, and see how it is struggling to acquire a new shape in order to render the cosmos in a new shape."

We are not living in the universe of Newtonian era. We have far larger, far deeper, far livelier and far more fascinating universe today than we had in the Newtonian era. We have to live in our times and have to create a universe for ourselves and for our worlds of the future. And such a universe is in the making. Let us hear Henryk Skolimowski sparkling our path towards a new dawn, new era and a new and real universe:

- ❖ *There is a new sense of the depth of the universe...* The depth of the universe is also the depth of our Mind. We cannot find new depths in the universe unless we find these new depths in ourselves.

- ❖ *There is a new sense of depth to the human person.* We have acquired a new sense of the beauty of the human condition. A new sense of meaning and purpose is emerging; and a new sense of spirituality which is not tied to past religions. We are increasingly aware that we live in a participatory universe, which means that a sense of responsibility is thrust upon us, a responsibility so great and joyous as no generation before us has experienced – the responsibility for our own destiny and for the future of the planet.

- ❖ *We are reclaiming meaning and spirituality as indispensable components of human life and the concept of person.* T. S. Eliot writes: 'Man is man because he can recognize supernatural realities such as truth, obligation, meaning, purpose and validity.' We no longer define universe as a clock-like mechanism; and we are less inclined to define man as a machine... Spirituality denotes an enhanced and fulfilled meaning. Within this form of logos, which I call Evolutionary Telos, the human being is defined as an unfolding field of sensitivities organized in patterns of meaning and spirituality.

- ❖ *Wholeness and connectedness are essential characteristics of Evolutionary Telos.* Almost each new paradigm that has emerged (during recent decades) emphasizes the importance of wholeness and connectedness.

❖ *Connectedness and wholeness are essential features for reading the book of nature in a new way...* Ecology conceived as the science of interconnected organic wholes has been of great importance in clarifying our understanding of the interconnectedness of all things, and in articulating the importance of holistic, connected thinking... Ecology and ecological thinking must be seen not as separate parts of a whole, not as another movement concerned mainly with the environment; but as an essential part of the process of the transformation of consciousness. Ecological thinking writ large becomes participatory integral thinking: thinking in accordance with the inherent laws of the cosmos.

❖ *We live in an open, non-deterministic universe...* We are opening up, the cosmos is opening up, evolution is unfolding. Our new spiral of understanding must be par excellence evolutionary... *Our path is creative transcendence.*

Summary

The Western Mind, throughout the history of humankind, has reflected many shades of light. It has undergone spectacular evolutionary changes passing through four major cycles Henryk Skolimowski calls *the four great cycles of the western mind.* These are:

1) The Mytho-poetic Cycle (From the tempestuousness of the Homeric heroes to the lucidity of Plato);

2) The Graeco-Roman Cycle (From the fall of the Roman Empire to the building of Chartres Cathedral);

3) The Medieval-Christian Cycle (The Renaissance: the Civilization that did not make it); and

4) Modern Mechanos (The engines of Mechanos beginning to run a new civilization)

The fifth cycle has begun to emerge and evolve. Henryk calls it Evolutionary Telos. These cycles of the Western Mind are not just cycles but an extravagant history of one of the best cultures of the world presented in a unique and fascinating way which we shall nowhere find in written or spoken history of the West. This history reflects fascination, charisma and enthrallment of the Skolimowskian Philosophy. Let us go through the Summary of the four great cycles of the Western Mind as written by Henryk Skolimowski:

> The Homeric heroes were rational. But their rationality was of different sort from ours. Each cosmology engenders its own distinctive rationality. Rationality is derived from the backbone of a given cosmology and it serves it in its turn. There is a wonderful rationality underlying the whole ethos of the Greek culture of archaic times. This rationality is expressed through metaphors, myths and takes rather than in discursive ways. It is powerful and clear, nevertheless.
>
> Around the sixth century BC the whole archaic formation slowly collapsed. The old tales of the universe and the old rationality were gradually replaced. The translucent Greek logos assumed its place in all its splendour. The achievements of this logos are supreme. Not only great temples were created, unsurpassed in their beauty and grandeur, such as the Parthenon and the Erectheion; new systems of thought emerged which were to nourish and inspire the Western Mind for the millennia to come.
>
> The lucid logos of classical Greece produced memorable and lasting achievements. It was light shining through everything the Greek Mind touched. Yet around the fifth century AD came the exhaustion of Graeco-Roman cycle,

and the whole civilization collapsed. A different form of reason emerged, ultimately leading to a new cosmology. We enter medieval times. The predominant form of reason is one which we call Theos – reason inspired and guided by the monotheistic Judaeo-Christian God. The achievements of the new civilization are copious and splendid in their own right. A great coherence exists in human and celestial realms, as both are guided and overseen by the benevolent, almighty deity. The Gothic cathedral is a visible symbol of hierarchy, and a central metaphor around which all earthly life is woven. Although medieval civilization was interested primarily in securing eternal salvation for its people, its earthly achievements were considerable. The first universities were established: the Sorbonne, Bologna, Oxford. The mechanical clock which measured time in the villages was a foretaste of great mechanical wonders to come. Medieval rationality differed from our own and that of the Greeks. It would be foolish to maintain that medieval people were irrational because they believed in God. Their God was the safeguard of their rationality. Given their assumptions, their civilization was a beautifully coherent one.

Botticelli's Venus emerging out of the foam of the sea marks the twilight of medieval civilization. The new motto of the Renaissance is: 'Man is the measure of all things.' Despite the creation of marvellous works of art, there is no unifying vision, no new logos which would serve as the foundation for the new cosmos. No new civilizational cycle emerges out of the Renaissance. The spiral of understanding of the Renaissance Mind was not distinctive enough, not strong enough, not enduring enough to produce a new outline of the cosmos.

The Renaissance merely represented epicycles over past Greek philosophy.

With the seventeenth century we enter the new cycle of our mechanistic civilization. The organizing new logos I call Mechanos. Starting slowly and inconspicuously, this form of reason creates a new blueprint according to which knowledge is power, the power to transform nature to our advantage. This knowledge should be expressed in mathematical equations. Working out the details of this blueprint, we have created a terrifying degree of power. The benevolent Mechanos is turning into a malevolent Moloch. The story of the sorcerer's apprentice is re-emerging in a new context. We have unleashed powers that we don't know how to turn back. In enjoying the spectacle of physical powers, we have sadly reduced ourselves in stature. In atomizing nature, we have atomized ourselves. We have complete freedom and seeming mastery over nature and our own lives, yet we are empty inside and crave meaning, even if it comes from phoney gurus. Our sterilized rationality has denuded our emotions and our spiritual life. Amidst the sulphur of toxic dumps, amidst the pollution of our rivers and our bodies, amidst the poison in our food and in our Minds – we courageously stare at a new dawn.

The dawn of new logos, Evolutionary Telos, can be seen in various places. We are refusing to die with the dying civilization. The new logos insists on the holistic nature of life and on the interconnectedness of all there is in the universe. The new logos is not afraid of mystery and asserts, along with Einstein, that 'The most beautiful thing we can experience is the mysterious. It is the source of all true art and science.' Our new journey is just beginning. We shall need all our courage, imagination and perseverance to make it a success. We have no choice whether to continue this journey or not. It is our evolutionary destiny.

CHAPTER 6

The Participation Methodology and its Consequences

Participation is the song of creation. . . Deepest form of participation is love.[1]
– Henryk Skolimowski

1. Problems of the Objective Mind

Henryk Skolimowski begins his story with Ludwig Fleck, a Polish microbiologist and an epistemologist, active before World War Two, who studied in depth what would be called the making of the scientific Mind in the field of microbiology, and elucidates the following:

- All perception, particularly sophisticated forms of perception, requires rigorous training and development.
- Students' perception is sharpened and focused to perceive according to the rules of one specialised discipline; their Minds are sharpened to recognize and identify the phenomena that are important for their discipline.
- It is the Mind that perceives, not the eye. The Mind provides the framework, specific knowledge and specific assumptions for the eye to see.
- The Mind constitutes the universe which the eye then sees. Put otherwise: our Mind is built into our eyes.

"The 'objective attitude' or 'scientific method' attempts to limit the perception of the world to what is assumed by science to be there; and attempts to deny what science's assumptions deny," warns Henryk. "Objectivity means clinical detachment and dispassionate forms of observation, the forms of perception that atomize phenomenon that we investigate. Objectivity assumes that things exist in isolation, that every phenomenon we examine is the universe in itself, independent of larger wholes from which it has been cut."

Henryk derives some other interesting and worth recognizing conclusions of the 'scientific method' or of the objective Mind:

- The scientific method has moulded the Mind to be its servant.
- *The scientific view of the world and the objective cast of Mind mirror each other.*
- In the scientific world-view the Mind has become a hostage to a selective vision of reality.
- *The Yoga of Objectivity is a gentle form of lobotomy.*

Counting the negative attributes of the scientifically trained objective Mind, Henryk sketches a picture of the Mind of a child: "Consider the Mind of a child. It is the 'magical Mind', as Joseph Chilton Pearce observes. Children are magical creatures. Their worlds and Minds are full of wonders, surprising things of great beauty. Consider the same magical child after fifteen years of schooling in *good* Western schools. What has happened to the magical Mind? What has happened to the sparkling imagination? They have become amputated by the relentless training in the Yoga of Objectivity."

Scientific training prunes all the dimensions of the Mind which, in natural mode of its development, attains fullness of its development and evolves into a vibrant, alive, conscious Mind, and a natural ally of the cosmos in the creativity in tune with cosmic designs of creativity. The objective Mind, through scientific methodology, is turned into a bonsai, to be allowed only limited or calculated growth. Yes, the specialized Mind is a Bonsai Mind. A specialized Mind is an ill Mind, for it cannot attain fullness of its growth. It is made to bypass its natural evolution. Turning a Mind into an objective or specialized Mind is an inexcusable and intolerable crime, crime against humans, crime against nature, crime against the cosmic evolution. Innumerable Minds – which could flower so intensively, which could spread their fragrance throughout the world, which could have changed the destiny of humanity and of our world – have been turned into Bonsai Minds, rendering limited services to limited people totally selfish and unconcerned with humanity and the world.

An objective Mind writes script of destruction, of disastrous consequences. Henryk further reveals such consequences of the objective Mind:

> The Mind trained in Yoga of Objectivity over a number of years becomes cold, dry, uncaring; always atomizing, cutting, analysing. This kind of Mind has lost the capacity for empathy, compassion, love… The objective Mind – when it begins to dominate the world – creates the atomic family, the atomistic society, the social and individual alienation; for alienation is a peculiar form of detachment. The atomized society and individual alienation (which are merely consequences of detachment) cause in the long run inner tension, frustration, anguish; which then give rise to extreme loneliness, anger and also violence… The objective Mind is so desensitized that it is oblivious of these consequences.

2. The Participation Methodology Overriding the Objectivity Methodology

Henryk Skolimowski opines that the idea of participation is among the most complex and beautiful ones in the history of the universe. "Nothing could happen in the evolution of life and the universe without participation," he adds. "Participation is at the core of our social life. Participation is a song of joy of our individual experience. The degree, depth and richness of our participation determine the richness and meaningfulness of our life."

Participation, in Henryk's words is an implicit aspect of wholeness. Participation is the means to conceive the structure of wholeness. He seems to be dancing; his words seem to be dancing when he presents his participation to us. A reader feels intoxicated by the lucid flow of Henryk's views on participation:

> All life is participation. The song of life is the song of participation. The sorrow of life is an estrangement from participation. When life has discovered the meaning of participation it has discovered the most important modus for growth. The process of participation is perhaps the most profound vehicle of the evolving universe. The participatory universe is merely another name for the unfolding life in organized forms… Deep participation means *empathy*, an almost complete identification with the subject of our attention. Empathy or identification is an aspect of the meaning of participation, thus an aspect of the meaning of wholeness… A meaningful participation, when it involves empathy, implies responsibility. We cannot truly participate in the whole, of which we are a part, unless we take responsibility for it… Participation is responsibility.

The four concepts of wholeness, participation, empathy and responsibility, which Henryk Skolimowski defines, co-define each other, partake in each other's meaning, and feed on each other. Henryk's concepts form a circular mandala, in which flow of meaning goes both clockwise and counter clockwise. The meaning of each concept, he explains, is not defined separately but in conjunction with other concepts.

There is a deep participation and shallow participation. The most tenuous form of the latter is what Henryk calls *linear* (or geometric) *participation*. Participation, as Henryk tells us, is a matter of context. For example, shallow, deep, intriguing, open and close contexts spell out shallow, deep, intriguing, open and stultified participations, respectively. "By engaging in deep participation, we create deep contexts. In brief, the depth and richness of the context depends on the depth and versatility of our participation, and vice versa," explains Henryk.

Henryk spells out other types of participation also: Pre-programmed participation could be *genuine* or *pseudo*-participation. He describes the other interesting levels of participation:

> Co-creative participation occurs when we are allowed the freedom of not only following the rules but also of making the rules... This form of participation, when we co-create with the universe, is the joy of our existence. It is here that our co-creative Mind blossoms fully. It is here that our being receives fulfillment... Yet there is still a deeper form of participation, which I call creative participation or creation. When great geniuses are involved in this sort of participation, great works of art bordering on miracles are created... Our status as human beings is enlarged by the degree to which we are allowed co-creative participation... Whether our participation is curtailed by a merciless king or computer, the consequences are the same: frustration, anger, emptiness and alienation. True participation is joy and fulfilment... *We are sitting at the feast of life. Its name is participation.*

Henryk Skolimowski summarizes his discourse in a Hymn to Participation. It is so enlightening and soul-soothing!

HYMN TO PARTICIPATION

Participation is the song of creation.
Participation is the whispering of life unfolding.
Participation is the common thread of all evolution.
Participation is the common prayer of amoebas and angels.
Participation is the oxygen fuelling the process of transcendence.
Participation is the song of our individual experience.

Whenever life emerges participation blossoms,
As the joy of life,
As the bond of solidarity,
As the pool from which all living beings drink,
As the yeast promoting growth and maturity.

When life discovered the meaning of participation
It had discovered its most important modus for growth.
Utterly simple and utterly profound is the meaning of participation.
Nothing happens in evolution without participation.
The language of solidarity is the language of participation.

To be aware is to participate.
To be asleep is to be estranged from participation.
To be alive is to sail on the wings of participation.
To be morose is to have one's wings of participation clipped.

Love is the deepest form of participation.
When there is love there is participation.
Loveless participation is an anaemic involvement.
To participate is the first step to loving.

How deeply can you enter into the immensity of the universe?

As deeply as you can embrace it in the arms of your participation.
Everything else is a mere shadow. The real thing
Is our immense journey of becoming through participation.

3. Participatory Research

The idea of research programme goes back to Popper, but it was Imre
Lakatos, who made it the central point of his problematic and put the
idea on the map, in 1970s. Lakatos's research programmes are a scheme
representing a mingling of three styles of thought, according to Henryk
Skolimowski. These are thought of:

- Popper (conjectures and refutations),
- Kuhn (the march of science through successive paradigms), and
- Feyerabend (the principle of cognitive fertility carried out by
  whatever method you apply – 'anything goes').

"Research programmes as conceived by Lakatos are mainly, if not entirely,
scientific research programmes: cognitive, objective, rational," Henryk unveils
the truth. "They are designed to handle the accepted scientific-cognitive
problems. In short, Lakatos's research programmes by and large accept the
underlying *context of science*, and in fact consider this context as sacrosanct."

Henryk emphasizes that the participatory universe requires new
research programmes which would clearly spell out for us new intellectual
strategies, new forms of perception, new forms of reasoning, new languages
and new apparatus. *Ascertaining a different universe requires a different
methodology* – a different spiral of understanding, he suggests, and outlines
the following characteristics for the same:

The participatory research is the art of *empathy* –
is the art of *communion* with the object of enquiry –
is an art of learning to use *its* language –

is the art of *using* its language –

is the art of *talking* to the object of our enquiry –

is the art of penetrating from *within* –

is the art of *in-dwelling* in the other –

is the art of *imaginative hypothesis* which leads to the art of identification –

is the art of *transformation of one's consciousness* so that it becomes part of the consciousness of the other.

In order to make it clearer, the participatory research progamme based on Skolimowski's concept (and slightly modified from the figure drawn by him) is shown in figure 1.

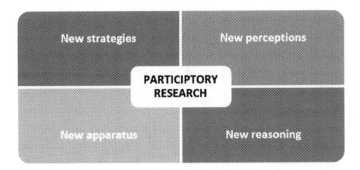

Figure 1: Participatory research progamme based on Skolimowski's concepts

Henryk Skolimowski gives very high importance and regards to art. "The work of art is a *sui generis* object," he opines. "In our language, the work of art is a participatory work. It signifies a highly complex participatory process." Henryk unravels the meaning of this process:

The work of art is endowed with the significance that transcends the material through which it was carried out. Each work of art has a material layer: the poem is printed with particles of printer's ink. The painting has layers of physical paint. Yet what is important is not the material underpinning but the significance that is expressed through these media. The artist *intentionally* endows the works of art with specific significance. We *intentionally* decipher or decode this significance. A deeply participatory process is going on. In brief, encoding (by the artist) and decoding (by the viewer) – of the meaning contained in works of art – is a participatory process par excellence... The artist works within the layers of participatory consciousness of human culture... Participation in art, by making it and receiving it, is among the most significant of human endeavours.

Further articulating is idea of participatory research, Henryk ponders over the crucial concept of empathy: "The aspects of empathy are to dwell; belong; share; give/ take. These are common sense concepts, colloquially used. Yet they also possess a deeper metaphysical meaning. We have to regain this deeper meaning in order to participate more deeply in the spectacle of the universe... Empathy, in brief, is a form of positive identification, a positive participation. To empathize is to become one with another, to beat the same rhythm with another, to understand through compassion and *from within*."

4. Participatory Strategies

NEED OF THE GROUNDS FOR PARTICIPATORY RESEARCH

In order to prepare the grounds for participatory research various strategies are needed, including what Henryk calls the Yoga of Participation. Henryk describes the minimal terms for practising participatory research, as follows:

- *Preparing* one's consciousness.
- *Meditating* upon the form of being of the other.
- *Reliving* its past, its present, its existential dilemmas.

- *Supplicating* to it for permission to enter it (just the opposite from cutting it with a surgical knife).
- *Praying* to the other to let us in (prayer as a form of empathic energy).
- *In-dwelling* in the other on compassionate terms.

"Our new strategies imply that we want to be on good terms with the cosmos, and understand things from within rather than crushing them," suggests Henryk. "To meditate, to supplicate, to pray is to create new strategies. These are some of the aspects of a new kind of *dialogue* which we want to carry on *compassionately* with the whole cosmos." There are some questions as part of our new intellectual strategies. These are meaningful and rational questions. We must reflect on some of these points which Henryk suggests before jumping to results:

- What is revealed? And in what language?
- How can I continue the dialogue?
- What are the levels, forms and terms of this dialogue?
- What kind of sensitivities does the other embody; operate through?
- How does the range and power of my sensitivities help me?
- Which of my sensitivities are most appropriate for the task at hand?
- I somehow understand how it works in its own terms…. how do I translate its terms into my terms, and then into intersubjective terms?

"We have to make a transition from objective consciousness to *compassionate consciousness*," Henryk aptly suggests. "This transition will be of momentous importance… The full articulation of the programme and a satisfactory validation of it will occur when we enact it collectively and create the compassionate consciousness as the vehicle of the new *participatory science*."

Henryk Skolimowski cites the description of Barbara McClintock, who received a Nobel Prize in 1983 for her investigation of chromosomes in the 1940s. She vividly describes the process of identification with the chromosomes she investigated. Skolimowski quotes: "I found the more I worked with them, the bigger and bigger the chromosomes got and when I was really working with them I wasn't outside. I was part of the [system]. . . it surprised me because I actually felt as if I was right down there and these were my friends. . . As you look at these things they become a part of you. . ."

"Indeed, 'As you look at these things they become a part of you,' Skolimowski infers what Barbara said. "But you have to acquire the art of empathy first so that you become a part of them, so that they become a part of you."

Quoting David Bohm's far-reaching book, *Wholeness and the Implicate Order* (1980), Skolimowski says that the story of universe is, for Bohm, the transition from an implicate order to an explicate one, and derives the following conclusion: Wholeness reveals itself as the implicate order becomes explicate. For the participatory Mind, this wholeness reveals itself in the multifariousness of its participation. Participation is the flowering of wholeness: wholeness reveals itself through participation and does not make sense without it. Thus *participation is the essence of the universe in its unfolding*. The universe has become what it is because of specific forms of participation in which it has expressed its nature.

5. Participatory Thinking

When the Mind is thinking it is talking to itself.[2] – Plato

Mankind came into being with thinking as an inevitable phenomenon. Henryk's thinking about thinking is so exciting, so prompting, so beautiful, so alluring, and so intriguing that, after reading his discourse on thinking, one is charmed by thinking and keeps thinking about thinking. He has so much in store for us to lead the thinkers to think about thinking a lot. "Thinking is a subject as old as mankind," He says triggering our thinking.

"The appearance of thinking may be considered as the threshold after which we welcome the emergence of human kind. We are so familiar with thinking, so well-trained in it. We think that we know what thinking is, and how to think well. All training in schools and academia is training in thinking."

Yet we are still novices in the art of thinking, says Henryk adding that great discoveries in ourselves and in the cosmos at large will depend on the invention of new forms of thinking. "Albert Einstein said that with the explosion of the atom bomb everything was changed except our thinking," Henryk says quoting Einstein. "For mankind to survive we shall have to evolve a substantially new manner of thinking."

Henryk reminds us that we have been slow in evolving this new thinking. He lists new types of thinking proposed in recent years. Main attributes of the four types of thinking based on his discourse are:

Systems thinking
- proposed in the 1960s, appeared to be of great promise, but ultimately it made itself a servant of scientific thinking;
- is objective, asserts only the phenomena recognized and sanctioned by science;
- has accepted the context of science and its cosmology.

Cybernatic thinking
- was the discovery of 1950s, now part of ordinary language;
- didn't deliver what it seems to have promised;
- as time went on, this thinking was monopolized by and incorporated into the scientific universe.

Holistic thinking
- appeared as aftermath of the ecology movement and the search for the holistic paradigm;
- we cannot provide a concise definition of it, its nature and characteristics may vary from context to context;

- ecological thinking is one form of it, purpose is not just to know, but to heal, maintain life, and to make life more vibrant.

Reverential thinking

- thinking infused with reverence: underlying assumption is reverence for life, reverence for all living beings, reverence for all living systems;
- foundation of right ecological thinking;
- recognizes human life as an intrinsic value, love as an essential and indispensable modality of human existence, creative thinking as an inherent part of human nature;
- joy as an integral part of our daily living, brotherhood of all beings as the basis of our new epistemological paradigm, participatory thinking as a crucial vehicle for mending the planet and maintaining its integrity, wholeness and beauty.

Henryk regards the participatory thinking at its best. He has many magnificent and delightful things about the participatory thinking, a corollary of holistic thinking:

> Participatory thinking is akin to Buddhist thinking, based on compassion. Participatory thinking is close to Christian thinking, when it is based on love in its pure meaning. Participatory thinking is also close to Taoist thinking, for right participation means following the right path. Participatory thinking does not impose a straitjacket on anyone but gives us freedom and encouragement to participate in the glories of the universe to the fullest of our potential... To think well is to co-create with the universe. To think well is to participate constructively in the well-being of your organism. Plato says that 'Health is a consummation of a love affair with the organs of the body.' *Mutatis mutandis*: Participatory

thinking is a love relationship between yourself and the evolving universe... Participatory thinking gives us freedom of opening up, of creation, of in-dwelling in the immensity of the universe on a scale unprecedented in history. It invites us enter where angels fear to tread... If mankind is to survive we shall need to evolve a substantially new manner of thinking – as Einstein proclaimed. Participatory thinking offers itself as first step, indeed as the necessary step in new design of the universe in which our individual liberation coincides with lasting peace on Earth.

From Henryk Skolimowski's discourse on participatory thinking can be elicited a vital suggestion which carries potential to promote peace on Earth. This goes like this: *Every culture must discover its own participatory thinking so that its people are not lost in empty abstractions or alienated from the vital pulses and rhythms of the universe.*

6. The Matter of Sensitivity

What is this world due to? Can we imagine the world without Mind? Henryk Skolimowski says that the world is the creation of the human Mind. The matter is not the world of physical dimensions, but 'the world as constituted in our knowledge'. Thus, we cannot imagine a world without Mind. The same is true of our cosmos. No Mind, no cosmos. The same is true of us. No Mind, no ourselves. No Mind, no world; no Mind, no cosmos – everything, indeed, is stalked in the Mind. Everything is imagined by Mind, perceived by Mind, conceived by Mind, processed by Mind, shaped by Mind, reshaped by Mind, monitored by Mind, transformed by Mind, revolutionised by Mind, sustained by Mind, sanctified by Mind, divinised by Mind. All the sensitivities are lying in Mind. Mind is such an organ of the evolution in which cosmos roots itself to acquire necessary shapes and rhythms of creativity.

Cosmology itself is a triumph of the Mind. Mind and cosmology are in reciprocal relationship both contributing to the development and evolution of each other. Therefore Mind itself is a triumph of a cosmology.

"The physical world has been made and remade many times in different cosmologies, each of which imposed on it its distinctive patterns, its distinctive sense of wholeness," explicates Skolimowski. "Each cosmology is a triumph of the Mind in moulding the diverse elements 'out there' into a clear recognizable structure. Each cosmology is also a triumph of the richness of the inscrutable cosmos which, in spite of our numerous attempts to capture and describe it, still eludes us, as if saying: 'I am capable of assuming ever new astonishing forms if you dare to come to me with new powerful insights.' The cosmos is standing there, an enigmatic entity, still inscrutable, still open to new creative dances,"

Henryk says that each system of knowledge finds the cosmos cooperative and obliging: "The reason lies in the very essence of the participatory universe. The participatory cosmos takes delight in assuming as many forms and configurations as our imagination is capable of conceiving. The astonishing power of the Mind brings out of the cosmos its astonishing characteristics."

On the matter and Mind relationship, Henryk has this, in short, to state: "Matter behaves as the Mind allows it. Let us put more precisely. If Mind is restricted, the behaviour of matter is restricted. If Mind is liberated, the behaviour of matter is liberated."

In Newtonian matrix, the matter does not reveal more of itself, says Henryk, adding that we did not want to reveal more of itself. Henryk illuminates when he says that "Minds have opened up and 'crazy' theories about the behaviour of matter have been welcomed and cherished… The Mind has vindicated its creative prerogative, by making matter sensitive, exquisite and extraordinary." Henryk imaginatively peeps across the times becoming conscious like evolution itself and says, "The future of evolution and of the human species belongs to the Mind that can conceive the inconceivable, and then find it out there, in the universe, as the universe and imagination blend together."

Summary

We possess an all-potent Mind whose impact is all-pervading. The universe which has evolved the Mind to this stage is a participatory universe. What type of the universe we own is also dependent on the type of the Mind we own. Participatory universe has a quest of participatory Mind. Participatory Mind and Participatory Universe – this is the destiny of everything there is in us, in the world, in the cosmos. This is the destiny of the evolution that constantly keeps generating the rhythms of creativity, keeps everything vibrant and in the mode of succession and transcendence.

Participation is not an ordinary process. It is an art. Our Mind imbibes with art of wonders, and wonders of art. Our life reverberates with art of wonders and wonders of art. How can our Mind articulate the art of wonders and express wonders of art, this really matters. The articulation would majestically depend on how we participate. Or, in other words, what precisely is the methodology we adopt and are accustomed to in order to participate holistically and meaningfully.

In this chapter, Henryk Skolimowski proposes and discusses right methodology of participation and its consequences. Making us aware of the pathology of the objective Mind, he stupendously describes the participatory research programmes, participatory strategies, participatory thinking and sensitivity of matter. Methodology must ensure interconnectedness, integrity and wholeness of everything else there is.

Henryk's call of participation, Henryk's methodologies of participation, Henryk's magic of participation, Henryk's philosophy of participation – as if the participation is a song of the universe, a song of human soul, a song of the evolution, a song of creation, a song of wholeness! Let us present a summary of the Skolimowski's Methodologies of Participation, in his own words:

> We do not live in a senseless, stupid, selfish universe, but in a connected and participatory one. We have the power in our Mind to make the universe stupid and disconnected.

But the Mind was not given to us for this purpose. The power of the Mind should be exalted for it is both beautiful and terrifying.

> The Mind is its own place, and in itself
> Can make a Heav'n of Hell, a Hell of Heav'n.
>
> – Milton, *Paradise Lost*

The methodology of objectivity turned out to be a mixed blessing. By pursuing it, we have been able to explore physical matter with a remarkable degree of thoroughness. Through it, we have also built immensely powerful technology. But the other side of the coin is menacing. We have created the atomized and decimated world – mainly as a result of the relentless pursuit of the Yoga of Objectivity which is imposed on us through the prevailing school system. The Yoga of Objectivity is a set of systematic exercises which the scientific method requires for the reification of its claims. The purpose of these exercises is to see reality in a selective way – according to the assumptions of science. The result of the Yoga of Objectivity is a gentle form of lobotomy – which we in the West all suffer; perhaps to the degree that we are not aware that we have been lobotomized.

We seek wholeness not for any capricious reason but because it is the foundation of our being. Wholeness is the matrix of meaning, and the basis for genuine understanding. The ancient Greeks knew these truths so well. For this reason they envisaged Harmony as an indispensable unifying principle bringing coherence to all. In the words of F. D. H. Kitto: 'A sense of the wholeness of things is perhaps the most typical feature of the Greek Mind. The modern Mind divides, specializes, thinks in categories; the

Greek instinct was the opposite, to take the widest view, to see things as an organic whole.'

The methodology of participation springs from one essential assumption: that the universe is one floating wholeness. Participation is the oldest methodology that has ever existed. *Participation is the methodology of life as growing and evolving.* All life is participation. The song of life is the song of participation. Participation is the song of joy of our individual experience. The deeper and more multifarious the forms of our participation, the deeper and richer the universe in which we live. The real journey is our immense journey to becoming through participation.

There are at least four basic forms of participation: linear, preprogrammed, co-creative, and creative. It is within the co-creative form of participation that the human being expresses himself or herself most fully. If true participation is denied to us, we atrophy and wither. Our modern times are afflicted with all kinds of mental diseases and disorders because human beings have been denied the right to participation. An outburst of various forms of therapy in our times is a hidden response of life to re-establish the right to participation. *All therapy is an attempt to bring the person back to meaningful form of participation.*

Life is an engagement, a continuous dance of participation; while technology, particularly high-tech, is disengagement, a dance of atrophy. Technology is damaging to our health primarily not because it pollutes our environments (including the mental one), but because it systematically disengages us from life, thus from participation, thus from meaning, thus from our essential nature. The prophets of technology triumphant are not even aware of the deep connection between healthy and meaningful life and deep forms of participation. Nor should we expect them to be so. They blindly serve the objective universe in which facile forms of linear participation prevail.

Participatory research is the art of dwelling in the other, is the art of penetrating from within, is the art of learning to use the language of the other; in short, the art of empathy. When empathy is writ large and systematically explored and applied, it becomes a new methodology, a set of new intellectual strategies. What clinical detachment is for objective methodology, empathy is for the methodology of participation. Just as we need to create right conditions for conducting research within the objectivist methodology, so we need to create right conditions for doing participatory research. Among these conditions is mediating upon the form of being of the other; supplicating for the permission to enter the territory of the other – not in the spirit of mindless praying, but in the spirit of reverence for the other. Ultimately the contrast between objective research and participatory research is that the former is based on objective consciousness, while the latter is based on compassionate consciousness. The contrast between the two should never be lost from sight. He or she who never developed compassionate consciousness will never be able to undertake participatory research in earnest.

Participatory research includes and articulates what is nowadays called the feminist epistemology, and the feminist sensitivities – which are an integral aspect of the union: reason/ intuition. Although I have not said so in so many words, this entire chapter, and especially the last sections on participatory thinking and the idea of the sensitivity of matter, is an articulation of the new sensitivities and new epistemology that the feminist movements postulate and attempt to justify.

The imperative of holistic thinking, of holistic perception, of the integrated being, is today perceived by many to be of importance second to none. Eco-feminism is one of the new important voices but by no means the only voice. Although we are travelling by different roads, the destination is the same – the creation of a new Mind, new sensitivities, new epistemologies which would be the cornerstone of genuine justice and equity in this world, and which would open for us a new chapter of our evolutionary journey.

An adjunct to participatory research, and indeed an integral part of it, is participatory thinking. Participatory thinking is a culmination of systems thinking, cybernetic thinking, holistic thinking and reverential thinking. Participatory thinking is the vehicle of the compassionate consciousness. Participatory thinking gives us the freedom of opening up, of in-dwelling in the immensity of the universe. Participatory thinking is the first step, and perhaps more than this, to what Albert Einstein admonished us to do – to evolve a substantially new manner of thinking if mankind is to survive.

As to the sensitivity of matter: the more sensitive the Mind, the more sensitive becomes matter – and the universe – handled by it. The more intelligent the Mind, the more intelligent the matter. The more obtuse the Mind, the more obtuse the matter. Things reveal their nature in participatory interactions with the participatory Mind. The magical child is always present in us.

CHAPTER 7

The Structure-Symbol-Evolution Axis

All are architects of Fate,

Working in these walls of Time;

For the structure that we raise,

Time is with materials filled;

Our todays and yesterdays

Are the blocks with which we build.

Build today, then, strong and sure,

With a firm and ample base;

And ascending and secure

Shall tomorrow find its place.[1]

– Longfellow

1. Structures as Footprints of Evolution

The universe of ours is a structure. The world we live in is a structure. Structures are not just physical entities. Symbols are not just expressions in physical terms. Skolimowski says that structures and symbols contribute to the process of becoming of the universe. The genius philosopher brings this to our knowledge that "Mind expresses its prowess and genius by inventing symbols which, on higher levels of the evolutionary Odyssey, become the carriers of life." In his philosophy, Skolimowswki provides a sacred space for the structures and symbols. He assesses the validity of structures and symbols on the basis of their participatory prowess: How deeply and significantly they contribute to our wellbeing. He extends the participatory Mind into the realm of structures and symbols and adds a unique chapter to the wisdom.

There is no dearth of the variety of structures in the available body of literature. Almost all disciplines have some telltale about structures. While technology makes the meaning of structures more technical, biology does make them less technical and arts and religion further simplify them. Skolimowski's definition of the structures is different from all, carrying deeper meaning and deeper and real purpose for life. It goes like this: *Structure signifies as organized wholeness which enables us to distinguish orders through which the evolutionary ascent has been maintained, perpetuated and perfected.*

Wherever there is a discernible structure, Skolimowski says, there is a:

- principle of organization at work;
- sense of identification of the whole to which the various parts belong;
- form of participation;
- purpose.

"The purpose of all structures is to serve life," Skolimowski elegantly suggests. "The purpose of all structures is to serve life."

About Simon's notion that hierarchical structures are of great importance, Skolimowski writes, "What Simon says is informative, but it does not go to the heart of the matter. And the heart of the matter is the relationship between structures and effervescence of life. Structures are recognized as organized whole not only because they help our perception but because they help life. This point is of great importance." Skolimowski adds: "Life means evolution. Evolution means growing complexity. Complexity means appropriate structures through which life articulates itself. *The origin of all structures is the articulation of life.* Thus the purpose of structures is to create orders that are life-enhancing."

About the considerations of structures in chemistry, Skolimowski says that "the chemical compounds in chemistry are analyzed and identified as structures because ultimately they are life-building-blocks." He also refers to them as 'part of the order supporting life.' However, neither nuclear bombs not black holes create order, and therefore, they are anti-structures. "Structures help life and are life-enhancing," says Skolimowski distinguishing structures from anti-structures. "Anti-structures undermine life and are destructive to life." He warns against the modern technology which has been 'quite prolific in devising anti-structures,' and reminds us of our ethical imperative: "We have arrived at an important ethical imperative: *in your work, in your behaviour, in your research do not engage in activities that result in anti-structures.* This alone could be the basis for a new, post-technological ethics."

Skolimowski's discourse on structures brings before us many imaginative things about the structures and about the nature-structure-evolution trinity. An excerpt:

> Structures should not be confined to the products of scientific activities only, be it chemistry or biology. Nature itself is a stupendous form of structure... Ecological habitats are distinctive structures. Evolution also can be seen as one enormous evolving structure. In truth, evolution is the greatest structure of all. It generates, articulates and nurses all life. This structure is so staggering in its complexity that we are often unable to see it in its totality. To see evolution for what it is: a life-supporting, life-giving and life-enhancing force, is a liberating experience... It is claimed, in feminist and anarchist literature, that *all hierarchy is bad and should be abolished.* This view is mistaken; or at least so partially formulated that it makes a caricature of the issue... Life, both biological and social, is pervaded with life-enhancing hierarchies without which the structure of human existence

would collapse... The mind (or the brain) is supremely hierarchical organ; and so is the eye. They coordinate our voyage through life in most subtle, cunning and beautiful way... Our life is hierarchical through and through. We make these choices and not other choices in the name of our preferences; which are based on our values; which are based on our hierarchies – which are often based on the hierarchies of life itself... In summary, the ascent of life goes hand in hand with the invention of structures. Hierarchies are vertical expressions of life-enhancing structures. So the equation is simple: no hierarchies, no structures, no articulation of life.

Skolimowski is of the opinion that political and ideological reasons are behind the so much resentment and animosity towards the very idea of hierarchy. The particular hierarchy, such as of Patriarchy, has brought about much grief and injustice. (For Skolimowski, even the matriarchy is a form of Hierarchy.) He stresses the need of having a close watch on political and ideological hierarchies as 'they have a tendency to become malignant.' Underlining the reason of the invention of Democracy, Skolimowski says that it was done so 'to rectify the degenerating shifts in political hierarchies, which are not based on participation.'

2. Looking into the Origin of Structures

Designing and building up new structures is going on at a very rapid pace and we appear to be too busy to deeply understand the origin of the structures. Henryk Skolimowski reminds us of this crucial aspect of the structures. He gives examples of two different shells with the common quality of accommodating and sheltering molluscs. Henryk regards the shells as 'magnificent examples of structures that are life-enhancing.' If one is asked whether there is something common between a shell and a temple? This question appears to be irritating. But Henryk magnificently shows commonality between the two seemingly mismatching structures. "On a deeper analysis we find that shell is not so small, not so frail. And not so different from the temple," explains Henryk. "Upon reflection we shall find that each is a form of shelter, although sheltering different forms of existence. The shell shelters the mollusc's forms of existence. The temple shelters aspects of man's spiritual existence."

Henryk goes deeper still. He regards *evolution* as 'the ultimate thread that unites these forms.' "In its unfolding, evolution created various kinds of spaces in order to shelter different aspects of its being," Henryk Skolimowski reiterates. "On the level of the human being, evolution created new kinds of spaces to accommodate the increasing variety of human needs, including cultural and spiritual needs. Now, although they look so different, both the shell and temple respond to the need for shelter; on different levels of evolutionary unfolding... The more we learn about the magic of the shell the more able we shall be to design our dwellings and temples."

Further unfolding the essence of structures, Henryk says that "When evolution made a transition from the physical to the cultural, and then to the spiritual, human beings, in response, started to build those new kinds of structures – temples and other monuments of art." About the temples, Henryk's beautiful saying in fascinating words goes like this: "Temples are among the most significant structures evolved by human beings. They embody and express the great rhythms and symmetries of life. The secret of structures and their greatness lies in their *symmetry*. We find these symmetries fascinating and irresistible because deep down it is evolution in us that responds to its own evolutionary epic."

The origin of all structures, according to Henryk, is symmetry: "Primordial symmetry is expressed through life-enhancing rhythms, which form the basis of structures." The following excerpt from his writings on structures bears in Mind a kind of rhythm arousing our interest in the evolutionary structures:

Life, as conceived in the universe of ours, has been carried on through the structures based on rhythms and symmetries. From the rhythm of pulsating stars to the rhythm of sexual intercourse, we find rhythms and symmetries pleasing and enthralling because they are the stuff of life, the bearers of life, the underlying harmony and unity of life. All art, and much of the life (when lived significantly), is an epic struggle of the Mind to weave the natural rhythms and symmetries into ever new structures.

3. Symbols for Our Glorification

Symbols symbolize almost all aspects of life. They show their robust presence everywhere and are part and parcel of our existence. Symbols speak. Symbols make us speak. Symbols sing. Symbols make us sing. Symbols dance. Symbols make us dance. Symbols define. Symbols make us define. Symbols make us. Symbols make us make ourselves. Symbols enlighten. Symbols make us enlighten ourselves. Symbols glorify. Symbols make us glorify ourselves. Symbols can destroy. Symbols can make us destroy ourselves. Symbols and human life go hand in hand. Symbols and human cultures go hand in hand. Symbols are lively. Symbols are full of life. Symbols are all-powerful. Symbols are all-pervading. Life devoid of symbols is no life.

Henryk's discourse on symbols is marvellous and heart-stirring. Symbols defy explicit definitions, he says, adding that they define us as much as we are capable of defining them. He brings to the fore very exhilarating account of the all-powerful symbols. "Symbols are the frail creatures," he says. "But they can possess explosive substance. Great revolutions have been fought in the name of and inspired by symbols. You cannot break a symbol. But a symbol can break you; or can make you."

Henryk regards the works of art as the best examples of 'organized and orchestrated wholeness'. He says that through their symbols, they (the works of art) integrate us into those realms which they express. Some of Henryk's views on works of arts, as follows, are so interesting to go through:

> Works of art, particularly great ones, are holistic in a double sense. They represent a remarkable unity and completeness within themselves. But, secondly, through their presence, through the relationships they establish with us, they draw us in – into their universe. The more significant the realm they symbolically represent, the more significant can become our integration... Indeed, works of art are among the primary vehicles of transcendence. Works of art are modalities of our existence... Works of art make us feel that we belong, that we participate... The symbols of art and religion make us belong not only to earth but also to heaven... Though they are mysterious, symbols should not be regarded as invisible ghosts. They are rather *intentional relationships*.

Henryk Skolimowski rightly calls *Homo sapiens* as *Homo symbolicus*. In fact, *Homo symbolicus* is a being wholly impacted by symbols, directed by symbols, chiselled by symbols, Sansktitised by symbols, proclaimed by symbols. Skolimowski reminds the *Homo symbolicus* of the symbol-related virtues: "Because man acquired the capacity to produce symbols much larger than his earth-bound existence, he could make something of himself. Our spiritual journey began when we started to project symbols and then attempted to live up to these symbols. Whether we take the restless, outward-directed Prometheus or the implacable Buddha, sitting serenely on the lotus flower, the symbolism emanating from each has inspired human beings to deeds and achievements that would have been inconceivable without these far-reaching symbols."

In order to respond to various questions relating to symbols and symbolism, Henryk has three different interpretations which 'overlap, and sometimes vie for dominance with each other':

- *Ontological* interpretation: symbolic form is related to (and not quite distinguishable from) Platonic ideas or Platonic forms.
- *Phenomenological* interpretation: the meaning of symbolic form is grounded in the quality of human consciousness – in the particular mode of an animated reality of the experience of the phenomenon under investigation, and the symbolic form underlying it.
- *Mythic* interpretation: symbolic form delineates the sacred form the profane; symbolic form stands then as a threshold to the realm of the sacred.

About the case of Ernst Cassirer and his followers who wrote voluminously on symbols, Skolimowski has the following to interpret: "Philosophy of Ernst Cassirer is a universe in itself and no perfunctory summary or critique can do it justice. The work of Cassirer and other writers of the twentieth century is a living testimony of the importance of symbols on the one hand, and of their profoundly mysterious, non-discursive character on the other."

Why some religions survive better than other religions, and some works of art and some cultures are more enduring than others? What is the reason? Henryk asks. "The reason must be that their symbols are more universal and more sustaining than other symbols," he explains. "For symbols do sustain, and often articulate, different aspects of our human condition – as can be clearly seen in the cases of Buddhism, Hinduism and Christianity."

4. Symbol Evolution in Buddhism, Hinduism and Christianity

Symbols have played significant role in the evolution of various religions and vice versa. The spread of Buddhism went hand in hand with the spread of unique symbols and symbolism became a unique artistic reality of the Buddhism. As many as 84,000 stupas in equal number of villages was a symbolic glory achieved by Ashoka the Great (273–237 BC) during his complete devotion to the Buddhism. The growth of the Buddhist art and that of the Buddhism itself went on inseparably. "It is at this time that the symbolism of Buddhist art was articulated, refined, and conveyed in thousands of statues," writes Henryk Skolimowski. "The symbolism is striking in its simplicity."

The symbols have a lot to narrate, a lot to spell meaning and light. Henryk explains the following in the context of the Buddhism: "The pervading symbol is that of the tranquil Buddha, sitting serenely on the lotus flower. The lotus flower came to signify the quality of the Buddha – the inner peace of Mind which is a precondition of real well-being and of happiness. The symbolism is simple. Yet it is powerful and universal... In this symbolism some of the noblest longings of the human race are expressed."

Symbols evolved in religions are potent sources of wisdom leaving a soothing impression on Mind. The impression produced by the Buddha statue at Kamakura has been thus described by C.F. Holland:[2]

> It tells of passion long subdued,
> Of wisdom's calm repose,
> Of patience born of pain and strife,
> And strength to him who knows.
> It tells an all-embracing love,
> Of joys that never cease.
> And how from sorrow, grief, and fear
> Emerged eternal peace.

Henryk mentions about striking parallels between Buddhism and Hinduism, that is, the same belief in reincarnation, in Nirvana, in Karma, in Dharma. Henryk also counts markedly different symbolism between

Hinduism and Buddhism: "The Buddhist symbolism emphasizes austerity. The symbolism of Hinduism, on the other hand, emphasizes the exuberance and sensuousness of life. The symbol of the Linga – which is the central symbol of Shiva temples, and which is a phallic symbol par excellence – only confirms the general élan of the culture. These lingas are an integral part of the religious faith… They do not just symbolize the worship of the primordial sexual urge, but rather the sanctity of life, the miracle of life; they gloriously encapsulate the life abundant, the art that must be cherished and held sacred in all its aspects."

Hinduism is one of the oldest religions replete with mythology and symbolism. What is the most outstanding symbolism the Hinduism embodies is the dancing Shiva, Nataraj. Henryk marvels various aspects of the Hinduism as follows:

> Hindu mythology is very colourful, very complex, and so are its symbols. The dancing Shiva is its most striking and perhaps the dominant symbol. It is the symbol of continuous metamorphosis, of the ceaseless becoming of life, also a symbol of fluidity and essentially indefinable character of life… It is an enthralling metaphor to conceive of the universe (and of our life in it) as the dancing Shiva… Many Western thinkers of our time, particularly those with a background of post-Newtonian physics, have sought in the dancing Shiva a new metaphor, congruent with the New Physics, which could help us to transcend the immobile, static and petrified aspects of the Newtonian world-view.

About the Christian symbolism, Henryk's views dismiss parallelism between Hinduism and Christianity on the basis of abundance of life in the Hindu ideal and Jesus' ideal of Life Abundant. "It is not this ideal that dominates Christian consciousness and Christian symbolism, but rather the conception of life as transient, full of suffering, lived in the vale of tears," argues Henryk. "The dominant symbol of Christianity is the cross: Jesus crucified on the Mount of Golgotha. This is this symbol that has ingrained in our consciousness. Through this symbol we are led to think of life on earth as misery. What a contrast to the Hindu conception of life! And also to the Buddhist, as symbolized by the serene Buddha."

Henryk Skolimowski further argues by raising a burning question about the dominant Christianity symbol 'always counting our sins and miseries':

> Are we morbid as a culture because the dominant Christian symbol, the cross, when interiorized, has been devastating to our psyche, and made us morbid individually – never accepting joy as a fact of life, and always counting our sins and miseries? There was *no necessity* to elevate the cross as the central symbol within Christianity. We may wonder why it was so elevated. This symbol has been haunting our imagination more than we are aware. It may be responsible for many of our neuroses. Our life is split in the middle by the growing awareness, emanating from the cross, that life is not for living… Can Christianity renew itself? It has tried but without much success. It would seem that the best path for renewal would be to switch from the cross as the central symbol to the idea of Resurrection as the central symbol.

Has the central symbol of the Christianity been responsible for inciting the fundamental Christians at certain point of time in the past for the blood bath of the Jews? May be, if we judge from Skolimowski's philosophical interpretation of symbols. A symbol wearing gloom, and only gloom is, no doubt, might throw one into an abyss of frustration, violence and vendetta. Henryk also seems to unveil this fact saying that "The cross as a central symbol is very harsh."

In conclusion, Henryk has the following to bring to the fore: "Hindu symbolism is overwhelming to us in its exuberance – too many gods, deities and tangential stories. Christianity, with its morbid symbolism, has been at a low ebb for quite a while."

As life keeps evolving, as religions keep becoming more and more mature, new symbols keep emerging and enriching the values of symbolism to life. Henryk brings to the fore a rather newly invented idea/ symbol/ image – that of GAIA, the living Earth. About the Gaia, Henryk writes: "Gaia has proved to be very inspiring to all sorts of people. Gaia, in the image of the planet earth photographed from a satellite, is a symbol of oneness, a symbol of unity, of interconnectedness of the planet earth – its oceans, continents, peoples... Gaia is at present the best symbol we possess of the unity of the human race."

5. Enigmatic Symbols of Scientific Knowledge

In this age of ours science is dominating our hearts, our Minds and our psyche. Therefore, science, like religions and art, is also vibrant with symbols. The scientific symbols are often regarded superior to those of religion and art. But Henryk Skolimowski attempts to demonstrate that they are not, that 'the reasons for their alleged superiority are shaky at best, and question-begging most of the time'. Scientific symbols, until recently, were considered more powerful on the basis of two sources of justification as Skolimowski brings to the kind notice of all:

- Pragmatic in character: The scientific symbols were related to the idea of progress; and
- Epistemic in character: The scientific symbols were related to the idea of truth, and the idea that science had a privileged access to truth.

Henryk Skolimowski deeply examines both the justifications on the basis of which the scientific symbols attempt to prove their validity, and puts the whole truth before us, to our disapproval of the customary justifications:

- Science's legacy of progress is now very mixed blessing. Progress is no longer treated as sacrosanct, a sacred cow, and is indeed viewed by thinking people with grave misgivings... We have all learned by now the meaning of the dreadful fall-out of progress: a sense of frustration and stress, and of the meaningless of life; the destruction of the environment and of many species; the loss of the sacred... Thus progress has turned out to be a double-edged sword. Whoever wishes to take credit for all the blessings that science has brought to us must also take the responsibility for the negative consequences of science and technology... Thus the argument seeking justification of the validity of scientific symbols in terms of progress is crippled nowadays... The pragmatic argument is further weakened by the fact that in the twentieth century, by splitting the atom, science has unleashed enormous destructive powers. The symbol of the atomic mushroom is now part of our mental landscape. The possible horror of nuclear war is still haunting our dreams and making us uneasy in our daily living.

- How well are scientific symbols justified as bearers of truth? What do they actually represent? Put otherwise, what do they symbolize?... Within the doctrine of empiricism, scientific, or more generally, cognitive and physicalist symbols are most important because *they give us supreme access to reality*, which is physical in character. Yet this position is now part of the story of the past. The simple-minded realism that holds that the world exists as we describe it in our scientific theories can no longer be seriously upheld... We now know that our Mind is built into our theories. Our instruments are built into our theories. Our specific human faculties and their limitations are built into the structure of our theories. Our sensitivities are built into our instruments and our theories... The outcome of these arguments is that the epistemic justification of scientific symbols also collapses. We have naïvely believed that scientific symbols correspond to reality because we *assumed* so from the seventeenth century onwards. After three centuries of scientific experience, we now know better.

"How can the validity of scientific symbols be judged?" asks Henryk offering a stupendous idea. "Ultimately all symbols are to be judged by their contributions to the well-being of life, to the well-being of the human species and the well-being of other beings." Henryk's following words of suggestion are illuminating a new path for the science to work upon: "The onus is at the moment on the shoulders of science to show that its enterprise, and specially its symbols, truly serve culture in the broad sense."

Henryk also attempts to weigh scientific symbols against the backdrop of the theory of participation: In what way do they make us participate, and what is the result of this participation – for our total universe, and especially for human meaning? He gives us this idea to conceive and practice: "How deeply can you enter into the immensity of the universe? As deeply as you can embrace it in the arms of your participation; as deeply as your symbols engage you in the spectacle of the intentional universe.

Skolimowski remembers one of the most indisputable symbols of science which ranges between our fascination and its most serious repercussions. It is interesting to quote him saying:

> Yet some symbols of science do exert a great fascination over our Mind. The equation $E=mc^2$ is a marvel of human invention. And what a terrific potency it contains! Yes, precisely. It is a Faustian delight that we experience when we contemplate this symbol – for it is a symbol of a great power, the power that can explode and destroy. If it is the most significant equation that has ever been formulated by the human Mind, it is also the most ominous – its visible symbol is the mushroom cloud over Hiroshima. Need we say more?

6. *The Mind as a God of Symbols*

Before projecting Mind as the creator of symbols, Henryk quotes a beautiful verse from ancient Indian scripture, *Prasna Upanishad*:

> *Seen and unseen, heard and unheard*
> *Felt and not felt, the Mind sees all*
> *Since the Mind is all.*

Mind is not only the creator of symbols, but also interpreter of symbols and a coordinating agency of all symbolic activities. The history of various cultures, says Henryk, is a compelling testimony of how versatile, inventive, powerful and creative the Mind is. Henryk emphasizes the variety of cultures, rather than cultural relativism, because in that lies a supreme manifestation of the great potency of the *universal Mind*. It is this potency that makes our Mind *a participatory Mind*. Henryk's discourse on Mind the creator goes on to the fascination of the Mind itself:

> The theatre of the Mind is endlessly inventive. It writes the script in which the actors are people as well as objects of the outside world… There is nothing that is excluded from the theatre of the Mind. If anything is excluded from the Mind, it is 'outside reality'. The theatre of the Mind sets the boundaries to reality, defines and redefines these boundaries. 'Reality' does not have fixed boundaries. Whatever boundaries we find in it, they are imposed by the Mind… The creation of symbols is one of the peculiar powers of the Mind. In the making of symbols we have found another way of augmenting ourselves. For symbols have facilitated a new, important stage of our evolutionary articulation. By developing symbolic codes we have brought art, religion and philosophy to fruition. In the process we

have articulated ourselves as social, cultural and spiritual beings.

Symbolism created by human Mind is the uniqueness of human beings sharply distinguishing *Homo erectus* from monkeys and other primates. "It is our symbolic activity, the power to conceive symbols, and to use them extensively in an extraordinary variety of ways, that separates us from our brothers down the evolutionary ladder," Henryk reiterates.

Our Mind, our symbols and our world make a single axis. Quality of our Mind determines the quality of symbols it creates, which determines the kind of the world we live in. Henryk puts it as follows: "The deeper the Mind, the deeper the symbols. The deeper the symbols, the richer the world we live in. Thus the richness of our life can be defined by the depth and richness of the symbols (and other forms of sensitivity) through which we can receive, decipher and transform the abundance of life."

Symbols are part and parcel of all human aspects. These do not exist in isolation. A culture is also constantly under the influence of symbols it is identified with. In other words, symbolism is an integral part of a culture. "Our psyche is structured by the symbols of our culture," says Henryk. "The structure of our psyche shapes our values. Our values shape our actions." Thus, the psyche-values-action axis shapes our present world and the world of our future. This axis is rooted into symbols. The whole matrix can be represented in the form of a pyramid (figure 1) in which action (the tip of the pyramid) generated (and controlled) by symbols through psyche and values shapes a society serving as a fuel for the karma of the society – always a visible attribute of the society.

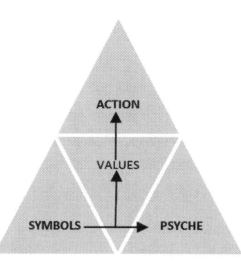

Figure 1: *The pyramid of culture* based on Skolimowski's theory of symbolism
(Action emerging from symbol through psyche and
values forms the visible tip of the iceberg)

As Henryk puts it, symbols are stronger than logic, and logic is often at their mercy. Symbols cannot trail behind logic. Logic cannot defeat symbols. Logic is often led by symbols.

Summary

Structures and symbols form integral constituents of life. Structures are for the whole life, and symbols for human life. Structures are articulation of life, and symbols that of human life. Structures are visible forms of the evolution which provide ever more hierarchical and ever more beautiful dimensions to life. Structures themselves have strikingly contributed to the ascent of evolution. On human part, an action leading to anti-structures is an activity countering the designs of evolution. An activity resulting in anti-structures amounts to killing light and advancing towards darkness. There is no dearth of such activities emanating from science. Therefore, science must contribute to support evolution in designing structures and structures in supporting the stupendous designs of the evolution. Rhythms and symmetries have been distinctive in the continuous evolution of structures. The ultimate thread that unites all forms of structures wonderfully serving to shelter life and create sacred precincts, such as temples, for the evolution of religious and cultural living is the evolution itself.

Symbols, as integral part of human cultures, impart to human life richness, vibrancy, resilience, beauty, prestige and sustainability. Buddhism, Hinduism and Christianity have led to evolve a variety of meaningful symbols many of which show parallelism and many are distinctive. These religious symbols have been pivotal to keep the dominant human cultures flourishing for centuries. A diversity of cultures with a variety of lively and deeper symbols is indispensable for the continuous flowering of humanity with right values leading to right action and contributing to the evolution of a new world. Symbols created by science are by and large dismal, not contributing to the enhancement of life. Symbols need to be valued in terms of their phenomenal contribution to the well-being of human life, of whole life and of the living planet. The Mind is the creator, interpreter and coordinator of the symbols. A religion or a culture through its evolution attempts to enrich itself with vibrant and meaningful symbols. Symbols phenomenally influence human psyche, which, in turn, determines the values, and values direct our actions. Thus the symbols, psyche, values and actions make a pyramid of culture in which only action is the visible tip of the iceberg. The more vibrant and meaningful the symbols the more resilient, creative and sustainable the religion and culture.

The Skolimowskian Philosophy is aesthetically fragrant with structures, symbols and evolution. Skolimowski eloquently taps the wonders the structures, the symbols and the evolution are laden with. Let us quote Henryk Skolimowski summarizing structures, symbols and evolution:

> The origin of all structures is the articulation of life. Structure is an open-ended scaffolding on which life can climb and flourish. All structure is a dwelling for life. The joy of structure is the blossoming of life woven around it.

Without structure or structures nothing would happen in evolution and in the architecture of human thought. For the evolutionary ascent has been carried through organized wholes, otherwise called structures.

Structures help life and are life-enhancing. Anti-structures undermine life and are destructive of life. This distinction enables us to see immediately that modern technology has been guilty of devising anti-structures, that is to say, *negative orders* whose purpose is to suppress the variety of life. We have arrived at an important ethical imperative: *in your work, in your behaviour, in your research, do not engage in activities that result in anti-structures.*

When life began to articulate itself, it burst into structures. When human life began to articulate it burst into symbols.

Symbols continue the odyssey of structures on the level of culture. They make life enhancing on the spiritual level. Symbols share with structures the importance of rhythm and symmetry, particularly symbols of art. Yet the ultimate religious symbols seem to address themselves to a sphere of their own – as they attempt to reach out in order to symbolize man's oneness with the Ultimate Wholeness. The ultimate religious symbols do not articulate. They integrate.

Religion integrates.

Art articulates.

Science describes.

We devour symbols, and our life is shaped by them. Tell me what your dominant symbols are and I shall tell you how you envisage the meaning of your life. If symbols were to be removed from us, we would spiral downwards to the level of monkeys. The greatness of our being is in proportion to the greatness of the symbols we contemplate, identify with, live by. Symbols are among the most profound inventions evolution has ever conceived.

The dominant symbol of Buddhism is the Buddha serenely sitting on the lotus flower – the symbol of eternal peace. The dominant symbol of Hinduism is the Dancing Shiva – the symbol of the universe in perpetual transformation. The dominant symbol of Christianity is Jesus dying on the cross-symbol of the impermanence and suffering of life. Are we morbid as a culture because the dominant symbol, the cross, has acted on our psyche so as to make us morbid, preventing us from accepting the joy of life as a natural phenomenon?

When we compare scientific symbols with religious symbols, the striking difference is that scientific symbols are non-intentional; they are only descriptive or denotative. We as human beings live in an intentional universe – this is where values reside, this is where our emotional life resides. Because scientific symbols are not intentional, they leave us cold, they do not partake in our intentional life.

The symbols of God in various religions were conceived as dynamic actors in the cosmic drama of becoming. Scientific symbols are pale shadows of the rich complexities that religious symbols unfold to us and enable us to participate in.

We do not know what symbols are. They are mysterious entities which relate us to the world, to each other, and above all to the life of the spirit. In the existence of symbols there is contained part of the mystery of being human.

Of all the mysteries of human existence, the Mind is the most intriguing. It is both transparent and inscrutably opaque. It is the maker of symbols. It is the interpreter of symbols. It is the ruler that decides what relates to what and why. Two billiard balls, hitting each other, do not know that they are related by cause and effect. Our Mind does.

We cannot unravel the complexity of the universe by looking at objects only. We can do it by looking most deeply into the Mind. The universe does not hold secrets; only the Mind does. All new insights are the flashes within. The contours of the outside world reflect the topography of our mind.

The deeper the Mind, the deeper the symbols. The deeper the symbols the richer the universe.

The glory of the universe is the unfolding epic of ever more penetrating symbols through which the destiny of the world is being realized.

CHAPTER 8

Understanding the Individual Spiral of Understanding

If virtue is one of the things in the soul, and if must necessarily be helpful, it must be wisdom: since quite by themselves all the things about the soul are neither helpful nor harmful, but they become helpful or harmful by the addition of wisdom or senselessness. According to this argument, virtue, since it is helpful, must be some kind of wisdom.[1]

– Socrates in *Great Dialogues of Plato*

1. The Individuality-Universality Interplay

We are individuals. Yet we are an integral part of the humanity. We are individual beings. Yet we are universal beings. Our individualism and our universalism are the two truths we as individual beings and as universal beings are existing. Henryk puts the two truisms in a more interesting way: "In spite of being highly individual, we are universal beings; and in spite of being universal, we are highly individual." He has explained how our individuality and universality coexist with each other; and how the phenomena of individual growth can be integrated into the fabric of culture and seen as congruent with the growth and manifestation of the universal Mind.

We record numerous examples in life wherein we find other peoples somewhat different or quite different from ourselves. Sometimes we find them as much different that they seem to us like a puzzle, and everything belonging to them looks weird, sometimes making us somewhat uneasy and indignant. Sometimes two peoples of different cultural background enter into conflicts. Why? Henryk Skolimowski has given very interesting, palatable and digestible reasons:

- because their spiral of understanding makes them understand the cosmos in quite a different way from ours;
- because their spirals of understanding and their cosmoses are often so different from ours;
- because their respective spirals of understanding may be so different that they interpret the phenomena in thoroughly different ways.

But the contrasts are possible to be overcome. Despite belonging to two different poles of culture, an understanding between people is possible. "Because we are one species, with common ancestry, and one Mind that unites us all; and this is in spite of, and in addition to, the endless variations and manifestations of this Mind," says Henryk fuelling hope into Mind.

2. Becoming with Pain

Physical growth of the body is important. But equally important, rather indispensable, is the mental growth. "When we grow mentally (intellectually, culturally, spiritually), our spiral of understanding grows," says Skolimowski adding that when one grows spiritually by developing the spiral of understanding to the point that his/ her Mind is seen as light.

"What happens when each of us grows in understanding, compassion, wisdom?" asks Skolimowski. "Our spiral of understanding enlarges. And the way it does so is very subtle, mysterious and complex... A radically new knowledge, as compared with that which the cone of our cosmos contains and is built upon, may shatter our world, and it may be traumatic and agonizing experience. Such an experience may even be tragic – if we are unable to resemble the pieces." However, the ultimate outcome is painless. Skolimowski adds: "Piercing through the walls of the cosmos may be a liberating and exhilarating experience, after which we are elevated and start to live in new dimensions."

How our individual growth takes place? Henryk Skolimowski attempts to explain many theories in this regard. However, he clarifies that none of the theories explains this growth satisfactorily, and that none probably will ever do. The two main theories he mentions about are as follows:

- Positive disintegration by K. Dabrowski: We do not grow mentally in a smooth, homogeneous, uninterrupted way. The process is discontinuous, at various times. There are some specific junctures at which a disintegration of the old personality (or of the old being) takes place. After a partial disintegration, we reintegrate on a new level, within a new spiral of understanding. When the process is completed, we call it 'positive disintegration'.
- Kaspar in *The Tin Drum*: We remain in a continuous state of disintegration, refuse to grow up, perhaps mentally ill for the rest of our life. It is a fascinating and awesome process, our journey through a partial disintegration, until, if we are lucky, we emerge out of the tunnel in a renewed shape.

The process of positive disintegration happens more than once in our life cycle, according to Henryk:

- The first occasion is the transition from babyhood to childhood. A three-year-old doesn't want to be treated as a baby any longer.
- Another transition of this kind happens when the teenager is in the process of becoming an adult. The whole personality changes. The whole being changes, often accompanied by all kinds of ridiculous tantrums. There is no rational or logical explanation for the erratic and inexplicable behaviour. Deep down the spiral of understanding is reconstructing itself.

- In our mature life too – if we are lucky – radical transitions occur when the old spiral is dismantled, and a new one is painstakingly reconstructed, and we become a new person.

Why are these transitions so painful? Skolimowski explains:

- Literally, *we have to rebuild our cosmos*. Our identity is modified in the process. The old psychic niches are upset and uprooted. This is a disquieting and painful process.
- In our development we do not grow smoothly and continuously. The discontinuities lead to tensions and sometimes to crises. These crises can sometimes be resolved within the existing psychic structure. Sometimes, however, they presage a transition to another structure. The crucial transitions are never easy and always painful. For what we experience is *the pain of becoming* – which cannot be alleviated, if we are to grow and mature.
- Becoming is not a logical process. It is an emergent process; and a creative one. The creative process of any kind means giving birth to something new. Like giving birth to a baby, it is full of pain. Such is the nature of our contingent universe: *to create is to experience the pain of becoming. To be in the process of becoming is to experience creative pain.*
- If pain is a precondition of real growth and real becoming, then we should not attempt to avoid it or try to escape it. For if we succeed in this escape, we may very well escape the process of growth itself. 'No pain, no gain.' To freeze one's development in order not to suffer is tantamount to psychic death.
- In periods of real growth and becoming, the foundations of our psychic structure are impinged upon. Our stability and identity are challenged and unsettled. We feel insecure. This insecurity extended over a period of time, particularly when it is acute, resolves itself in pain.

- Our being is in pain because it wants to stay where it is, while our becoming unanchors it and says: Come on, we must keep moving, we must fly. *The tension between being and becoming is a fundamental one in all evolution*, and in our individual lives as well. The result of this tension is always pain.

When growing old, we feel like Teilhard: "Growing old is like being increasingly penalized for a crime you have not committed." Henryk's philosophy, however, does not haunt us with the fear of growing older and older, or creates a fear of death. Pain is an inevitable ingredient of the process of becoming and thus worth being felt. "It is not the suffering that crushes and destroys, but the suffering of becoming that is part of the unfolding structure of evolving universe," says Henryk suggesting that we must look at suffering from a larger evolutionary perspective.

3. Truth Embedded in a Person

Our Mind is uniquely not ours own. And yet it is ours own. Henryk Skolimowski exposes us to our Mind, which is not ours, and is ours own: "Our Mind is made of the Mind of evolution, of the Mind of the species, of the Mind of the culture, of the Mind of our family. Each of these larger Minds is grafted on to our own, and so deep and pervading is the influence of these Minds that it seems astonishing that as individuals we still have a Mind of ours own."

Our Mind imbibes with sensitivities which Henryk regards as 'outreach tentacles of our Mind'. And the Mind cannot escape influence of any aspect of life. Family background, culture, society, system of education, even a system of governance, etc. profoundly influence our Mind. But, Henryk says, ultimately the spiral of our understanding is uniquely ours own; just as our face, so similar to many other faces, is yet unique. He reiterates, "It is therefore possible and justifiable to speak of the unique forms of perception of an individual; and also his/ her unique world-view which, although it is shared with many other individuals, yet may possess some features that are utterly singular."

Despite utterly singular characteristic of the Mind, can there something like personal truth, or truth can only be universal (the truth of a given culture)? There can be, and there is, of course? Like unique Mind there is unique spiral of understanding too. "There are some aspects of our own spiral which are unique and not reducible to the universal spiral," argues Henryk.

There are some questions stirring the Mind in its deeper layers. Henryk raises them: Why do we, each of us, have a different and unique spiral of understanding? Why is the cosmos so diverse? Why is it so that each snowflake is different? Henryk's simple and Mind-satisfying answer is: "The cosmos delights in variety. Life needs variety for its exuberance and resilience. The human body, and the body of every animal, is a miracle of complexity. The human brain is one most complex creation of nature and of the cosmos. This complexity, when translated into individual Minds, resolves itself in a myriad of different spirals of understanding. Those aspects of our individual spirals that are outside the universal spiral are the ones that make our world-view a little different, our perceptions a little different, and finally our truths a little different – not in all aspects but in some aspects of our perceptions of the world."

The consequences of the personal truth can also lead to a clash. When? Henryk lets us know: "There are times when the idiosyncrasies of our individual spirals of understanding (expressed as personal truths) become especially important for the individual. There are times when the individual does not wish to or is unable to suppress his/ her truth. As a consequence a clash follows."

We recognize our personal truth and often attempt to superimpose it on the truths upheld by religion and science. The personal truth infuses in us a feeling of cheerfulness and pride. But it is not digested by the religion, culture and science, and often remains unrecognized. Sometimes the individual truth throws one into controversy, sometimes even in trauma.

Why is the personal truth regarded as inferior, and unfit to be recognized as truth? Henryk makes it clearer: "The reason lies in our established philosophies, and particularly the ruling epistemologies, which can be very dictatorial and overpowering masters."

What does the science-oriented Western philosophy assume? Henryk presents three assumptions:

(1) It assumes that we are all possessors of the universal Mind, which is somehow embodied in each of us in the same form and apparently in the same degree; because of this, it allows us to operate as the same universal beings.

(2) It assumes, moreover, that reality is knowable or accessible to us and can be adequately described in our theories; it assumes that we can equally well comprehend these theories – because of the first assumption.

(3) It assumes furthermore that our Mind does not change historically and individually. We are supposed to have the same structure of Mind – unchanging and fixed, yielding the same kind of knowledge through the eons of time.

Henryk concludes that these assumptions strike us rather crude. "It *cannot* be legitimately claimed that we all have the same universal Mind embodied in us in the same form and degree," says Henryk. On the basis of his arguments about the personal truth and universal truth, Henryk derives his own conclusion:

> I have argued for the legitimacy of personal truth, but I do
> not wish to enshrine personal truth as all-important. Nor do
> I wish to eulogize the individual spiral of understanding as
> all-important. We are evolutionary creatures, social creatures,
> cultural creatures. To that degree our truths are common.
> Yet the individual Mind and its truth – as reflected in the

unique aspects of its spiral of understanding – must not be ignored. Therefore a distinction must be made between shared (universal) truths and personal truths.

4. The Meaningful Transformation

Skolimowski's delighting views about transformation make a room in the heart and leave an aesthetic feeling. "Transformation is a beautiful term. It embodies a multitude of virtues. Whatever aspect of evolution or of our lives we take, transformation has been at work… In our shattered world we all desire transformation, if only in order to heal ourselves, and become whole again. Since so many people desire transformation and wholeness, this demand must somehow be met."

A new change our being undergoes is a meaningful transformation. However, as Henryk says, it can be no easy, weekend affair. "The Illustrious Ones knew better when they exhorted us, sometimes gently, sometimes not so gently, on the necessity of discipline – which often includes the path of austerity," he reiterates.

Henryk narrates the experiences of his second visit to Dharamshala, a little mountain village in the foothills of the Himalayas in northern India to see the Dalai Lama: "I had been moved by his simplicity and his genuine concern for all sentient beings. I was also impressed by the way Tibetan monks are trained, or should we say, train themselves: endless memorizations of classical texts… and at the end of the process – the Mind breathing universal compassion, which they call the Great Compassion."

Henryk, during the debate at Dharamshala raised the question he simplified after giving deeper thought: "Is the Mind inherently compassionate or is compassion acquired?" To Henryk, the Tibetan Lamas seemed to be saying in response to the question: even if the Mind is not compassionate, we can make it compassionate. The endless Tibetan techniques of controlling the Mind are created for this purpose. "In the Buddhist framework human nature is assumed to be noble," adds Henryk.

"Our Mind has almost infinite capacity," Henryk explains. "But the development of this capacity is an arduous process, and so is the process of the transformation of the spiral of understanding that accompanies it. No shortcut to glory."

Henryk Skolimowski attempts to provide some the principles that can help one in embarking on the path of genuine transformation. For this he emphasizes the Yoga of Transformation and illustrates ten principles of it:

(1) Become aware of your *conditioning*.

(2) Become aware of *deep assumptions* which you are subconsciously upholding.

(3) Become aware of the most important *values* that underlie the basic structure of your being, and of your thinking.

(4) Become aware of *how these assumptions and values guide and manipulate your behaviour, action, thinking*.

(5) Become aware *which of these assumptions and values are undesirable* because they dwarf your horizons or arrest your growth in one way or another. Each of these assumptions may be held at a deep subconscious level, and from there may be controlling you.

(6) *Watch and observe the instances of your actions and behaviour* while they are manipulated by the undesirable assumptions/ values. Identify clearly the causes and the effects.

(7) *Articulate alternative assumptions and values* by which you would like to be guided and inspired.

(8) *Imagine the forms of behaviour, actions and thinking* that would follow from the alternative assumptions/ values.

(9) *Deliberately try to bring about the forms of behaviour, thinking and action* expressing the new assumptions. Implement your new assumptions in your daily life. Watch the process. *Repeat the process*. Practice is important.

(10) *Restructure your being* in the image of these assumptions; which is to say, restructure your spiral of understanding.

The Yoga of Transformation that Henryk Skolimowski has developed and taught genuinely serves as a set of strategies for the individual Mind that is on the path of self-transformation. Henryk gives us a tip: "The gift of transformation is not one given to you from heaven, but one that you give yourself at the end of the long, arduous but exciting journey."

5. Meditation in the Spiral of Understanding

Exquisitely defining meditation, Henryk Skolimowski describes the spiral of individual understanding during the process of meditation. First, let us meditate on Skolimowski's stupendous definition of meditation: It is a process of deep relaxation combined with a process of deep reflection – a process of going into the depths of ourselves that enables us not only to rest deeply but somehow detach ourselves from the busy ticking of our Mind – according to its usual routine.

To harvest some of the nicest feelings about meditation and the real taste of meditation, let us hear Skolimowski saying more about meditation:

> If meditation is successful we gain during the course of it a capacity to look at ourselves; and more importantly at our own Mind – from a distance. During such moments we can really see how conditioned our Minds are and how conditioned are the forms of our thinking. We are looking then, as it were, at our own spiral of understanding from a vintage-point outside the spiral – which does not often happen in our busy lives.
>
> Now during prolonged periods of meditation we cannot step out of our spiral but actually enlarge it. This happens when we are able to find in what way it constrains us; more specifically which assumptions our spiral holds and how these assumptions affect us. Reasoning with assumptions is a most difficult task. They invariably control our thinking from a

hidden layer below. Now during the process of meditation, when the discursive and coldly rational functions of the Mind are suspended, it is easier to 'talk to our assumptions', to question and examine them, than during normal periods when we simply act these assumptions out. Meditation can thus be used as an aspect of the yoga of transformation.

Our cosmos goes on enlarging with the increase of the angle of our cone if we intend to do so. Skolimowski asks what happens if we keep enlarging this angle, and gives a fabulous response himself: "Extraordinary things happen! If during meditation, or through some other means, we succeed in transcending all assumptions, liberating ourselves from all spirals of understanding, then we become infinite, our understanding is infinite, our cosmos is infinite... This is the state when the Atman meets the Brahman, when one is united with the One, the state of ultimate oneness of the individual consciousness with . . . there are no words to express this state."

6. The Two Hemispheres of the Brain

Can there be something more absurd than analyzing the functions of a Mind in a piecemeal manner? Sharp division of human brain into two parts, viz., left hemisphere and the right hemisphere by neurophysiologists, and then ascribing different functioning to the two parts, is yet another case of reductionist thinking.

The neurophysiologists generalized different functions of the different parts of the brain in 1970s. For example, as Henryk mentions, the left side of the brain is predominantly responsible for abstract, discursive and analytical thinking and action, while the right side of the brain is predominantly intuitive, emotional, artistic, integrative.

Referring to the splitting of the brain into two distinctive hemispheres as 'part of the heritage of Cartesian dualism and also of Cartesian crispness' Henryk Skolimowski decries the separation of the brain. "Now we decry

Descartes' separation of the Mind from the body, Henryk criticizes. "We also decry Descartes' analytical method, which neatly and clinically separates all things into isolated compartments, for the method is responsible for much of the process of atomization, and following it the process of alienation. Yet deep down we seem to love this Cartesian-clinical sorting out! The separation of the brain into two *distinctive* hemispheres is essentially a Cartesian exercise, a split that divides what we know as working in a unitary way in our own lives."

There is too much craze, too much enthusiasm, too much curiosity amongst scientists to know the specific functions of the two hemispheres of the brain. To them the two hemispheres look like a wonder. Explanation of the brain in terms of its physical dimensions again becomes a matter of physical science, which is addicted to look at everything as a machine. Brain's structure is no exception. Henryk is baffled by the fact that 'we are so conditioned to accept as genuine only *physical* explanations'. And he is worried also, when it comes even to the Mind which should not be victimized by false interpretations. "It boggles the Mind how absurdly reductionist we have become – even when we attempt to explain the highest mysteries, such as the Mind," he explains.

In splitting the brain into two hemispheres, according to Henryk, we have finally found the scapegoat: "It is the left hemisphere that is the culprit. It is the monster in our midst that paralyzes." With this physical explanation of the brain, we have discovered the real culprit. We have always been right; what can we do if one of the two hemispheres of the brain is culprit. "Our two hemispheres are out of balance," Henryk ridicules the reductionist theory. "The left hemisphere is an ogre intimidating and suppressing our right hemisphere. We are the innocent victims."

Henryk also attempts to bring to the fore some more facts which deeply affect our life and our role in life in the context of the explanation of the Mind:

> There is indeed a grave imbalance in our life if we allow
> abstract analytical modes of our Minds to dominate our

being to the point that we become dry sticks, devoid of emotional life and withering in the straitjacket of objectivity, logic and functional rationality.

But another form of imbalance is possible and often occurs, namely when we try to live by the right hemisphere alone. We then end up in emotional messes. Our emotional life runs rampant and we become a slave to it. The reasoning by pure brain is a mistake in the long run. But reasoning by blood alone is equally dangerous. Emotions running loose may be as dangerous to our balance as excessive rationality freezing it.

Henryk recognizes the need of imposed emotional control: "These controls are called ethical codes, codes of honour, duty, obligation. They often include the process of sublimation of our sexual urges, and other manifestations of our imperial ego."

Do we need to give too much emphasis on the functioning of or increased dependence on the right hemisphere? Henryk has this crucial tip for us: "The right balance is a proper articulation and the right orchestration of our sensitivities. The heart and emotions have to be cultivated in the form of appropriate sensitivities. Only then do we become masters of our own life... Through articulateness of our sensitivities we weave patterns of meaning. Unarticulated emotions can become a torrent that messes up our being. Articulated emotions, when crystallized in enduring works of art, are things of beauty, the joy of human life, and the pride of evolution."

Thus we need not be dependent or swayed away by the synthesis of the brain's two hemispheres. This is immaterial to life. What is important is the right path to wholeness which needs, as Henryk tells us, the cultivation and articulation of human sensitivities, including wisdom and compassion.

7. Modelling the Self-integrity

Mind alone is the course of bondage and liberation for human beings.[3]
– Amritabindu Upanishad

Henryk Skolimowski looks at the three basic models of the self-integrity and then proposes his own which is compatible with our times. "Each model of the self not only reveals what it considers to be the essential meaning of human life but is in fact a *disguised form of religion*," says Henryk.

The Hindu Model

- The individual self receives its meaning by participating in the Absolute self. When the Atman (the individual self) completely merges with the Brahman (the Absolute Self) and dissolves in it, the individual self is completely redeemed, fulfilled and at peace. The strife is ended, and the Nirvana achieved.
- Individual self acquires its significance by the presence in it of the Absolute Self. The individual self is sustained by Absolute Self, and finally dissolved in it.

Henryk chooses the Hindu model as the exemplar one because 'within it the relationship between the individual self (the Atman) and the cosmic self (the Brahman) is very clearly spelled out; while the relationship is often confusedly spelled out in Abrahamical religions'.

The Plato Model

- The individual self (the soul) is imprisoned in the prison of the body; or at least limited and constrained by the body.

- The process of liberation and of self-actualization is one of overcoming the coarseness of the body. This occurs through the process of Enlightenment.
- The individual self then merges with the Form of the self.
- The liberation consists of the realization of the god-within, which is identified with the absolute Form.
- The meaning of life and the meaning of the self are related to the essence of man – the Form underlying our existence.

The process of liberation in the Hindu and the Plato models is different. According to Henryk, "In the Hindu model the self (Atman) is liberated by *dissolving* in the Brahman (the Cosmic Self). In the Plato's model (as well as in the Buddhist one), the self is liberated through its own effort, until the self reaches the very core of its being – the god-within."

The Existentialist Model

- There is no absolute. There are no essences. The self is conceived as a drifting monad without a higher aim or purpose.
- Since the individual existence is wretched and meaningless, the best we can do is to enjoy it perversely.
- God is dead. The universe has no purpose or meaning; nor do we. Existential despair is a natural state. There is no abode for our hopes and higher aspirations. There is only brute matter out there. And *us* – freaks from the standpoint of the vast, mute and cold universe.

The Existentialist model of Sartre and his followers is overtly aesthetic, but, according to Skolimowski, the model possesses its curious ideology. About this model Skolimowski concludes: "Viewed historically, the existentialist model of the self is a derivation of other models representing the philosophy of resignation such as Epicureanism, cynicism, hedonism – all born at the time of the shrinking of man."

The Participatory Model

Skolimowski reaches highest possible horizons of human thinking and moulding human actions accordingly encompassing everything in man and man in everything, proposes the fourth model of the self. It is the Participatory Model. Basic features of the model are:

- The individual self and the cosmic self are in the process of continuous evolution, each contributing to the other as evolution goes on.

- The individual self does not merge with the absolute self or the form of the self that is ready, out there, and waiting for us.

- The self is *projected* into Omega, which is the cosmic self at the end of time. In continually upgrading itself, the individual self contributes to the cosmic self.

- Meaningful life is the life of continuous becoming. Continuous becoming signifies continuous creativity; it also signifies continuous liberation from the shackles of old being, which wants to hold us back. Thus, meaning = becoming = liberation = creativity. And conversely, creativity signifies liberation; and also signifies becoming and ultimately the attainment of meaning. The four concepts co-define each other; they form a mandala pattern (figure 1).

- The four concepts outline a new theology. The name of this theology is: 'We are God in the making', through our creative potential, through the process of continuous becoming.

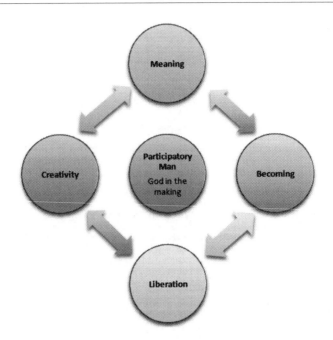

Figure 1: The mandala of the life of continuous becoming
(slightly modified from Henryk Skolimowski)

The Skolimowskian Model of the self, the participatory model, has two major attributes which have enormous implications for the holistic development of the self, and consequently of the entire humanity. These are: Being at peace, and being whole. Henryk explains as follows: *Being at peace,* means attaining the optimal state of being; not grumbling, not being torn by ever new desires, ambitions, envy, jealousies. *Being whole* means not being fragmented, decimated, scattered. Above all it means being guided by coherent pattern of meaning.

The two attributes of human life Henryk describes – being at peace and being whole – are difficult to be achieved in our contemporary times. Henryk ascribes the overall meaninglessness of the technological world – its frantic drive for efficiency, and its violence as the main reason. "Meaninglessness and violence are built into the very structure of the technological world," Henryk looks deeper into the crises of all sorts associated with the meaningless development of heartless and mindless technology, the notorious daughter of science. "The modus operandi of this world is efficiency, fragmentation, control and manipulation, which are hardly prerequisites for an integrated life."

"The key to meaningful reconstruction lies in the idea of participation," claims Henryk. How deeply can you enter into the immensity of the universe? As deeply as you can embrace it in the arms of your participation. Everything else is mere shadow. The real thing is the immense journey of participation... The integrated self is one of the high attainments of the human species."

The integrated self, Henryk tells us, is accomplished by the positive construction of the self: "The positive image of the individual self that is harmoniously merging with and meaningfully participating in the social self, and then the universal self (figure 2)."

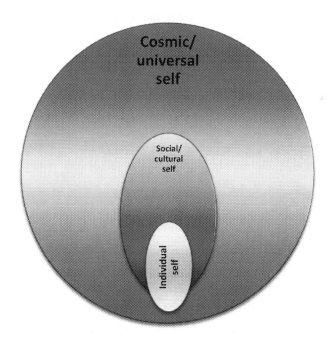

Figure 2: Positive image of the self (modified from Skolimowski)

A model of the integrated self, i.e., the participatory model, is distinctive and evolutionary. It not only augments integrity at individual level, at social/ cultural level and at cosmic/ universal level; it helps humans discover new horizons to work at. It is life-enhancing and happiness-ameliorating. Henryk's model truly cultivates karma and creativity vital for the becoming and keep nurturing. He makes a soul-touching suggestion:

> To be truly integrated, you must participate in the interest of the human family and of the cosmos at large. If you only cultivate your own garden, if you don't participate in some kind of heaven which is above you and beyond you, you cannot be genuinely whole and integrated... The universe of participation is immensely powerful, if we make participation an inherent part of our universe.

8. The Space of Grace for the Participatory Mind

Infinite is the source of joy. There is no joy in the finite. Ask to know the infinite.[4]
– Chandogya Upanishad

The universe is endowed with meaning. The universe is endowed with grace. The universe is endowed with a purpose. The universe is endowed with everything it is meant for. The universe is endowed with all sacredness. The universe is endowed with everything, every process, every phenomenon it has been created for.

Upholding the universe's endowment of sacredness as the most significant aspect of human life amounts to understand the real and the deeper meaning of life. "The meaning of the sacred cannot be understood unless the meaning of life is understood," advises Henryk. "The 'meaningful' and the 'sacred' are inherently connected. They present two facets of the same phenomenon. 'Sacred' is a religious term for expressing the ultimate depths of human meaning. On the other hand, 'deeply meaningful' is an existential expression for those special reverential moments of our life that we hold as sacred – although we do not use the term."

Henryk quotes Gregory Bateson, who in his *Mind and Nature: A Necessary Unity* writes: "The *sacred* (whatever that means) is surely related (somehow) to the *beautiful* (whatever that means). And if we could say how they are related, we could perhaps say what the words mean. Or perhaps that would never be necessary."

Arriving at the meaning of sacred space, Skolimowski questions before responding himself: What is the meaning of sacred space? Does it exist of itself, independently of the Mind, by its 'objective' characteristics, so to speak? Or is it created by human Mind?... Can sacred spaces be declared as such *without* the participation of the participatory Mind? Is it not the participatory Mind that makes spaces and geometries sacred of its depositions and powers?

Skolimowski's answer to the questions he raises about the sacredness is as follows: "We become God when we experience some spaces as sacred, at whatever brief moment of time. Or more precisely, we assume the characteristics of God when we enjoy a spiritual experience. Alternatively, we experience the world as sacred because God dwells in us at the moment of these experiences." Skolimowski flows his ideas so marvellously:

'He who thinks becomes God' (Upanishads).

He who participates in God becomes God.

He who participates in the context of God becomes God.

He who is capable of creating the context of God becomes God.

Being at one with God is participating in God's plan. (God's plan when spelled out means: he/ she who has the power of empathy and of deep identification (on the emotional, spiritual and intellectual levels) with those attributes through which we conceive of God – becomes God.)

He/ she who lives in grace inhabits sacred spaces.

He/ she who lives in Grace possesses the reverential frame of Mind and is guided by reverential perception.

"*When the participatory Mind enters the space of grace, it becomes the reverential Mind,*" says Henryk. "The reverential Mind is the form of the attunement of the Mind that allows us to enter the space of grace." Henryk also presents the Christian and the Hindu views of the space of grace:

- According to the Christian view, grace is considered a gift, God's gift. It is bestowed on us whether we deserve it or not.
- Within the Hindu framework the state of our individual grace is a gift of the Brahman, is bestowed on us by the Brahman – conceived as the absolute everlasting ground of being from which everything springs and by which everything exists and moves.
- In both the traditional Christian framework and the Hindu framework, grace is explained as *dues ex machina* – by the intervention of divine powers residing outside ourselves. Participation in God is then an act of divine mercy bestowed upon us from outside.

When we read Henryk Skolimowski's talks on the sacred space, or the space of grace, his ideas begin flowering in heart; and our Mind undergoes natural process of magic (which is a rare experience), and begins flowering with wisdom:

> *Within the framework of the participatory Mind, (as with Plato and Buddha) it is our Mind which creates the attributes and structures that enable the Mind to become reverential. Through this act we create the space of grace. . .* The space of grace, or sacred space, is created by the condition of the Mind that experiences 'ordinary' spaces in an extraordinary way. *The divine Mind is part of evolution divinizing itself.* The experience of divinity is part of the natural process. There are no occult forces, no supernatural interventions, no magic – except the magic of becoming. Thus magic is part of the natural process. The point is that the natural (at

certain pivotal junctures) manifests itself as magical. . . The Buddha has taught: Be forever awake. Be forever watchful. Keep your Mind clear. A well controlled Mind is a source of great joy. . . Through its natural magic, evolution has created Mind. Through its natural magic, the Mind co-creates with reality. A part of the process of co-creation is the creation of reverential space. When one lives permanently in reverential spaces one lives in grace. Participatory Mind is a vehicle of divinity. For there is no other vehicle to deliver us to divinity.

Summary

Henryk Skolimowski's theory of the spiral of understanding attempts to quench human thirst of understanding to understand the 'limits' of Mind and the 'limits' of the universe the Mind extend into and plays its role within. Henryk does churning of thoughts evolving from the spectacularly evolving Mind and makes us understand how the spiral of understanding works at individual level in determining the expansion of the universe at individual level. Our individuality is an integrated entity of our universality. The phenomenon of individual growth is connected with the fabric of the culture the individual has been nurtured into and with the universal Mind the individual Mind is the manifestation of. 'There are endless variations and manifestations of the Mind'. What a wonderful essence of Henryk's interpretation of human Mind!

Becoming is not an ordinary phenomenon, not a logical process. It is extremely complex and extraordinary phenomenon which does not go on without experiencing pain. The pain is inevitable to keep the phenomenon of becoming going and helps us accumulate some of the nicest experiences. We are ready to bear the pain, as we have lure to becoming. The becoming helps us to break the walls of the cosmos, thus helping our cosmos expand its boundaries. Becoming and creativity go hand in hand. There is no creativity without becoming; and there is no becoming without creativity. Creativity makes us feel the experience of pain of becoming. The pain itself is creative in nature. As pain is part of the phenomenon of natural growth, we must not avoid it.

Our Mind is not just our own, not just as it looks to be. It is no individual property. It is made up of many other illuminated Minds – the Mind of the evolution, the Mind of the species, the Mind of the culture, the Mind of the family. An individual Mind is grafted with so many larger Minds. Therefore, in a sense, an individual Mind is a Universal Mind with certain degrees of sensitivity of the 'larger' Minds it integrates into itself. What is significant for acquiring knowledge is the Universal Mind each individual Mind is grafted with.

Transformation is a continuous process. The whole life is in transformation. We all seek transformation, for that is the precondition of our becoming, of our entry into heaven. Even the Buddha will seek his transformation. Without transformation we cannot realize our complete cycle, our salvation. Undergoing transformation, we elevate our being, enlarge our spiral of understanding and, consequently, our universe. Compassion may be acquired or it may be an inherent trait of our Mind – it might be difficult to conclude, but a compassionate Mind, rather than an aggressive Mind, is a boon for humanity, and we have enormous 'ammunition' in our Mind to ignite compassion and transform us into a complete compassionate being.

Clear-cut division of the brain into two hemispheres by neurophysiologists is an attempt to categorize the wonderful organ of the body as a physical entity. They also ascribe specific functions to the right and to the left hemispheres of the brain. This kind of reductionist approach itself attempts to strike an imbalance in the delicate phenomenon of the Mind. The Mind astonishingly reveals the mysteries of everything there is in the universe.

There are four important models of the integrated self: The Hindu model, the Plato model, the existentialist model, and the participatory model. In the participatory model, proposed by Henryk Skolimowski, the meaning, the becoming, the liberation and the creativity complement each other and complete the cycle of continuous becoming. The integrated self is realized with meaningful participation of the self with the society and the culture and with the cosmos.

The participatory Mind, upon entering into the space of grace, becomes the reverential Mind. A sacred space or a reverential space is a result of the co-creation of the Mind with the reality. The participatory Mind serves as a chariot to lead us to divinity.

The theory of Individual Spiral of Understanding propounded by Henryk Skolimowski can be delightfully articulated in individual development of humans following the participatory Mind approach. Let us read Skolimowski summarizing the Individual Spiral of Understanding:

> Our individuality and universality are engaged in a continuous eternal dance. We are not monads. We are not carbon copies of the same universal Mind. We share vast realms of our experience with others, including language, symbols and the appreciation of art. Our individual spiral of understanding merges with the universal spiral, but not completely. It is shaped and determined by the universal spiral, but not entirely. We are the guardians of our own spiral. It alone determines the meaning and the shape of our life.
>
> The individual spiral of understanding evolves continuously. In its evolution there are discontinuous jumps. When they occur our cosmos is in disarray. The recomposition of the spiral of understanding in our own life is always a painful process. These are the pains of becoming. We must not avoid them. For in avoiding them, we would avoid our greater destiny.
>
> Becoming is not a logical process. It is an emergent process, and a creative one. To create is to experience the

pains of becoming. To be in the process of becoming is to experience creative pains. As we evolve, we change. As we change, we leave behind the old shells. As we reconstruct within, we suffer a temporary dislocation of our identity. As we suffer the inner dislocation, we are in pain. All this is natural and inevitable. Pain is a part of individual growth and of evolutionary growth. We must not try to avoid it. But we must not court it either.

Truth is a sublime subject and a difficult one. When we talk about truth, we often imagine it to be something given from above, something so mighty and universal that we simply must bow to it. Yet truth is a matter of understanding. Truth is indeed a form of understanding. All understanding is a function of our spiral of understanding. When we recognize universal truths it simply means that our individual spiral sings in unison with other spirals. At such a time universal truths prevail.

However, our individual spiral of understanding cannot be entirely expressed through the universal spiral. There are aspects of it that are unique, idiosyncratic, singular. These aspects are usually suppressed, since we are encouraged to conform. Yet there are times when the idiosyncratic aspects of the individual spiral surface and assert themselves – against the prevailing opinion. At such times the individual expresses his/ her personal truth.

Personal truth is not a contradiction in terms. It is as justifiable an epistemological product as universal truth – if we comprehend the meaning of the spiral of understanding (individual and universal) in any depth.

There are instances when personal truths become universal ones. It happens when other individuals 'begin to see our way.' Those individuals have reconstructed their spiral of understanding which now enables them to comprehend the new truth/ vision. This happens in religion and in science. Every new insight, whether religious or scientific, begins with a personal truth. Every new great philosophy starts as a personal truth. Every new religion starts as a personal truth. Every new social design starts as a personal truth.

We all desire transformation – even if we are Buddhas. To seek transformation is to seek an entrance to heaven, however small this heaven may be. From genuine transformation, which changes our being and our spiral of understanding, we must separate out a variety of superficial ego-messages which abound in our times and which are but weekend-long transformations. A cosmetic message is better than nothing, one might maintain. But the other side of the coin must not be overlooked. In opting for a superficial message we may be actually preventing ourselves from attaining a genuine transformation.

Whether our Mind is inherently compassionate or whether compassion is an acquired trait is an open issue. What is clear however is that the existence of the compassionate Mind is as much a part of human nature as is the existence of the aggressive Mind.

Universal compassion is not limited geographically among the world's peoples. Tibetan monks are not unique in being able to tune to it: Western Europeans can accomplish this feat as well. That the young Mr. Dreyfus could become a Tibetan *geshe* eloquently testifies to the fact that the human Mind is almost infinite and that almost anything is possible for it. The potency of the Mind does not actualize itself without an effort. Transformation is work. Sometimes it is a Herculean task.

Whatever route to transformation you choose, be aware of the power of the assumption of the system in which you grew up. Deliberately try to bring about the forms of behaviour, thought and action embodying the desirable assumptions. Try to implement the new assumptions in your daily practice. *To become a Buddha, you must behave like one.* This also applies to the model of the integrated self. To be a part of the process of God in becoming, to be at peace and whole, you must hold strong images of your wholeness in your Mind – your wholeness as part of the overall harmony with yourself and with the larger cosmos. The integrated self is one of the highest attainments of the human race. The art of living is second to none. The art of sculpting yourself is as difficult as the art of carving *David* out of raw marble.

Basic models of the individual self are not numerous.

(1) The Hindu/ Christian Model. God exists outside; He infuses meaning into our lives.

(2) The Plato/ Buddha model. Godhead exists within; the realization of meaning is the actualization of our divine potential.

(3) The existential/ hedonistic model. No God; alternatively – we are god unto ourselves; meaning is limited to our ego-based, self-contained journey.

(4) The participatory/ evolutionary model. Evolution is God-in-the-making; meaning emerges in the process of our evolutionary becoming.

Meaningful life, in the evolutionary model, is the life of continuous becoming. Continuous becoming signifies continuous creativity; it also signifies continuous liberation from the shackles of the old being. Thus meaning = becoming = liberation = creativity. We should become used to thinking in concepts that organically feed into each other. Holistic thinking and participatory thinking transcend atom-by-atom arrangements. *Mandala thinking* is another name for holistic thinking.

To participate in the highest realms of human experience is to participate in the sacred. This form of experience is a form of magic. But it is natural magic. We create this magic, or the space of grace, by cultivating the reverential Mind. When one lives permanently in reverential space, one lives in grace.

We were born in difficult times. We can feel sorry for ourselves. And justifiably so. But being sorry for ourselves will not help us to take our evolutionary destiny into our own hands. Critical times such as ours break many lesser souls. Yet such times are a challenge to our ultimate substance. Those who have it will prevail – to give testimony to the indestructible fibre of the human condition; to the qualities of endurance, perseverance, courage and hope upon which will be built a new spirituality – a positive residue of the anguish of the country.

Hope will be very important in this endeavour. Hope is the spring eternal. Hope is part of our ontological structure. Hope is the scaffolding of our existence. Hope is the nourishment that sustains us daily. Hope is a precondition of our mental health. Hope is the oxygen of our hearts and souls. Hope is the ray of light that separates life from death. Hope is the eternal flower that blossoms against the snow.

Hope is a reassertion of our belief in the meaning of life; and in the sense of the universe. Hope is a precondition of all meaning, of all strivings, of all actions. To embrace hope is a form of wisdom.

We should not forget meditation either, for it is an invaluable mirror in which the spiral of our individual understanding can be beautifully reflected upon. The rational man does not shun meditation, for it can be a powerful tool of self-transformation.

CHAPTER 9

Understanding the Universal Spiral of Understanding

To follow knowledge, like a sinking star,
Beyond the utmost bound of human thought.[1]
– Odysseus

1. The Culture-Spiral-Perspective Diversity

Henryk Skolimowski spells the culture so exquisitely! "Our culture is our bondage. Our culture is also our liberator. Our culture is our nourisher. Our culture is also the mesmeriser – keeping us transfixed in the mould it has established, and hardly allowing for alternative perspectives."

There is a close relation between the cosmology of a culture and the knowledge this culture has produced for the understanding of the world, for its interaction with other cultures of the world. Every culture considers, or tends to consider, its world-view superior to others; often it regards its world-view as the only true one. A culture teaches its people to consider themselves to be superior to others, to be the only true people in the world. Skolimowski refers the people as 'happy victims of their culture's perspectives' because they 'acquired them with their mother's milk'.

Until 20th century, Henryk says, most Western anthropologists tried to understand various cultures by imposing their matrix, their spiral of understanding, on different matrices and different spirals of understanding. They also projected those cultures as irrational and primitive. "Only in the twentieth century, and particularly the second half of the twentieth century, have anthropologists begun to understand other people in their own terms: by submerging themselves within these other spirals of understanding, by seeing them within," Henryk maintains. "And then things started to appear differently. Many of these 'primitive cultures', when we try to understand them from within, exhibit an extraordinary degree of unity and connectedness."

What happens when two radically different cultures interact with each other? Henryk Skolimowski has the following explanation:

-   Their universes and consequently their spirals of understanding do not match each other; they usually partly overlap, but there are areas in which there is no overlap.
-   The areas that do not overlap are usually difficult for each other to comprehend. . . If two spirals of understanding do not overlap at all, then we are in real trouble – there is no communication possible. We have so far been unable to establish a communication with extra-terrestrial intelligences. Perhaps they are willing to communicate with us. But our respective spirals of understanding may be so different that there is no point of overlap. Therefore we have nothing in common, we cannot communicate; we cannot enter into each other's cosmos.
-   When the gap between two incompatible cultures is somehow bridged, it simply means that those parts of their respective spirals which were once not overlapping are now somehow calibrated, translatable into each other.
-   Our spiral of understanding attempts to manipulate the situation and convey it in its own distinctive terms.
-   In every culture there are invisible forces and presences which interact and interfere with the visible realities. They make the deep underlying matrix. They are a part of our mythology which

nourishes and controls. We all live by the invisible. *It is the invisible that controls the visible.*

- When two different spirals of understanding meet each other, what is at stake is not just different interpretation of certain facts, but the validity of cultures that these respective spirals represent. What is at stake, on other level, is the validity of our own cherished Mind. *We never think little of our Mind.*

Explaining the phenomenon of Qi (Chi), the Chinese term for vital energy, Skolimowski concludes that "Reality is not a figment of our imagination. But it is at the mercy of our mythology, and especially of our spiral of understanding." Briefly mentioning about the history of science, Skolimowski concludes: "The more imaginative the Mind, the more interesting the conjectures. The more interesting the conjectures, the richer the reality around us. *The ascent of Mind is making the unbelievable the believable.*" About the spiral of understanding, he concludes: "*The spiral continuously pulsates with life, for it is an embodiment of life itself.*" His conclusion about knowledge goes like this: "All knowledge is normative. Its purpose is to help men to live and to promote harmony between human kind and the rest of creation. Understanding for the sake of understanding is really based on the desire to comprehend the cosmos at large, is to satisfy man's sense of wonder, is to provide him with a sense of psychological security. In the ultimate analysis, these are normative quests. In every act of human understanding, human values are concealed."

Who could be the proponents of the new ideas, of the articulation of new logos, which Skolimowski calls Evolutionary Telos? Skolimowski has the following advice to seriously ponder over and follow:

Perhaps the road to renewal leads through convincing the young, who are not entirely conditioned by their culture's existing spiral of understanding. The road to renewable particularly leads through addressing ourselves to children.

For children, anything is possible. The world is magic. The more magic the better. Magic is for children part of the natural order of things. Children are truly divine beings. They cooperate with the universe effortlessly. Their fall starts when one rigid orthodoxy is imposed on them. Their magic world then wanes. Their imagination dries up and infinite options are reduced to a few pedestrian choices. This is what we call 'realism'.

2. Brains, Minds and Computers

The Brain, which is the physical organ of the Mind, is one of the two precious products of the aeons of Evolution: the other is imponderable "social instinct".² – Har Dayal

Henryk Skolimowski tells us about the 'complex and problematical' relationship between the brain and the Mind: If the brain is studied within the realm of neurophysiology, we try to understand the functioning of the brain in the language of chemistry; subsequently, we use the results of the brain's chemical study for understanding the 'subtle, cognitive, emotional, volitional and spiritual' functions of the Mind. At this point, says Henryk, we want to use the chemical nomenclature for explaining the 'higher intellectual functions' of the Mind.

However, the chemical, or neurophysiological, terms are not capable enough to explain human meaning, as Henryk explicitly explains giving various examples which we experience in our daily life. "You may give me all the chemical reactions that happen in my brain, you may map all the neurophysiological relationships that occur when I say to another person, 'I love you,' and you will never, if you stick to your scientific terms only, be able to *explain* the true meaning of 'love'; of 'justice'; of 'goodness'; or of 'truth'," Henryk reiterates. "The fundamental conceptual point to be borne in Mind is that within the present scientific endeavour there is nothing in the universe of, and in the language of, chemistry that can begin to give us the meaning of such concepts as 'justice', 'truth' or 'love'. So the very idea of explaining higher intellectual attainments of the human Mind by reducing them to their underpinning neurochemical components is, quite simply, nonsense."

In our contemporary world, haplessly, the Mind is *explained* through brain which is owing to the shadow of Western culture. Henryk repents on the way the Western culture attempts to *explain* the Mind. He categorically says, "The cognitive imperialism of Western physical science has so pervaded our Minds that almost instinctively, we demand explanations for nearly everything in physical terms. Henryk also gives an example how the reductionist physico-chemical analysis of the Mind fools everyone, even the ordinary people: ". . . because neuron gamma-223 hit the neuron alpha 26-k a love relationship occurred." Henryk adds that "many reductionist explanations such as we see aplenty in current specialist literature are *au fond* just as much of a parody as this."

"The necessary material basis of the brain is not sufficient explanation for the higher functions of our Mind," infers Skolimowski adding that "descriptions and explanations are different things altogether."

The brain and Mind are different entities. While brain is an organ of the body, Mind is a system that pervades externally and, through outreach tentacles, it is connected with everything else we see, perceive and imagine. Our Mind is as much extensive as much the universe it creates to accommodate itself in and work out its creativities. Brain is part of the Mind, but Mind is not a part of the brain. The brain is an organ of the body, but Mind is a lucid organ of the universe. The Mind is both an organ and a system – organ of the universe, system of a human being anchoring functions of human beings with those of the universe. Mind is shapeless whereas brain has a structure (or, we can say that structure of the Mind is akin to that of the universe).

The structure of a brain can be both described and explained easily (by biologists and neurologists, for instance), but Mind is indescribable in its invisible structure. Whatever is out there is all Mind. Understanding Mind's functions through conventional means – biologically, or neurophysiologically, for example – is impossible. Mapping Mind's functioning through mapping brain's functioning is inappropriate. By making big claims that they understand well the functions of the Mind, the neuro-physiologists are living in fools' paradise. Understanding the mystery of Mind is mysterious in itself. Science cannot work out a simple scientific explanation of the Mind. Nor should it try, for then it would be a great injustice to humanity gifted with the most evolved organ of the universe.

Skolimowski rightly says, "It is a (reductionist) mistake to assume that it is only by understanding the brain that we shall understand the Mind." He gives a mantra: "*We shall understand the Mind by understanding the Mind.*" The participatory Mind is optimistic: Time will come when we shall understand the brain and the Mind together. "But this understanding will come about *when increasingly we shall comprehend more and more of the behaviour of the brain through the categories of the Mind and not conversely –* by attempting to reduce the Mind to the stuff and the categories of the brain," explains Skolimowski.

The third ally of the brain and the Mind is the computer. By the lovers and proponents of science, it is often claimed that we are living in the computer age. It is also often said that computer is the most intelligent thing in the world. In general discussion of the scientists we often hear statements like this: this or that person's brain is computer; he or she is smart like a computer, and the likes. In universities and colleges, we find smart rooms; a smart room is the one equipped with computer facilities for teaching. Thus, computer has virtually been superimposed over human brain and Mind in almost all spheres of life. None is parallel to computer – such feeling has been inserted deep into us. Computer, in essence, is regarded (by the scientific Minds) as the supreme.

Henryk refers to Roger Penrose's book *The Emperor's New Mind* (1989), in which 'he shows (actually *proving* it mathematically) that the computer can never become an adequate analogue for our brain/ Mind.' However, says Henryk, the young computer Turks have kept going undaunted, as '*they want to believe in their brave new world.*'

3. A Historical Perspective of Interactionism and Participatory Mind

Mind forms knowledge, or knowledge forms Mind? To an ordinary Mind, it appears to be a simple question; and its simple answer by such Mind would be: the Mind forms knowledge. But, what is the other way round? Can knowledge form the Mind? What is the nature of the interaction between knowledge and Mind? Or, such an interaction is possible at all? Let us understand the complexity of such interaction from Henryk Skolimowski himself.

Skolimowski presented a paper on *The Interaction between Knowledge and the Mind* at an international conference on Biology, History and Natural Philosophy in Denver in 1966. What Skolimowski presented at the conference reveals a phenomenon worth understanding:

> The conceptual structure of the Mind changes with shifts and developments in the structure and knowledge. . . There is a parallel conceptual development of our knowledge and of the Mind. Knowledge forms the Mind. The Mind formed by knowledge develops and extends knowledge still further, which in turn continues to develop the Mind. Thus there is a continuous process of interaction between the two. Although they are independent categories as far as their meaning is concerned, viewed in overall cognitive development, knowledge and Mind are functionally dependent on each other, and indeed inseparable from each other. They are two sides of the same coin; two representations of the same cognitive order. The concept of Mind must include the knowledge that has formed it and that it possesses. . . *The conceptual development of science is paralleled by the conceptual development of the Mind*. The conceptual arrangement of the Mind with its

specific patterns of thought thus mirrors the development of the conceptual net of science with its complicated mesh of concepts. . . The continuous interactions between the Mind of a scientist and the science he engages in are actually interactions between the Mind of an individual scientist and a particular science. But the result of these individual interactions constitutes a new stage in the development of science and a new stage in the conceptual development of the Mind.

Henryk says that this was an earlier formulation of his idea of participatory Mind and that he did not then have the idea of the participatory universe as the background. He maintains that this idea was proposed for the first time by John Archibald Wheeler in 1974, while the outline of the whole participatory model appeared for the first time in his paper of 1966. In the conclusion of his essay, Skolimowski states explicitly:

The model of the Mind outlined in this essay is a dynamic matrix which allows for the study of this interaction, and thus for the study of conceptual change. Latent in this model is the idea of evolutionary epistemology. Evolutionary epistemology is the discipline which provides a new perspective on the nature of our problems concerned with the growth of science and conceptual change. This discipline when worked out in detail will be an alternative to the logico-empiricist epistemology that has been for too long dominant in twentieth-century philosophy.

In 1974, eight years after his presentation of the above-mentioned paper, Henryk wrote an essay on 'Karl Popper and Objectivity of Scientific Knowledge' to a volume on the philosophy of Popper, in which he says in conclusion that "there must be a relationship between Popper's third world (the world of ideal objects, including the meaning of scientific concepts and theories – the cognitive reality, existing independently of our Mind) and his second world (the world of mental processes)." Henryk's interpretation directly dissolves into Mind: "*It is only by recognizing the Mind as a part of the growth of knowledge that we can arrive at a consistent idea of objective knowledge and thereby a consistent justification of the objectivity of knowledge. . . As knowledge grows so does the Mind; one reflects the growth of the other.*"

Skolimowski subscribes to everything Popper says, except his identification of evolution with Darwinism. Darwinism, especially the social Darwinism, for Skolimowski serves as a tool of exploitation and oppression. "Evolution is cooperation par excellence, not vicious competition as the Darwinian model would have it," Skolimowski argues. "The models we choose determine the nature of the world around us. Let us therefore choose well so that the models we have created do not limit us and do not oppress other people." In the context of evolutionary knowledge or evolutionary epistemology, Skolimowski's disagreement is on the following ground, as he writes: "His (Popper's) evolutionary knowledge is too narrow and almost exclusively limited to scientific knowledge, and it is marred by an unexamined adherence to Darwinism. My evolutionary model of knowledge has been one claiming that the three – Mind, knowledge and reality – are intimately connected with each other. We cannot do justice (in any truly evolutionary model) to any of these three concepts without simultaneously examining the other two, and by seeing how they really are aspects of each other."

4. Deriving Inspirations for the theory of the Participatory Mind

We have a distinct voice of ours. Our own voice amounts to our individual spiral of understanding. At the same time, we are not alone. Many voices become our voice. Our own voice is shadowed in the voice of society. In other words, we speak by many voices and these voices impart an impression on our own voice. Many voices speaking through us can be equated with the universal spiral of understanding. What is not that doesn't mingle in our voice? And what is that doesn't touch our voice, our soul? In a sense, we are everyone, for numerous voices embody us. Our genes, our culture, our religion, our civilization and our cosmos – all speak in full volume through us. "To recognize this is both chastising and exhilarating," admits Skolimowski. "It is humbling to know that one's voice is so small. It is exhilarating to know that one's voice contains so many other voices." Skolimowski adds value to a number of voices speaking through us by saying the following: "Amidst the symphony of other voices, we add a little melody of our own."

Skolimowski's Philosophy of the Participatory Mind has been influenced by many great voices. Plato, his beloved philosopher who inspired him to swim in the ever flowing stream of philosophy, is the first voice to have blessed him to create his philosophy. In the twentieth century Skolimowski considers himself 'a continuation of Bergson, of Teilhard and of Popper.' To these, he also adds another name, that of Jean Gebser.

About Jean Gebser (1905–73) Skolimowski says that he is one of those solitary thinkers who are important for the twentieth century, and at the same time almost completely neglected. "He was a poet, a man of letters, a philosopher," Henryk maintains. "Above all, he was the creator of a new synthesis. His magnum opus is entitled *The Ever Present Origin* (1985). But this is a difficult, tortuous book to read. A concise rendering of Gebser's philosophy can be found in Georg Feuerstein's *Structures of Consciousness: The Genius of Jean Gebser: An introduction and Critique* (1987). . . Why is Gebser important? Because he has the courage to think large. He has the imagination to pose great questions."

Skolimowski brings to the fore many facets of the Gebser's philosophy that inspire us and that inspired Skolimowskian Philosophy of the Participatory Mind:

- Gebser is an important part of the process of repossessing ourselves by understanding rationally the prerational stages of our consciousness.

- Gebser's scheme is ambitious, vast, panoramic, as he attempts to reconstruct the structures of human consciousness from the time around one million years BC to our time.
- Gebser is right that the immense burst of creative energy in the Neolithic period needs to be duly appreciated.
- Gebser lumps the three periods together under the label of 'objectivised consciousness.'
- The strength of Gebser's model is that it allows for the future development of consciousness.

Skolimowski shares Gebser's view that our Mind and our consciousness are far from completed. He makes us realize that the evolutionary journey is going on. "What new structures of consciousness or new forms of Mind the future will bring as evolution unfolds, not even God may know at present."

5. The Human Subjectivism on the Canvas of Participatory Universe

Henryk Skolimowski narrates his experiences of the times when he had not imagined the lively universe he later on attempted to unfold: "When I was a student of engineering in 1950s, we still believed in the hard palpable universe 'out there'. When I started teaching in the 1960s, the scientific world-view was still considered the only rationally justified one. This world-view proclaimed that science adequately describes reality existing objectively and independently of us 'out there'. However, the confidence of science as the arbiter of all that exists started to wane in the 1970s."

Henryk counts the many causes of such waning of the confidence: e.g., conclusions of quantum physics fundamentally challenging the principle of objectivity; and the revelations of astrophysics conveying to us that we do not know much about the nature of the universe, including the nature of the laws of science.

Henryk elicits some realities about science. Earlier science claimed that its theories were about reality. But in the 1980s, science found itself derailing from its earlier claims. Science began proclaiming that scientific theories are in fact *models* which might or might not relate with reality. He adds that gradually reality has been relegated to the domain of the subjective experience of individuals. He narrates some of the experiences he underwent, to arrive at the meaning of reality:

> The most telling test of this overall transition came for me in the spring of 1990. I was teaching at the time a class on 'Technology and Man', at the University of Michigan, to a group of graduating seniors in engineering. A bright group it was. We finally broached the subject: what is reality? Much to my amazement none of them opted for an objective or even a semi-objective concept of reality. All declared, one by one, that reality is a substratum of our experience. . . What took me twenty years to learn – that reality is not independent of my Mind – they learned painlessly during their undergraduate education. . . Deny the meaning of human history (the history of human kind has been the history of human striving for *meaning*), and this history is nothing. Deny the meaning to human life, and human life becomes nothing. . . Thus in order to maintain the meaning of human life and of human history, we must transcend the tenets of shallow subjectivism.

The glories of the participatory universe in its unfolding journey, Henryk emphasizes, should be recalled to rescue our subjective feeling of what reality is. "The grandeur of evolutionary becoming is not a subjective figment of our imagination," Henryk enlightens. "Evolution is the canvas of our perception and the participatory universe has been the weaver that has woven this canvas."

Henryk, in his discussion, extends a beautiful and soul-delighting thought, which works to unite and integrate the humanity: "*The whole underlying structure, the structure of the human Mind, is common to us all*, is the same for the whole human species." He adds: "For this reason also, we humans, have a similar sense of beauty. And for this reason we share similar values."

Our evolutionary journey in this participatory universe assures that we all are one. Our participatory Mind co-creating with the participatory universe makes us realize that *All is One*. This is the fundamental universal law the Skolimowskian Philosophy emanates, the fundamental universal principle this philosophy projects before the humanity to awaken and augment human consciousness vital for solidarity and integrity. The *All is One* principle the Skolimowskian Philosophy is pregnant with works at individual level, at socio-cultural level, at global level and at universal level. The *All is One* reflects the core truth of the integrated universe. Disintegrated, the universe can have no meaning, no existence. Integrated, the universe has meaning and intensive existence. Integrated humanity, integrated life, integrated world are meaningful and glowing with existence. Such is the power of reality dwelling in the philosophy of Skolimowski.

"On the canvas of the participatory universe, we – as individuals – weave our own little universes of meaning," says Skolimowski. "Our subjectivity is important and through it we express the world of human differences." However, as Skolimowski stresses, our evolutionary bond is even more important. He elaborates: "Through it we express the magic of being human, the values that enhance and elevate the human condition, the indelible sense that in spite of all agonies it is thrilling to be alive, to be on the journey of becoming, to have other living beings as our brothers and sisters in creation, and to have mountains and brooks and forests and clouds as our companions in the unfolding tapestry of evolutionary becoming." He elucidates beautiful things, which are worthy, for us to know, to understand, to grasp and to articulate:

> The universe is not my ego, although it has been filtered through my ego. What must not escape our notice is the

fact that this very filter, which is my ego, is a refined product of the whole evolutionary process. Our subjectivity is thus universal. Scratch its veneer and under its façade you will find the universality of evolutionary grandeur. Let us therefore beware of the glib expression: 'The universe is my own creation.' No, it is not. You are its creation. You are the mirror in which the universe is contemplating itself. You are the yeast out of which universe is making thoughts. You are one of the myriad atoms out of which the universe is making its mosaics, including the mosaics of human meaning.

Henryk Skolimowski wishes glory to human subjectivity, 'for it is a miracle of creation', to the participatory universe, 'for it is a trans-subjective canvas out of which human subjectivity can arise', to God 'Who is making His footprints through the workings of our own subjectivity and through grand designs of the participatory universe'.

Summary

The Skolimowskian theory of the universal spiral of understanding attempts to widen knowledge from individual to universal level. The individual spiral as well as universal levels of understanding are connected, not separated from each other; and they contribute to each other's development. There is enormous diversity in the culture–spiral–perspective axis on which is built systems of knowledge. Each culture considers its world-view to be superior and often there are clashes between different cultures over the superiority issues. There exists a certain degree of intolerance in each culture against other cultures. It depends upon how much is the overlapping between two cultures. If there is enough compatibility between two different cultures there is enough possibility of these cultures to exist in unison. An enlightened culture is capable to reconstruct its spiral of understanding, and therefore its perspective, and it dissolves the differences, which can help bring the two different cultures in good terms with each other. The enlightenment thus helps create an environment of peace and tranquility. The Skolimowskian Philosophy is pregnant with the ideas that sparkle peace, tranquility, and creative dialogue amongst different cultures of the world.

Henryk attempts to resolve the dichotomy between the Mind and the brain. He dismisses the anatomical and neuro-physiological analyses of the brain that attempt to divide brain into two parts – the right and the left hemispheres – and ascribe unique functions to each. This, he says, is ridiculous and reductionist approach to understand the mysteries of most important aspect of human life. Mind is the most mysterious phenomenon and it can be understood through an understanding of the Mind's intricacies, of the Mind's miraculous functioning, of the Mind's co-creativity. The brain cannot serve to understand the mysteries of the Mind. The Skolimowskian Philosophy outlines a theory in which the Mind plays its all-pervading role and co-creates with the universe. It is also unjust to compare Mind with the computers. Computers cannot equate Mind. Comparing Mind with computer amounts to downgrading Mind and underestimating the liveliness of the universe. It also amounts to counter the value of evolution, which has the evolutionary Mind as one of the most beautiful outcome of its unceasing journey.

Skolimowski opens the historical record of the interactionism and the participatory Mind. The conceptual structure of the Mind changes with the shifts and developments in the structure of knowledge. There is a parallel conceptual development of knowledge and Mind. Knowledge forms the Mind. And the Mind formed by the knowledge further contributes to develop knowledge. A relationship between Mind and knowledge which Skolimowski beautifully sketches is interesting. The both are in continuous interaction with each other. Although they are separate entities from the viewpoint of their meaning, they functionally depend on each other and are the two sides of the same coin and inseparable from each other.

Skolimowski mentions some forerunners of his theory of the participatory Mind. We have a voice of ours own, but many other voices also speak through us. Voices of some great people speak through us. Our genes speak through us. Universe speaks through us. We are our own person but we are influenced by a number of factors. Henryk's participatory theory was inspired by Plato, by Bergson, by Teilhard, and by Popper. He especially mentions Jean Gebser, whose impact on his spectacular theory was enormous. Gebser attempts to reconstruct the *structures* of human consciousness starting from the time around one million years BC to our time.

Henryk took about twenty years to learn that reality is not independent of Mind. Human life, throughout the course of history, continuously strived for meaning. On the canvas of the participatory universe, we – as individuals – construct our own little universes of meaning, and on this canvas arises the human subjectivity.

Let us go through Henryk Skolimowski's own summary of the Universal Spiral of Understanding:

> We never think little of our Minds. We are conditioned to think that our culture knows best. For these reasons, when we meet people of different cultures, conditioned by radically different spirals of understanding, our first reaction is – they must be crazy.
>
> Until the twentieth century, Western anthropologists and Western people in general, while trying to understand other cultures, attempted to force them into the boxes of Western understanding, with the result that these other cultures have been grossly misinterpreted and impoverished. So often, we deemed those other cultures irrational as they did not conform to our criteria of rationality.
>
> The picture has been changing in the twentieth century, particularly in the second half of the twentieth century, when we have tried to understand other cultures through empathy and by merging ourselves with the context of

these cultures. Thus we have come to realize that different cultures may, and often are, based on different forms of rationality.

It is the invisible that controls the visible. This is so in all cultures, including our own. The quality of the invisible determines the quality of our lives. If your invisible is a benevolent god which showers blessings on you and guides your life daily, then your life is going to be more happy and connected. If, on the other hand, the controlling invisible are electrons and quarks which do not give any guidance or blessings to your life, then your life, inspired by and controlled through this invisible, is going to be less connected and happy.

The spiral of understanding not only provides the cognitive structure for our intellectual understanding. It also provides a normative matrix which and against which things are evaluated. Taken in toto, the spiral is a normative agency. It never sits objectively and guides us with its objective commands. *The spiral continuously pulsates with life.* For it is an embodiment of life itself. For this reason alone it is a normative agency.

An enlightened culture can imaginatively reconstruct the premises (the spiral of understanding) of other cultures and can demonstrate that the ways and paths that at first appear 'odd' and unacceptable from the view point of our standards are perfectly normal and acceptable within those other cultures. Thus one of the consequences of understanding in depth the meaning of the spiral of understanding, within our own culture and across cultures, is *tolerance*. Tolerance is the fruit of understanding.

It is never easy to accept the spiral of understanding of another culture, for it requires, in a sense, renouncing the spiral of understanding of our own culture, or at least significantly altering it. Such changes are invariably seen as a threat to our identity. Therefore, such changes are vigorously if not vehemently opposed, particularly by the guardians of the status quo, who have vested interests in keeping things as they are. For this reason we should be aware that we may never be able to *persuade* the guardians of the status quo about the necessity for new departures, for they do not want to see changes and specifically *they do not want to believe in the validity of new phenomena* and new forms of knowledge which contradict the old. And if you do not want to believe, no evidence will convince you. Children are our hope. For them, magic is natural. They co-create effortlessly with the universe.

As to the claims that Minds are computers, we should not fear; not yet; and not for *quite* a while. When the computers do catch up with us (if ever) we shall by that time be on a higher level of evolutionary development. The fact that *some* people are so eager to reduce us to the machinery of electronic automata is not so much an insult to the glory of the human Mind but rather a profound comment on their mentality. Who are those people who are so eager to see us as machines? What is their conception of heaven?

I did not devote much space to the findings concerning the mechanisms of the brain. But this fact in no way invalidates my findings about the Mind. It is a fallacy to assume that by understanding the brain we shall understand the Mind. We shall understand the Mind by understanding the Mind.

Concerning the predecessors of the participatory theory of Mind, there were many: from Heraclitus to Bateson; from Meister Eckhart to Jean Gebser. Although I freely admit my indebtedness to Popper, I do not consider his interactionism as a predecessor of my participatory Mind for the reasons I have explained. My interactionism precedes Popper's by a decade.

Bateson's ideas, on the other hand, are beautiful anticipations of the participatory Mind; and partial articulations of it. The idea of healing epistemologies, the idea of the ecology of Mind, the idea of the universal or the cosmic Mind, the idea of relational thinking (which I prefer to call participatory thinking) are all parts and aspects of the participatory Mind – although differently expressed in my philosophical system.

Jean Gebser, whom we discussed only briefly, is a friendly soul, and we salute his cosmic quest. Although I find his programme fascinating and important, his Mind I find less understandable and less attuned than the Minds of Bateson and Teilhard.

Our age is one of spiritual search. With evolution truly recognized, our spirituality and our God are parts of the becoming of the universe. This is the only viable alternative that has thrust itself upon us after we have awakened to the nature of the participatory universe and the nature of the participatory Mind. There are no mysteries of the universe, except for the mystery of the Mind. As the Mind is, so is the universe. This is the mystery of the Mind as the key to the becoming of the universe.

CHAPTER 10

Prevalence of Participatory Truth

The face of Truth is covered
with a brilliant golden lid;
that do thou remove,
O Surya (Lord of intelligence),
for the law of Truth, for sight.[1]
– Isha Upanishad 15

Truth is that kind of error without which a certain kind of living being cannot live.
–Nietzsche, quoted by Henryk Skolimowski

1. The Correspondence Theory of Truth

Truth is the crux of human life. Mind came into being to live in, live with, live for and live by truth. Evolution of human beings was to survive with truth. Without truth human existence itself appears to be non-existent. Without truth a society would go blank with knowledge and wisdom; and knowledge and wisdom would stay as *good* as ignorance. Without truth justice would go unjust. What happens when truth is abandoned? Henryk asks some questions: "What happens to society and our concept of justice? What happens to our quest for knowledge, which is so often identified with the quest for truth?"

Henryk regards truth as a sublime subject, 'an intersubjective entity which holds good in transactions among people'. Discussing universal truth in contrast to personal truth, Henryk brings into light the correspondence theory of truth. "From Aristotle on, we have inherited the correspondence theory of truth or the classical theory of truth, which claims that truth is the correspondence between reality and its faithful (or adequate) descriptions," Henryk goes on explaining. "These descriptions, which are faithful, or adequate, we call true. Truth resides in these descriptions. Truth is an attribute of descriptions or linguistic utterances."

Henryk maintains that a glimmer of this concept of truth can be found in Plato and Socrates, and perhaps also in their predecessors. But in Plato, he finds 'equally forcefully expressed another concept of truth – truth as a living dialogue: words and utterances are made true in virtue of the total situation, of the total context within which they are embedded at a given time'.

The correspondence or classical truth began prevailing since the times of Aristotle. The living truth in Plato thus becomes less important. The correspondence theory of truth, according to Skolimowski, becomes known as objective truth, which has become a backbone of Western rationality. Looking into the hidden structure of the correspondence theory, Skolimowski says that we often do not realize that it presupposes a number of things. It, according to him, presupposes:

(1) the existence of an objective, unchanging reality out there;

(2) that this reality is equally available to each of us, under the same aspects;

(3) that language, and specially present language, can describe this reality adequately;

(4) that we can judge – each of us equally – the adequacy or the correspondence between our linguistic descriptions and reality itself;

(5) the same spiral of understanding that resides in each of us.

These insights have, by and large, been dismissed as 'not sufficiently rational and gone on believing in the *transparency of reality*'. This belief has been widely held both in science and religion. "The whole body of Christian philosophy is in fact a rather rational and discusrsive enterprise – upholding and cherishing Aristotle's idea of the correspondence between reality and its description," says Henryk Skolimowski. ". . . While (in Western knowledge) we adhere to the correspondence theory of truth, we assume that the universe is static, permanent, unchanging. Only when we assume the universe to be unchanging can we happily go on believing in the correspondence theory of truth."

In medieval times God's design (of the fixed and unchanging universe) was believed to be true knowledge; and the church propagated and maintained this 'truth'. In modern times, science is doing the same, and the knowledge of these laws (of fixed and unchanging universe) is considered to be the true knowledge of reality.

At the close of the nineteenth century, we witnessed serious crises in the foundation of our knowledge. The Newtonian physics *damaged* the image of our universe, and with it, established truth and reality were at stake. Henryk reminds us of the efforts to save reality or at least to save traditional knowledge as made by some receptive Minds, such as those of Henri Poincaré (1854–1912) and Ernst Mach (1838–1916).

"We are somewhat afraid that truth by convention may lead us to the idea of subjectivity of all truth: if the acceptance of basic axioms (basic language) is up to us, then the determination of truth is up to us," suggests Skolimowski. "We don't like this consequence. And for good reason. For then all truths somehow become personal truths. . . The idea of truth by convention may lead us in another direction: to look at all knowledge in a new way. This new direction will almost certainly lead us to revise the entire edifice of objective knowledge and the objective view of reality which we have cherished so much. We don't like this consequence either, for it gives us much to do. And we may be too lazy to rethink it all." Skolimowski has also a complaint, rather concern, about philosophers:

> Indeed philosophers have become lazy nowadays. They don't like deep, searching questions which are all-consuming and all-important. Instead they occupy themselves with little analytical, often facile problems which give them the satisfaction of doing the work really well – even if it is of a purely technical nature. They like to cling to the traditional notion of empiricism and refine it over and over again. As a result, the whole notion of empiricism has become meaningless if not ludicrous. Thus we have 'robust' empiricism, 'hypothetical' empiricism, 'good' empiricism, 'tentative' empiricism, 'plain' empiricism, 'conceptual' empiricism – you name it. All these labels indicate a sort of desperation to preserve something that is untenable. For empiricism is a doctrine based on: (1) the acceptance of correspondence theory of truth; (2) the acceptance of reality as postulated by science.

Henryk is optimistic and attempts to implant hope in our hearts: "Empiricism, of whatever variety, is not the only issue that is at stake. Indeed, the whole civilizational formation is collapsing – and by this I mean the philosophical foundations of the modern Western world-view. This world-view was based on the doctrine of metaphysical realism – the belief that things are as they are and science describes them best. The collapse of this metaphysical realism is now acknowledged. . . Putnam and others have embarked on a new notion: 'contextual relativity' or 'internal realism'. Both labels are misleading but they are groping in the right direction – towards participatory truth."

2. The Coherence Theory of Truth

Henryk cites reference of Ernst Mach from *Science and Mechanics* (1893): He went to another direction. He found that reality has become somewhat elusive. So he decided: 'Let us not talk about reality, perhaps we don't know what it is.' Henryk asks: How do we save knowledge in these circumstances? And then he responds himself: By quietly abandoning the correspondence theory of truth in favour of the coherence theory of truth – whether explicitly or implicitly formulated. "The coherence theory of truth maintains that it actually does not matter whether we can describe reality or not," Henryk elaborates. "What matters is that our knowledge is coherent, that every new theory and new description fits with the rest. Thus a new theory or proposition is true if it is coherent with the rest of our knowledge."

But, says Henryk, we have never been happy with this conception of truth, for it somehow abandons reality – which has been too precious to us for the millennia of rational inquiry. He clarifies further that, besides this, the coherence theory of truth makes it difficult to distinguish coherent fiction from coherent knowledge. He cites the glaring example of the *Alice in Wonderland*, 'a wonderfully coherent fiction; so coherent in fact that you almost want to believe in the truth of its reality.'

Giving an example of Karl Popper, one of the twentieth century philosophers, Henryk says: "Popper incisively concluded that if it is the case that even such well-established theories as Newton's are limited and cannot be claimed to provide absolute and permanent knowledge, then *all knowledge is tentative.* This was an epoch-making step. . . The crux of the matter is that, while accepting the tentative character of knowledge, Popper refused a possible conclusion that all knowledge is subjective or personal. . . Popper invented the notion of approximation of truth, which tried to save – at the same time – both the traditional concept of reality as objectively existing out there, and the correspondence concept of truth. There exists objective truth, Popper held. It happens when we describe reality adequately, faithfully, thus truly." Raising certain doubts Skolimowski dismisses this description to arrive at truth. His following discussion makes the things more interesting and revealing:

> . . . *we never know, and we can never know whether our descriptions of reality are ultimately true or only approximately true. We, the seekers of truth, are like mountain climbers, scaling high mountains in perpetual dense fog. And the fog is so dense that we do not see our way around. Even if we are at the top of the peak, we do not know it, for there may be another peak higher up which is covered by fog.* Thus even if we had arrived at objective or absolute truth, we have no way of knowing it for certain.

Henryk considers this both 'a romantic and a cunning concept of truth'. He also considers the problem of truth as 'a thorny one indeed for Popper'. "The idea of approximation to truth was meant to be the solution in the following way," Henryk maintains. "We propose theories. They are, in time, refuted. New theories represent a closure approximation to truth."

Skolimowski now cites the reference of Thomas Kuhn in his *The Structure of Scientific Revolutions* (1963): "Kuhn hardly discusses the notion of truth. . . If we don't know how to talk about reality coherently, how can we talk about truth coherently? . . . Kuhn's reconstruction of science (through the notion of paradigm) is a two-faced affair. On the one hand, claims are made that science is about reality and somehow about truth. On the other hand (when we come to specific arguments), truth is paradigm-bound. Since reality is paradigm-bound, so must truth be."

The universal truth has been our *target* of search for last several decades. But, Henryk says, *we have been unable to do so.* The classical or the correspondence theory has in particular been unable to be maintained. He, therefore, feels a need of thorough re-examination of the notion of truth. His proposal of the participatory truth attempts to show us the light of the true truth truthfully. It has been reviewed in the next section.

3. Truth of the Participatory Truth

The earth is supported by the power of truth; it is the power of truth that makes the sun shine and the winds blow; indeed all things rest upon truth.[2] – Chanakya

The participatory truth propounded by Prof. Henryk Skolimowski, in true sense, is universal truth, but not objective or absolute. This truth is trans-subjective and does not abandon truth as such. However, he suggests, the inter-subjectivity and this universality must be delicately handled and not confused with old-fashioned objectivity, and especially with the absolute notion of truth.

Henryk Skolimowski reveals, "Participatory truth is not an entity in itself, but a consequence and an articulation of the whole edifice of the participatory Mind, including the notion of the participatory universe." He presents five characteristics of the participatory truth:

(1) It is species-specific.
(2) It is culture-specific or culture-bound.
(3) It is evolving.
(4) It is determined by the spiral of understanding. (Since it is participatory) it is *happening*.

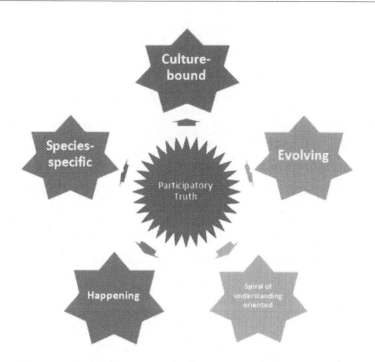

Figure 1: Participatory Truth illuminating with its essential
characteristics (inspired from Skolimowski)

Light of the Skolimowski's participatory truth can be shown in its five
specificities in the form of a mandala (figure 1).

(1) PARTICIPATORY TRUTH AS SPECIES-SPECIFIC

We live in a participatory universe. Our knowledge is participatory
knowledge. Therefore all truth must be species-specific. Skolimowski puts
it ecstatically: *"If there is no species, there is no truth. If there is no consciousness,
there is no truth.* The truth of the stars or the truth of God is quite
different from ours – as their consciousness is different. Our participatory
Consciousness changes with time; and so does our participatory truth."

Henryk's theory of the species-specific truth implies that truth is not
a monopoly of human beings. When he explains the species-specificity of
truth, he attempts to complete Nietzsche notion about truth: 'Truth is that

kind of error without which a certain kind of living being cannot live.' What emanates from Skolimowski's species-specificity of the participatory truth is that every species lives with its own truth. It is also true that we – the certain kind of living beings – enjoy the truth of our species in our own way and can also interpret the truth associated with all other species in our own way.

Thus, the species-specificity of the participatory truth can be interpreted in the context of non-human living species also. Skolimowski also brings to the fore a wonderful attribute of the Mind: *Truth is an attribute of the Mind.* Since other species too owe Mind, the truth must also be an attribute of their life. It is a different thing that owing to be the owner of more evolved Mind, truth exists more intensively with our (human) species than with all the rest. Even plants (which *may not* be having Mind) demonstrate certain kind of consciousness and, therefore, must be existing with certain kind of truth. It also makes distinction that our species (of humans) cherishes truth differently than all other species, which is because of different level of consciousness – an attribute of the evolution itself.

Truth of plants, of hippopotamus, of lions, of whales is different from that of our human species, for their consciousness is different from ours. A whale knows truth about the vastness of oceans better than humans. For humans, truth is mainly linked with the statistics of different aspects of the oceans. Similarly green plants' ethology is determined by environmental factors, especially the light, and plants are conscious enough for these factors. For human species the knowledge of physical nature of the environment (in conventional context) is more than satisfactory. The Skolimowskian theory of the participatory truth links truth with all species' truth confined to the species themselves. Of course, truth of other species is not independent of us. Different level of our consciousness, our language, our expression and our Mind are attributable to the reason why their truth is not independent of us. On the basis of Skolimowski's species-specific truth, we can correct Nietzsche as follows: *Truth is that kind of error without which all kinds of living beings cannot live.*

(2) PARTICIPATORY TRUTH AS CULTURE-BOUND

Skolimowski considers that amongst human beings truth is culture-specific. For it is culture that determines the rules of participation. "There is no truth without participation," says Henryk. "Participation is determined by rituals, myths, cognitive strategies, a variety of forms of praxis."

He further makes it clearer: "In a sense culture is the maker of truth – specific for a given epoch. . . The context of a culture is not subjective, is not personal, is not relativistic. What this statement asserts is that all truth occurs within human discourse. There is no truth without language. There is no language without participation. Language is property of culture, a property of participation. In outlining the boundaries and the matrix of participation, culture also determines truth, which is bound by its context, which is intersubjective within a given culture."

Participatory truth, thus, is not only determined but also 'limited' by a given culture. It seldom breaks boundaries of a given culture. Within the boundary of a specific culture truth always claims to be universal, and often discards any *parallel* truth emanating from the boundaries of another culture. A culture sometimes, rather often, regards other culture-specific truths rather antagonistic to its own integrity. Nevertheless, the culture-specificity of the participatory truth enhances integrity of its individuals. Individuals of a given culture sometime break the boundaries that make the participatory truth limited, and thus attempt to make the participatory truth intercultural in its nature.

(3) PARTICIPATORY TRUTH AS EVOLUTIONARY IN NATURE

Truth is not static. Truth does not freeze itself. Truth blossoms intensively. When truth blossoms, it means it is evolutionary in nature. "If something is true, it is true, because it is true," Henryk removes layers-upon-layers enveloping the evolutionary nature of truth. "But this way of looking at truth leads us back precisely to the absolutist framework within which reality is fixed and unchangeable, and our knowledge of it is a strict photographic representation of it – as based on the old idea of correspondence."

Stressing upon the evolutionary nature of truth, Skolimowski says, "When we say that truth is evolving we mean to say precisely that evolution itself is evolving; as it does, so must our truth of it. . . If our understanding is evolving, our truth is evolving. *For our truths are only the distilled fragments of our unfolding knowledge.*"

If evolution is the fundamental truth of the universe, the universal truth, or the participatory truth, must stand boldly on the foundation of evolution. Truth does not come from outside the universe. It has to be implanted in the universe. It has to grow in the universe. When it grows in the universe, naturally it has to be evolutionary in its nature.

Skolimowski brings out the three stages of the discovery of evolution propounded by three scholars, viz.:

(1) Geological evolution (Lyell)
(2) Biological evolution (Darwin)
(3) Epistemological evolution (Popper, Kuhn et al.)

The consequences of what Henryk terms 'the evolution of knowledge', or 'epistemological evolution', are far-reaching and not yet fully drawn, as he himself admits. Henryk spells what has been inferred by whom, in the context of the discovery and articulation of epistemological evolution:

> Popper: All knowledge is conjectural.
> Kuhn: All knowledge is paradigm-bound.
> Ilya Prigogine: The nature of the laws of nature changes.
> David Bohm: The known and the knower merge as the implicate order unfolds.

The articulation of Popper and Kuhn, thus, has been furthered by thinkers as Ilya Prigogine and David Bohm, according to Henryk Skolimowski. He prettily evolves the idea: *The participatory Mind is epistemological evolution writ large.* "One of the consequences of epistemological evolution is noetic monism," explains Henryk. "*Nous* pervades the universe. At least the universe that we can reach. Any other form of universe is not the universe for us. At the very least we have to recognize that nous pervades all human knowledge. For nous is built into the very structure of this knowledge."

Evolution of truth goes on with the evolution of Mind and that of knowledge. Henryk concludes why truth is evolving: "It is evolving because our Mind is evolving, our knowledge is evolving, and our universe is evolving. *As the universe is evolving, so it creates more knowable Minds. As the Mind becomes more knowable, it begets a more intelligent universe.* In this process, truth does not remain static and frozen, but evolves with our evolving universe and knowledge." In essence, no phenomenon and no object can drift away from evolution. And all evolving things and phenomena are interconnected in the tapestry of universal evolution.

(4) PARTICIPATORY TRUTH AS DETERMINED BY THE SPIRAL OF UNDERSTANDING

We have been exposed to Skolimowski's theory of the spiral of understanding. We know that the spiral of understanding is always evolving. As it evolves, our universe also evolves, and so do the epistemological patterns of our Minds. Then it immediately follows, as Skolimowski elaborates, that truth must be seen as evolving and not static; as participatory, not absolute; as determined by the characteristics of the Mind and not by absolute reality existing independently of us.

(5) PARTICIPATORY TRUTH AS A 'HAPPENING'

As already established by Skolimowski, truth is neither static, nor in the state of a frozen being. It also doesn't go without doing anything. It is not something that goes without happening. The participatory truth in fact is happening. "Perhaps the time has arrived when we realize that truth is one of the most playful of concepts," alerts Skolimowski. "It always *happens* in the framework of some participation, never by itself." We need to enlarge the scope of our participation. For, Henryk says, when we so limit our participation, we limit the universe at large, and the consequences are disastrous.

"All truth is participatory," Henryk stresses. "In the strict sense, there is no such thing as *physical* truth. All truth is noetic, is a property of or an attribute of the Mind." He adds that "Participatory truth is always partial, is always fragmentary, is always incomplete, for every context of participation is fragmentary and incomplete." Henryk asks some questions before he tries to respond to them: "Is there ultimate, objective or absolute truth? And if so, what is the most fruitful way of looking at it, of thinking about it? Furthermore: how is this ultimate or absolute truth related to our participatory truth? Let us try to grasp the following Skolimowski offers to us in the light of these questions:

> *There is absolute or ultimate truth. It is one gigantic truth about the whole universe, in its totality, in its unfolding, in its realization.* . . Such a truth even God cannot comprehend. And yet this may be the only objective or absolute truth. We cannot even hope to grasp this total truth. Yet we can envisage each context of participation is a fragment of this enormous evolving truth. Is this then a reassertion of the relativity of truth? No, it is an assertion of participatory truth.

4. Searching the Completeness of the Universe through Participatory Truth

Truth of the universe, according to Skolimowski, is not independent of us. "The kaleidoscopic fragments of truth created through the intervention of human imagination and human participation are real," he explains. "There is nothing subjective about them. These fragments of truth are aspects of the gigantic absolute truth about the whole universe in its totality."

Skolimowski, by posing questions and giving their answers, tries to satiate our inquisitiveness: "How do we know that these fragments, which we entertain as partial truths, fit, that they are integral aspects of the total truths? We cannot know this for certain. For to know this would mean to have a glimpse of the total absolute truth. Are we therefore groping in darkness, from one participatory context to an another, without any signpost to absolute truth which alone can vindicate our fragmentary truth? In short, is there no guiding light on the road to Truth? We cannot be sure that there is, as this absolute truth is so enormous that it exceeds the bounds of our reason and our science. Yet there seems to be a guiding light. This is the light of our intuition, the light of the special insight that so often flares up to illumine our destinies."

What does the light of intuition, in this context suggest? "The light of intuition suggests that the more meaningful the participation, the more truth it reveals," Skolimowski attempts to reveal. "The deeper the participation, the deeper you enter into the mysteries of life – until you arrive at the deepest contest of participation, which is God."

Henryk ultimately concludes that *Truth* (the ultimate total truth) *is the realization of God*. He also tries to make us realize that "Religion can be seen as the search for paths leading to God, to the absolute reality, to that scene of the cosmic drama in which the universe is consummated and fulfilled."

Henryk lets the holy Ganga of religion flow into hearts and from hearts it flows into the whole universe: "Religion, in addition to bring a ritual (sometimes empty), a ceremony (often significant), an opiate for the masses (not entirely insignificant), has often been a profound search for the ultimate wholeness of the universe, for absolute truth, for the ultimate completeness of the universe."

5. *The Participatory Context and its Consequence – the Truth*

Truth, in fact, is the consequence of the participatory context. Henryk feels the need to emphasize this. He denounces the 'physical' truth of the universe. "There is no physical truth in itself and by itself – unless there is an appropriate context of participation," He adds. "Physical contexts are important. But they are not the only contexts... a great variety of contexts are value-laden. Their purpose is life-enhancing. We know that not all contexts are equally life-enhancing, or under the same aspect, or within the same time-frame. The criterion of what is life-enhancing must be delicately balanced. It should be seen against a larger panorama. What is this panorama? The liberation of life in the long run, the realization of our evolutionary potential, the realization of the God-within."

Henryk considers that participatory truth is close to *religious* truth. He stupendously defines various kinds of truths, which evolve in different contexts, e.g.:

> ➤ *Cultural* truth: Participatory truth when envisaged as part of the process of the realization of human meaning within the cultural context.
>
> ➤ *Physical* truth: Participatory truth employed in the physical framework within which we search for the regularities in the physical universe – which are then recorded in the annals of science and of history of knowledge.
>
> ➤ *Formal* truth: Participatory truth that is created when we construct new logical and mathematical theorems and proofs.
>
> ➤ *Practical* truth: Participatory truth that emerges out of contexts in which we inquire (e.g., whether DDT accumulated in sprayed crops can be harmful to human beings over longer periods of time).

"All these forms of truth – religious, cultural, physical, formal, practical – are intertwined with each other; are woven together in one magnificent symphony of human participation, which is continually played in this universe of becoming," says Skolimowski.

Ultimate falsehood could be the opposite of the ultimate truth. When could this state come? Henryk explains so enchantingly:

> The Ultimate Truth is equal to self-realization of the universe – which some people without apologies wish to identify with God – then *the destruction of the universe would be the ultimate falsehood.* If one could imagine a black hole, which grows exponentially, and devours the entire universe, while the human species is still present, then this would signify falsehood indeed. For then all grounds for participation would be annihilated. No universe – no species; no species – no participation; no participation – no culture; no culture – no language, and finally – no truth. . . Falsehood is thus an annihilation of the participatory context that bears and enables participatory truth. Actually, the annihilation of the *whole* context prevents us from talking either about truth or falsehood. No context – nothing. . . Usually falsehood occurs when there exists a violation of some features of the context, some discrepancy, some dissonance between what we expect to find, within the established and accepted context, and what we *do* find in it. This discrepancy/ dissonance/ violation may manifest itself in different ways, depending on the nature of the context. . . If instances (observations) clash with a theory that is considered valid and true, these instances are called falsehoods. . . A false icon is one that disagrees with accepted symbolism of a given religion. A false prophet is one who undermines the accepted faith. False gods are ones that question or undermine the authority of the established God(s).

Henryk also explains what a false behaviour is. "Strictly speaking, behaviour cannot be false – if truth is the property of statements or linguistic utterances," he says. "Yet the expression ('false behaviour') can be seen as valid when we allow the notion of language to be conceived broadly. For *behaviour is a form of language that we can read with great subtlety.*"

The following extract from Skolimowski's discussion on *Truth as a Consequence of the Participatory Context* aims at the purpose of truth: "The arbiter of truth is life itself. Truths should be judged in accordance with their life-enhancing powers. The more significant the context, in the overall pursuit of life, the more significant truths it contains. Any given proposition, thought or action (each of them is a life-form) should be judged in accordance with how much it contributes to a given life-enhancing context. The production of nuclear bombs is the production of evolutionary lies."

Summary

Truth is the essence of human life. Many philosophers have worked on various aspects of truth. Truth, for centuries, could not capture roots in our Mind. Henryk Skolimowski attempts to bring us face-to-face with truth. He presents two old theories of the truth: the correspondence theory of truth, and the coherence theory of truth. Discussing striking shortcomings of these two theories, he devices his own theory – the Participatory Truth. According to this theory, worthy of being universally acclaimed, truth is neither absolute nor objective but intersubjective and universal. He finds participatory truth embracing five characteristics, viz., species-specificity, culture-specificity, evolution-following, spiral of understanding-oriented, and happening.

Participatory truth is vital in the sense that it strives to search the completeness of the universe. Truth, in fact, is indispensable for completing the very essence of the universe. And participation is at the core of it.

Truth itself is the consequence of the participatory context. Skolimowski summarizes his philosophy of the Participatory Truth as follows:

> With the collapse of the Newtonian world-view, we witness the collapse of the doctrine of metaphysical realism – which was its philosophical justification. Simultaneously we witness a collapse of a variety of empiricisms from Locke and Hume to Russell and Quine. These empiricisms have been merely more refined versions of metaphysical realism.
>
> On another level, the collapse of the Newtonian world-view signifies (at least a partial) collapse of the correspondence theory of truth – which in modern times has been uniquely bound to the scientific world-view. The correspondence theory of truth did not originate with the Newtonian world-view and therefore does not need to be entirely tied to it. Yet modern Western philosophy is inconceivable without the tie between the correspondence theory of truth and the scientific world-view.
>
> Some have tried to rescue the correspondence theory while foregoing the notion of permanent knowledge which Newton's physics stipulates. Among the bravest of these was Karl Popper who introduced the notion of approximation to truth – an ingenious idea but ridden with the irresolvable difficulties: if we don't know truth, how can we ever handle an approximation to it? What is the meaning of an approximation if we don't know that which it approximates to?
>
> Others have tried to replace the correspondence theory of truth with truth by convention (Poincare, early Quine). Yet others have tried to find an escape in the coherence theory of truth (Mach, Kuhn). Others again have opted for the pragmatic theory of truth – American pragmatists on

the one hand, and Marxists in the communist world on the other. Although I have not discussed the pragmatic theory of truth in any detail, it is fair to say that this theory (as a replacement of the correspondence theory) does not fare any better than other new candidates of truth. The pragmatic theory of truth can be social disaster when it becomes a weapon of advertising men and of politicians.

As we construct the cosmos and the meaning of this illusive term called 'reality', so we need to revise our old idea of what truth is, or what is the most judicious way to use the term. Participatory philosophy outlines the participatory concept of truth, which is neither objective nor subjective; neither absolute nor relative but intersubjective and universal – within the boundaries of the species (truth is species-specific); within the boundaries of culture (truth is culture-bound and language-bound); within the boundaries of the spiral of understanding. As evolution unfolds so does the Mind unfold, so our knowledge unfolds, so our truth unfolds. By saying that truth is unfolding we are saying that truth is a *happening* or simply that truth is participatory.

The concept of participatory truth enables us to recognize the validity of the religious concept of truth – which is determined by the specifically religious context of participation. By recognizing religious truth, we are able to shed a new light on spiritual seekers, the Illustrious Ones, who gave us religious and the moral law, and who, at times, identified God with truth. They were not half-baked, confused philosophers but envisaged truth as the realization of God, as the consummation of the destiny of man.

Yes, there is absolute or ultimate truth. It is the truth about the whole universe, in its totality, in its unfolding, in its realization. This may be God's truth; or the truth that even God cannot comprehend. Some simply say that ultimate truth is God.

We human beings must be satisfied with partial truths – always fragmentary. Fragmentary truths are not relative or subjective. Each turn of kaleidoscope called the evolving cosmos produces a specific pattern. When we enter this pattern and participate in it, a fragment of truth is created. Truth does not exist before we enter the cosmos or kaleidoscopic configuration of it, but only within human language, within the context of participation.

It is difficult to live with truth. It is impossible to live without truth. As a human species we need guidance as to what is right and what is wrong; what is justice and what is injustice. Truth has historically served as the basis of justice, as the yardstick of goodness – even if it was so in an indirect way. We now know that the only truth we can know is human truth – man-made truth. The human condition is frail but not arbitrary. And so is our truth.

No species – no truth! Participatory truth does not describe things as they are. Participatory truth is a vehicle of becoming. Participatory truth is the Promethean fire of transformation.

CHAPTER 11

Revisiting the Grand Theory on the Participatory Ground

No matter the phenomenon investigated, it could always be slotted into a wider theoretical scheme. Nothing would be left out; everything would be explained.[1] – Barnes and Gregory

1. Grand Return of the Grand Theory

Discussing the Grand Theory in the participatory key, Henryk Skolimowski narrates the following story: "In 1959 the American sociologist Wright Mills published his celebrated book *The Sociological Imagination*, in which he tried to bury and to ridicule what is called Grand Theory. Grand theory insists that framework is more important than particular facts. For facts receive their meaning from an underlying framework – a general theory, or a paradigm. Mills and his followers thought otherwise. They advocated the 'scientific' study of human nature, and of human institutions, in which particular empirical facts – their analysis and detailed examination – predominate, and are the only important thing. . . This was, of course, positivism applied to social science. This was the era in which not only social scientists became captive to positivism. The whole epoch was in the clutches of narrow, atomistic, positivist thinking. . . . The grand theory is flourishing again. If not flourishing, at least alive and making a significant comeback. There are, of course, many contenders to grand theory and quite a bit of confusion concerning the meaning of the term, as the school of hermeneutics and deconstructionism quarrel with each other."

Henryk further insists that what is important is not the differences between various schools but the fact that large normative thinking has returned. "It is again clearly perceived that our frameworks *do* determine the nature of the facts we examine, that the meaning of the whole determines the meaning of the parts," he elaborates. "Thus holistic thinking is in, while atomistic thinking is waning, at least among prominent grand theorists of the last decade."

Henryk cites an example of Quentine Skinner's *The Return of the Grand Theory in the Human Sciences* (1958) which adequately documents the 'new developments concerning the re-emergence of grand theory'. He enlists some of the main characteristics of grand theory as follows:

(1) It attempts to meet the challenge of the problems of the epoch.

(2) It attempts to offer an original interpretation of the multitude of phenomena, while at the same time it is capable of maintaining the value of tradition.

(3) It attempts to serve as a model or a paradigm for other fields of inquiry.

(4) It attempts to be consistent with scientific progress, or more generally, with the progress of knowledge.

It will now offer participatory philosophy as a candidate for a new grand theory, as Henryk says. One of the ironies of science is that it boasts of its own progress vertically, often leaving human beings aside. Henryk, in this context, suggests that scientific progress must be interpreted broadly, as a progress of human understanding, of which scientific understanding is but one aspect.

Skolimowski sketches an outline of Grand Theory in the Participatory Key. He also tries to provide some of the missing links of the participatory grand theory. He transforms reality by co-creatively participating in it. To the journey from one reality to the other he calls the Great Circle of Knowledge; this circle is open, not closed – in the nature of a spiral. The movement around this Great Circle is what Henryk calls the process of *reality-making*. Some crucial inferences Henryk draws are:

- Reality impinges upon experience.
- Experience, in its turn, gives rise to knowledge.
- Knowledge bursts with new insights.
- New insights change the nature of existing reality, and create a new reality.

Henryk writes a lot about experience. He refers to Greek poet Archilochus of the seventh century BC who wrote: 'Life is short. Art is long. Experience is difficult.' He writes: "We are but bundles of experiences. Experiences and experiences accompany us whatever we do."

2. Significance of Experiences

Experience is not what happens to a man; it is what a man does with what happens to him[2].
– Aldous Huxley

Experiences constitute treasure of life. Not just ordinary experiences. Rather the extraordinary experiences. Henryk Skolimowski calls such experiences as significant experiences. Each significant experience is like a golden chapter in life. A life replete with significant experiences is a happy, vibrant, creative, and exemplar life.

Experience, according to Skolimowski, includes at least three components, viz.:

- 'Reality' out there.
- Psychic dispositions to experience it.
- Appropriate sensitivities to articulate the experience.

He says that 'reality' is usually indispensable as the basis of an experience, or of experiences. But not always, he makes clearer. "Some of the greatest experiences we experience inwardly," Henryk maintains. "They are the soul-trips or the Mind-trips, not derived from or inspired by the outside reality."

About some other experiences, Henryk tells us that they appear to be beautiful or at least pleasant at the time they are experienced. But these are short-lived ones. "They float through us and disappear," he adds.

Significant experiences are extraordinary. They, as Henryk says, are *memorable, articulate* (or at least articulable), and *transformative*. He expresses these characteristics in the language of participatory Mind: *Significant experience is that kind of event, or that series of events, which leads to recognizable transformations of the spiral of understanding – either personal or universal (cultural).*

Is there any connection between knowledge and experience? "Knowledge and experience are deeply but subtly connected," Henryk explains. "Sometimes new experience leads to changes in our knowledge. After we have undergone some experiences, we know differently. Our knowledge has been somehow rearranged." Is the converse also true? Yes. "Not infrequently, new knowledge that we have acquired changes the nature of our experience," asserts Henryk.

We seek the experiences which lead to our own enhancement. We wish to undergo experiences which are enriching. We wish the treasure of experiences which lead to our transformation. This form of new and significant experience Skolimowski calls *S-experience* (S = significant). Only the S-experiences affect and change our spiral of understanding, others not. What is the sphere of the S-experiences, and which factors do lead to such experiences? Henryk gives some important tips:

- The spiral of understanding can only change through S-experience.
- S-experiences require courage, openness, making oneself vulnerable.
- The creative process is one open to S-experience.
- Unarticulated experience is a mist.

- Significant experience is one that somehow changes our being.
- The nature of our logos and the nature of our experience are twin sisters.
- Our sensitivities are ultimately the artists that give a distinctive shape to our experiences, and are the sculptors of our experiences.

What is the role of Mind? "The role of the Mind is all-important in shaping the nature of experience and in bringing out those distinctive forms that we sometimes call the delight of life, sometimes revelatory illuminations," Skolimowski marvellously explains. "By the Mind, of course, we do not mean the abstract brain, but the entire universe of sensitivities. What senses and sees and thinks is the entire body – not just the abstract brain. Our body, as the repository of the sensitivities of evolution, is doing the knowing and the thinking."

Henryk's participatory theory of Mind draws a delightful conclusion: *There is nothing in the senses that has not previously been in the structure of our sensitivities, thus the structure of our (evolutionary) Mind.* He adds: "The web of our sensitivities is all-pervading. It touches and refines everything that enters our being, whether through the senses, whether through intuition, whether through divine revelations. Divine revelation cannot descend upon the Mind that is not sensitive enough to receive it, and somehow make sense of it." Henryk concludes by saying: *Glory to the sensitive Mind, for it is the maker of all knowledge, of all experience.*

3. Experience-Knowledge Relationship

There is a difference between experience and knowledge. There is also a strong relationship between experience and knowledge. Experience translates into knowledge not always but under certain conditions. What kind of experiences qualify as knowledge? Skolimowski proposes that knowledge is:

- a significant experience;
- an articulate experience;

- a distilled experience (and a significantly filtered one);
- a communicable experience;
- a sharable experience;
- a linguistically structured experience;
- a repeatable experience.

He explains interesting relationships between experience and knowledge, which make us transform our own experiences *happening*, i.e., translating into our own empowerment by equipping us with knowledge:

❖ *Knowledge is a significant transformation of experience.*
❖ *Knowledge is a structuring of the significant and distilled experience; which we subsequently legitimize by expressing it in sharable and intersubjective patterns and forms.*
❖ True knowledge is a refined and sharable experience.
❖ *Knowledge is light. Knowledge is igniting sensitivities that can see,* in the manifold senses of the term 'see'.
❖ Knowledge consists of significant new experiences that lead to new illuminations.
❖ We cannot define knowledge because knowledge is doing defining.

4. New Illuminations, New Realities

From a reality, via S-experience, we arrive at knowledge of this reality. What does our Mind do? "Our Mind does not remain static or frozen," Henryk reveals. "In its explorations it conceives new ideas, is haunted by new insights or new flashes of imagination. . . The emergence of a new insight is usually preceded by the following three dialogues: of the Mind with the existing reality; of the Mind with the existing knowledge; and of the Mind with one's own experience."

The knowledge that emerges may be a small extension of the existing one; or may be a major breakthrough, according to Skolimowski. In the latter case, he says, it may even lead to a new picture of reality. *"It is at this point of new illuminations or new insights that the closed system of reality-knowledge becomes an open system,"* He explains with the help of his Great Circle of Knowledge.

Henryk queries about absolute knowledge: Why is absolute knowledge (whether of religion or of physics) a threat to our freedom? "Because – although it gives us a sense of security – it imprisons us in the static and frozen universe," he resolves himself. "On the existential level, absolute knowledge is a severe stumbling block to new experiences, and S-experiences. For if reality is completely fixed and known, then there is nothing to be known beyond it."

Henryk raises two more questions to arrive at right conclusion: (1) Why is the notion of experience, and particularly new experience, so difficult to handle via objective knowledge? (2) Why, in general terms, this tension and uneasiness between solid, articulated knowledge and fluid, volatile experience? "Because knowledge is the guardian of the status quo, is the servant of the existing cosmos; whereas experience is an inspired agent of becoming, is the harbinger of the things to come, a herald of the new world which by its very nature is unsettling to the status quo. Ultimately, being and becoming have to accommodate each other... so that they are a coherent unity."

New experiences are capable to 'outstrip the capacity of the established knowledge'. In such case the established (old) knowledge also attempts to defend itself by accusing the new knowledge as 'crazy, lunatic, or at least irrational'. The existing knowledge cannot be the yardstick of all knowledge. Henryk's discourse illumines our Mind:

> ... while the guardians of the status quo within the universities consider the innovators crazy, rash, irrational and irresponsible, the innovators think that these guardians are slaves to vested interests, insensitive to new realities, petrified in their reason, and ultimately irresponsible. So

who is responsible? And by what yardstick shall we measure this responsibility? Obviously we have two different spirals of understanding clashing with each other. We have the realm of being – established reality and established knowledge. And corresponding to them: form, structure, immanence, intersubjectivity, established language. On the other hand, we have the realm of becoming. And corresponding to it: new illuminations flourishing amidst creativity, fluidity, change, questioning, transcendence. This is the old eternal conflict between being and becoming.

5. *Reality and Meditation*

Henryk Skolimowski puts seemingly ordinary things in an extraordinary and interesting manner: "Every scientist knows, and especially every philosopher knows, that knowledge does not generate itself, that there is a human agent involved in the process; that the human Mind and the human experience are a necessary interface between reality and knowledge. However, the history of knowledge, and particularly of scientific knowledge, is often presented as if reality were having a direct intercourse with knowledge. Reality, as it were, lays its eggs in the basket of knowledge, which in its turn produces little chickens called scientific theories. In this model of direct liaison between reality and knowledge, the human mind, and especially human experience, seem to be dispensable."

Thus, the so called scientific method attempts to attach least, rather no, importance to the observer. The self-posing scientist claims that only he/ she, as Henryk puts it, 'can help reality and knowledge mate with each other successfully'.

"Let us realize that experience *always* meditates between reality and knowledge, regardless of how much we want to diminish, neglect and negate its role," Henryk elaborates "The direct axis between reality and knowledge is a fiction. The two never commune, never cohabit; they never have an affair with each other. Only we, through the versatility of our experience, have endless affairs with each."

About the axis of meditation (the horizontal axis in figure 1), Skolimowski says, "It often happens that new insights or new flashes of imagination spring, as it were, from our inner experience. New illuminations seem to be visiting us regardless of reality, and of existing knowledge we possess."

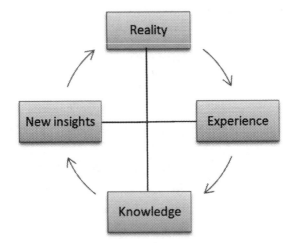

Figure 1: The reality-knowledge axis and the axis of meditation: vertical line is the axis of knowledge; horizontal line is the axis of meditation (modified from Henryk Skolimowski)

Based on his description of the reality-knowledge axis and the meditation axis, Henryk draws two fabulous conclusions:

1. *Do not deify or reify (or objectify) the reality-knowledge axis as if it were something existing out there independently of us.*
2. *Do not deify the axis of meditation as if it were independent of knowledge and reality.*

In the first conclusion, the axis is one of the expressions of the myth of objectivity. The second conclusion implies that in the act of illumination, our knowledge and our reality are firmly embedded.

6. *Knowledge as Power and as Liberation*

All things are subject to interpretation; whichever interpretation prevails at a given time is a function of power and not truth. – Friedrich Nietzsche

Knowledge by conventionalists and power-crazy philosophers is regarded as a source of power. Criticizing Jürgen Habermas remark about the production of knowledge, Henryk says that we cannot have factories for producing knowledge. Thus talk of *production* of knowledge is nonsense. 'Knowledge as power' is a Baconian-Faustion syndrome. Knowledge is no source of illumination for them. Henryk dismisses such remarks: "The production of knowledge is a *vulgar* endeavour. The knowledge-power quest is a pathological venture. Knowledge is illumination and there is no better term for describing its nature than that. Knowledge is not a hatchet for destruction or an instrument of domination, but a torch of light."

Knowledge is a fruit of enlightenment and a source of liberation. Knowledge as a source of liberation, according to Henryk, is also a foundation of our existence. Henryk's beautiful and enlightening thoughts about knowledge as a source of liberation go as follows:

> As we grow, we acquire knowledge. As we acquire knowledge we are gradually liberated – from the bondage of babyhood, from the bondage of our original egotism. And this liberation is proportional to the depth of knowledge we acquire. *We grow through the knowledge we acquire. And through knowledge we are liberated.* Thus knowledge is liberation. As societies grow and mature, they are liberated – from old taboos, fears, restrictions, hang-ups of various sorts.

The most glaring, sparkling and beautiful attribute of life and light – i.e., knowledge – should not be reduced to its lesser meaning. For, says

Henryk, 'to reduce knowledge to power is to challenge evolution at its very core, is to challenge the ascending spiral of understanding, is to challenge the spiritual heritage of humankind. . . to reduce knowledge to power is to create existential Hell on earth.'

We need to embark on the Great Journey, suggests Henryk. We need to bypass the old power-crazy epicycles and strive to unfold new dimensions of reality by pursuing the quest for knowledge-illumination. Such, in the words of Skolimowski, is our evolutionary destiny. "The idea that 'the reality of power is the only reality' is a somnambulist intoxication of those who have lost their souls," warns Henryk. "The addicts of power are pushing a lunatic course. They are stuck in a self-destructive epicycle. The pursuit of power ultimately destroys those who pursue power."

Summary

Prof. Henryk Skolimowski splendidly attempts to explain the Grand Theory in the Participatory Key. The Grand Theory, which is as old as human knowledge, is exhibiting its significant comeback and seems to be flourishing again. Quentin Skinner in his well-quoted work *The Return of Grand Theory in the Human Sciences* (1985) documents new developments concerning the re-emergence of grand theory. Meeting the challenge of the problems of the epoch, offering an original interpretation of the multitude of phenomena while maintaining the value of tradition, serving as a model or a paradigm for other fields of inquiry and being consistent with scientific progress or with the progress of knowledge are some of the main characteristics of the grand theory Henryk Skolimowski deeply looks into and fabulously interprets.

Reality, experience, knowledge and new insights exist in a definite relationship. Knowledge flowers into new insights. New insights make the existing reality change its nature leading to the creation of new reality. Experience finds new face of its own, though it is very difficult to be bound in exact words of definition. Henryk reveals three components of the experience: (i) 'Reality' out there; (ii) Psychic dispositions to experience it; and (iii) Appropriate sensitivities to articulate the experience. He talks about significant experience, or the *S-experience*: that only the S-experiences are transformative; that creativity has its windows open to S-experience; that vulnerability is also an essential precondition for the sweet realization of S-experience; that experience needs be articulate or it is just *dumped* into past and stays in our memory only like a mist; that a sensitive Mind is the maker of all knowledge and all experiences.

Henryk regards knowledge as a significant transformation of experience. Knowledge consists of significant new experiences that lead to new illuminations. Human condition is indefinable, for this condition defines ourselves. Knowledge is also indefinable, for it is knowledge itself that engages itself in defining everything else. Nature of the Mind is unexplainable, for Mind itself explains everything else – seen, unseen, what is on Earth, what is there in the universe, what has happened, and what is going to *happen*.

Our Mind is not an ordinary one. It is something most extraordinary. It is always active. It is never static; it is never frozen. It unceasingly conceives new ideas, is encountered by new insights and new imagination. Henryk underlines three dialogues that precede the emergence of new insight: i) of Mind with the existing reality; ii) of the Mind with the existing knowledge; and iii) of the Mind with one's own experience. The existing knowledge may assume some extension, or it may assume a breakthrough. The participatory Mind co-creates with reality. Absolute knowledge is not good, for it is a direct threat to our freedom.

Skolimowski gives us a soothing experience by making us visit what he calls Great Circle. Knowledge is not something that could be generated by itself. A human agent is to be involved in this process. Our Mind and our experiences serve as necessary interface between reality and knowledge. The objective or the scientific method calls for removing the observer from the reality-knowledge alliance. Experience always mediates between reality and knowledge. The direct axis between reality and knowledge is a fiction.

New illuminations visit us regardless of reality, and of existing knowledge we possess. Henryk puts forth two conclusions, based on his explanation of the reality-knowledge axis and the axis of meditation: i) *Do not deify or reify (or objectify) the reality-knowledge axis as if it were something existing out there independently of us*; and ii) *Do not deify the axis of meditation as if it were independent of knowledge and reality.*

Knowledge should not be used as power. If it is done, it will be a misuse of knowledge, and an insult to knowledge. Knowledge is an inexhaustible source of our liberation, of our illumination, of our right evolution, of our creativity, of our motivation of our holistic development.

Let us now glance through the summary of the Grand Theory in the Participatory Key as presented by Prof. Henryk Skolimowski himself:

> Grand theory is as old as human knowledge. When Moses brought his Tablets from the top of Mount Sinai, this was one example of grand theory. When Thales declared that all is water, this was another. When Plato insisted that Forms explain all, this was another. When Newton formulated his Laws of Nature, this was yet another. To be coherent, our thinking must follow some patterns. The master-patterns determine the meaning of particular words and events – whether we call these patterns grand theories or not.
>
> The Participatory Grand Theory reveals and analyses the process of reality-making. In trying to understand this process, we need to reflect on the nature of experience; and on the relationship between knowledge and experience.
>
> Experience is such a difficult term to define – yet such an easy phenomenon to acknowledge on the existential level. We float in the endless sea of experience. However, unarticulated experience is but a mist. Articulated experience leads to knowledge, art, philosophy. Each of these great realms of the human universe – knowledge, art,

philosophy – is but a *crystallized form* of human experience. But how exquisitely crystallized! Let us be aware – this power of crystallization or articulation of experience is a form of experience itself. But it is a second order experience. Though a vital one. Without this form of experience – ordering and structuring all other experiences (the first order experience) – we would live in a perpetual fog. Intuition will not help us.

Significant experience is that kind of event, or that series of events, which leads to recognizable transformations of the spiral of understanding – either personal or cultural. Those experiences that are significant and have far-reaching consequence I call *S-experiences*. Courting an S-experience is a creative act. The creative act requires courage, openness and vulnerability. Those are the very attributes and also preconditions of new experiences. Playing for safety does not lead to new experiences. On the contrary, it leads to stale forms of life – dull, repetitious, predictable. No risks – no S-experience.

Knowledge is structuring of the significant cognitive experience. We legitimize this experience by expressing it in intersubjectively sharable patterns. Yet on another level, knowledge is light. Knowledge is igniting sensitivities that can see. Knowledge consists of new significant experiences that lead to new illuminations. The incompleteness of our definitions of knowledge does not come from the deficiency of our linguistic or intellectual resources. Rather, it comes from the incompleteness of our being, the incompleteness of our truth.

Traditional theories of knowledge postulate, if only implicitly, that there is a firm axis reality-knowledge. Knowledge reflects reality, while reality feeds into (and tests!) existing knowledge. The presumption is that it is the same knowledge and the same reality that feed into each other in a circular way. This whole picture is fundamentally inadequate. The direct axis between reality and knowledge is a fiction. The two never commune, except through us. We are the point of connection. We are the point of communion. Therefore, we should not deify the reality-knowledge axis, as if it existed independently of us. To unduly stress the importance of this axis is to perpetuate the myth of objectivity.

Neither should we deify the axis of meditation, as if it were independent of knowledge and reality. In the acts of our illumination – whether we call them the phenomenological method or not – our knowledge and our reality are subtly embedded. Intuition should be recognized, but not deified.

The path of becoming is all-important. It integrates the axis of reality-knowledge with the axis of meditation; and creatively transcends them. Becoming is a benevolent god that devours being and transforms it into ever more effervescent forms. Becoming is a continuous fire of creation. Becoming is an endless transcendence, for only in this way does the world realize itself.

CHAPTER 12

Participatory Philosophy for the New World

You can cultivate gracefulness, but graciousness is the aroma of friendliness which emanates from a love-saturated soul.[1] – The Urantia Book (171:7.1)

1. Philosophy for Grace in Life-style

And we should consider every day lost on which we have not danced at least once. And we should call every truth false which was not accompanied by at least one laugh.[2]
– Friedrich Nietzsche

Philosophy is eternal spring of hope. Philosophy is inexhaustible energy of karma. Philosophy is the finest architect of our world. Philosophy is light extraordinary enlightening human soul. Philosophy is the stupendous art transforming human species into humane and compassionate humans. Philosophy is the cosmic boon rearing humans as guardians of all life forms and as custodian of the universe. Philosophy is a song of beauty. Philosophy is a phenomenon of sustainability flowing through human cultures.

Everything else dies. Philosophy is always alive. Philosophy is immortal like light, like soul. Philosophy, like all cosmic phenomena, has been in evolution, always keeps in evolution. A philosophy that does not imbibe with evolutionary ideas only serves to keep our world cool, inert, indifferent, devoid of creative ideas, and on the path of wrong karma.

Henryk Skolimowski has evolved a philosophy which is distinctive in itself – the Participatory Philosophy whose promises are infinite. This is the philosophy, which is rooted into the realities of our Earth, and which seeks new horizons of life-styles of grace and dignity. This is the philosophy that revives our spiritual concerns and that cultures a right karma. It elevates us to the cosmic scales of living: caring for the living earth to care for the cosmic sustainability.

Skolimowski brought this philosophy – as Eco-philosophy – into existence in 1974. He kept evolving his philosophy; and on the fertile ground of eco-philosophy he evolved the Participatory Philosophy which came into being in the last decade of the twentieth century. At that time he had given this call:

> Our times call for a new holistic philosophy, integrative par excellence and not shy of spirituality; capable of addressing far-reaching cosmological problems concerning the origin of the universe and existential problems concerning the destiny of mankind – all in the same framework.

So, the Skolimowskian Philosophy of the Participatory Mind is here – as a wonderful present to the humanity, at this juncture of time. In the evolution of human Mind, one essential characteristic has been that we became accustomed to live with wonders. Encountering wonders is an evolutionary quest of human Mind. The Participatory Mind keeps us engaged in unravelling all the cosmic wonders. Even the Mind presents itself as a wonder – in fact, the greatest wonder of the universe cultivating all other wonders to the satiation of its evolutionary quest.

"Philosophy feeds on its past, as does human soul," Henryk argues. "It may be of some value to remind ourselves of some forms of philosophy practiced in the past – very different from our discursive philosophy; yet very nourishing to the soul." The philosophy Henryk has created and evolved intensively blossoms in our times but it also feeds on its past. Almost all kinds of philosophies humanity has encountered in the past speak in the philosophy of Skolimowski's Participatory Mind.

Skolimowskian Philosophy deeply examines the lives of the illustrious ones, such as Buddha, Jesus, Socrates, Plato and many others. He says that when we do so we realize that 'something strange is at work. Some great alchemy is taking place.' Those illustrious ones were more than philosophers. They were made for something much higher. "If you live aright, you don't need philosophy," says Henryk looking into the great values the illustrious ones set out for humanity.

Henryk lets us realize the importance of philosophy. "It gives a structure of support to your life; that is if you cannot do otherwise," he maintains. "If you can do it otherwise, you don't need philosophy." Eliciting example from the illustrious ones, he adds that in their lives, philosophy is *transcended* in favour of effortless grace. The art of living, as Henryk regards, is a form of philosophy. "The art of living in effortless grace is ultimate philosophy," he reiterates.

In Socrates' time the discursive thinking began to dominate the Greek Mind, says Henryk. "It is at this point that we witness the rise of the supreme architect of human thought, Plato," he adds and explains why we call Plato a supreme architect. "Because he was able to construct a system of thought of staggering beauty, lucidity and depth… He appeased the discursive reason and, at the same time, to fly with the angels beyond the realm of logic and reason – on to the land of Enlightenment and spiritual salvation."

About the philosophers who phenomenally influenced our world, Henryk writes: "Socrates' quest is unmistakably that of liberation. Plato wants to have it both ways – liberation as the spiritual salvation and the discursive satisfaction. Aristotle clearly abandons the idea of liberation. His ideal is the possession of knowledge. Aristotle wants to *know* everything (where is the wisdom we have lost in knowledge?), he wants to classify all phenomena, put them in boxes, label them. This was the beginning of the analytical disease."

Giving his view on the illustrious ones, Henryk Skolimowski arrives at this conclusion: Indeed, *philosophy is a mental substitute for our inability* to *live our life in continuous grace.* The actual act of living in effortless grace is the only convincing ultimate philosophy."

The thought that the illustrious ones did not write does not surprise us. "They knew that there is a special form of truth which is the living truth, and which can only be conveyed and expressed through the light that emanates through one's life," Henryk maintains. "Hence 'the life-cycle of effortless grace' is the right description of this ultimate philosophy which has left words and dwells in light."

Henryk cites an example of Plato about written philosophy: "Plato was actually apprehensive that his written philosophy was a betrayal of the living truth. He wrote with misgivings, as if apologetically, pointing out that his written philosophy was a form of entertainment, diversion rather than an expression of the living truth. In his famous Seventh Letter Plato writes: Owing to the inadequacy of language . . . no intelligent man will ever dare to commit his thoughts to words, still less to words that cannot be changed, as is the case with what is expressed in written characters."

With this example of Plato, one of the greatest philosophers of all times, Henryk makes assumption that 'philosophy put on paper is dead.' He adds: "The only way of practicing philosophy is the living dialogue. And this living dialogue can be carried out only with living beings. . . The methodology of participation informs us that dialogue with our cells, and even with oaks and rocks, may not be far-fetched – if we release and activate appropriate sensitivities."

2. Philosophy from Perennial to Scientific Stream

History of philosophy has been very twisty. "From the mystical exaltations this path has led *some* philosophers in the twentieth century to the realm of ruthless logic, which alone was meant to secure reliability and respectability for philosophy," writes Henryk. He attempts to trace many events relating to philosophers and their philosophy explaining several twists in the philosophical history of the past:

- Since Descartes philosophy has been fixated upon method. In his Discourse on Method (1632), he introduced his famous analytical method which proposes to divide and subdivide every single problem until we arrive at problems which are so simple and rudimentary, and so clearly defined, that we can indubitably resolve them without any ambiguity.
- With the introduction of powerful tools of modern mathematical logic, especially from Gottlob Frege (1848–1925) on, philosophers and logicians thought that at least they had obtained language and conceptual apparatus powerful and precise enough to tackle all philosophical problems and resolve them to their logical Minds' content.
- In 1910 Bertrand Russell announced the idea of scientific philosophy. This was an indirect result of his work (together with Alfred North Whitehead). The fruit of their joint venture was the monumental work in three volumes (1910–13) entitled *Principia Mathematica*.
- From this point on we witness wave after wave of the new philosophy, which attempts to be as sharp as a knife and as dry as a bone.
- First is of Wittgenstein, with his Logical Atomism, a metaphysical application of the logical tools of the *Principia*.
- Then came the programme of scientific philosophy of the Vienna Circle with Rudolf Carnap's *The Logical Structure of the World* (1928) as a forerunner of other similar ventures.
- Simultaneously was witnessed the emergence of the Polish school of logic and of analytical philosophy, Jan Lukasiewicz announcing his programme of scientific philosophy in 1927.
- Then the centre moved to England, first to Cambridge, then to Oxford.

- With the refugees fleeing from Austria and Germany, analytical or scientific philosophy reached the United States, particularly after Carnap, Hempel and Reichenbach settled there.
- A new philosophical orthodoxy was established in the United States under the inspiration of the ex-philosophers of the Vienna Circle who settled in America; this philosophy being in the image of logic.

Henryk tells us that orthodoxy is still controlling the departments of philosophy in major English and American universities. In a sense recent development of philosophy presented the philosophy as if it was meant to be *ultimate philosophy*. However, Henryk concludes, analytical philosophy has failed to help culture and to be a genuine part of culture.

"What does it mean to say that a given philosophy has been creative and a given philosopher has not been creative?" asks Skolimowski and presents three criteria that offer themselves for a philosophy to be called creative:

(1) A given philosophy must be novel; better still, original.
(2) A given philosophy must offer a new interpretation of the cosmos and/ or life.
(3) A given philosophy must prove sustaining to the culture from which it has grown, and to succeeding cultures.

Skolimowski considers the third criterion 'quite critical'. "Philosophy must be like yeast. It must enable other things to grow," Skolimowski adds. "If nothing grows out of it, then it is not a creative philosophy." He presents many interesting, stimulating and inspiring aspects of philosophy, such as:

❖ This kind of philosophy has a peculiar power to inspire, to fecundate, to renew, to sustain, and the great philosophical systems of the past, both in the East and the West, possess this kind of power.

❖ Philosophy is part of culture. It expresses and sustains culture. Great philosophy sustains not only the culture that engendered it but also succeeding cultures as well. A philosophy cannot be creative if it does not sustain a culture; or worse still – if it contributes to the atrophy of a culture.

❖ A culture not guided by intrinsic values is like a ship without rudder.

❖ The moral detachment is immoral.

What is the cause of the sickness the analytical philosophy is transferring to the society through some of the analytical philosophers? About the philosophers, Skolimowski has this to say in the context of the zigzag advancement of philosophy from the perennial philosophy to the scientific one:

> Philosophers of the present time are not the causes of our plight. Just as we are, they are sad victims. Being brought up in a morally desensitized environment, being simply brainwashed by the ideology of technicism, they suppress their moral impulses and the spiritual aspects of their being – only in this way could they have completed their studies and obtained their PhDs. Who is to be blamed? Our crass materialist culture. Which simply must be changed. This materialist pig of a world must go!

3. Philosophy for Courage

Courage is a grace under pressure.[3] – Ernest Hemingway

Courage makes us what we are—the human beings. Courage is knowing what not to fear, says Plato. Wonderful art, religion, all epics, great preaching, great philosophy are all attributable to courage. Henryk Skolimowski considers emergence of philosophy as 'continuous act of courage'. He describes several historical events concerning human courage that led to the beginning of philosophy:

- In the Homeric universe gods ruled supreme. . . It was perfectly rational to assume that gods were in command and responsible for the vicissitudes of human destiny. From generation to generation myths formed the underlying structure of explanations of the world and of the human struggle for meaning. Greek tragedies of the fifth century BC supremely exemplify the strengths and shadows of the mytho-poetic world-view.
- A new form of Mind started in earnest with Thales (634–546 BC), who speculated that all is water.
- Then came Pythagoras (585–495 BC), who postulated that all is number.
- Then came Heraclitus (535–475 BC), who was possessed by the idea of *partha rhei* – all is changing, wearing out.
- In the process of new thinking a new form of explanation evolved. No longer were the new thinkers satisfied with the constant intervention of gods in man's daily affairs. They now wished to explain both the visible and the invisible in the cosmos through natural reason.
- Thus the translucent logos was born, which marks the beginning of philosophy and beginning of the liberation of man from the bondage of myths.

"Where is the place of courage in all this?" asks Henryk with a beautiful answer underlying the substance involved in the act of courage. "Indeed, it took tremendous courage to conceive of an altogether new way of looking at universe, and a new way of thinking about it, particularly from inside a cocoon of myths. *Every new philosophy that breaks away from the cocoon of the established orthodoxy is an act of courage.*"

Ideas are so dear to Henryk Skolimowski! "Ideas are elusive things – not clearly expressed, they are lost," he gives his idea about ideas. "New ideas are gift of God. But to convey them in such a way that they can be understood by other requires skill and courage. For new ideas go against the grain of established orthodoxies. . . In so far as great philosophy is a continuous challenge to the established order – as philosophy continuously reinvents reality, the existence and continuation of great philosophy is a monument to human courage. It is in this sense that philosophy is courage."

On the basis of ideas being created and articulated by Mind, philosophers have contributed to philosophy which Henryk distinguishes into two kinds: 1) philosophy of creation and 2) philosophy of justification.

Henryk identifies the philosophy of creation with early Greek philosophers, with Socrates and Plato, as well as with Berkeley, Descartes, Galileo, Kant, Hegel and Marx. They all attempted to redesign reality, says Henryk adding that they all combined exemplary courage with exemplary imagination.

Henryk identifies the philosophy of justification (the philosophy that serves the existing order rather than attempts to change it) with great philosopher Aristotle, who painstakingly classified, sorted out and justified philosophy. "Aristotle is the beginning of the reign of the discursive reason that got the better of the Western Mind, particularly during the last three centuries," argues Henryk. "There is no question that from Aristotle on, the Western Mind is split, is caught between the desire for rational explanation and the desire (suppressed but still existing) for illumination and liberation." Augustine and Thomas Aquinas, both the saints of Roman Church, also represent the philosophy of justification. The modern times philosophy of justification is represented by Locke, Mill and all variety of empiricists, according to Henryk. Henryk also identifies the present-day analytical philosophers as philosophers of justification who 'endlessly justify, often quite forgetting what it is that they set out to justify and whose philosophy is without courage and without imagination'.

4. Participatory Philosophy

Philosophy is a mirror in which deep structure of a given society and culture are reflected. It is also a mirror in which the cracks of these deep structures are reflected.[4] – Henryk Skolimowski

Participation is one of the greatest attributes of philosophy. Deviated from participation, philosophy becomes a *property* of a privileged few. Such a philosophy can *elevate* some people to the status of elites living in vertical relationship with the society. Philosophy confined to a few turns into a private property. Such a philosophy is devoid of light. Such a philosophy is not evolutionary one. Such a philosophy is not everyone's. Such a philosophy attempts to impose its *private realities and truths* on masses. Such a philosophy emits its firefly-like light only in the castles of a few. Participatory philosophy, on the other hand, is like light of the street lamp that enlightens path for all. When participatory philosophy reaches its highest form of participation, it becomes a cosmic light – photosynthesizing, delighting and life-enhancing.

Participatory philosophy is the Skolimowskian Philosophy spreading the light of Universal Oneness. This oneness begins from individual oneness ensured by integrity of the self. The participatory philosophy strengthens individual integrity, and from individual integrity it works on higher integrated forms of life – integrated society, integrated world, integrated universe, and finally the Universal Oneness.

Secret of participation that reins in the Skolimowskian Philosophy is not new. Its discovery dates back to early Greek philosophers. "They (the early Greek philosophers) redesigned their world by co-creatively participating in it," writes Skolimowski. He has so beautifully revealed the secrets of participation and evolved a whole art of participatory philosophy. The latter half of the 20th century and the beginning of the 21st century – or the connecting decades of the second and the third millennium – have been pivotal in the evolution of a philosophy that is par excellence in designing new living, in empowering human Mind, in constructing a new world, in designing new cosmology, and in preserving the delicate cosmic balance. The credit goes to Prof. Henryk Skolimowski, the Father of Eco-philosophy, the Father of the Philosophy of Light, and the architect of Lumenarchy and Cosmocracy.

"Participatory philosophy is a potential powerhouse of ideas and energies," Henryk nicely claims. "To begin with, it implies a rediscovery of participation – as the vital process of being in this world, of having a Mind in this world, of creatively contributing to this world – and thereby shaping one's meaning and one's destiny in this world." Henryk presents many more fascinating elements of the participatory philosophy:

> The idea of participation is a true gift. It opens the gate to a new metaphysical paradise. When you follow the idea to its ultimate conclusions, it reveals a new world and new, exciting dimensions of our individual lives. Participatory philosophy implies a rediscovery of courage – the courage to behold one's destiny without a grudge and with dignity; the courage to uphold the rational Mind and at the same time to admit its limits in this mysterious universe; and above all, the courage of having a Mind – so illustrious and so frail an instrument, which is our torch, our delight, our only bridge connecting us with God.

Technology has been enemy No. 1 of the Mind. Mind, during its evolutionary journey, has been conferred upon so much power. And it is yet to gain more power of comprehending, for the evolution is going on unceasingly. "It is a curious facet of our technological society that while releasing so much new power, we have been reducing the significance of the Mind," Henryk reasons. "Indeed *the consumerist society is a mindless society.* It continuously replaces our ingenuity with expertise, our self-reliance with new gadgets, our capacity to govern ourselves with technological crutches. The destiny of human species requires releasing more and more of the resources of the mind, not the mindless consumption that reduces the potency of our Mind."

It is a matter of some relief that the mindless society has not yet dominated the world. Courage is still alive despite the economic globalism and omnipresent consumerism. "There is a courage to behold and celebrate," says Henryk with deep breath of satisfaction. The enormous gap that exists could be filled up by the participatory philosophy. Henryk suggests us to hold the participatory key:

> To understand the role of the participatory Mind in the participatory universe is to receive the key to participatory philosophy. To apply the participatory Mind while we converse with the universe is to weave new ontological designs out of the half-given cosmos; is to outline new epistemological strategies, as well as elicit and sharpen new sensitivities – our windows to reality – through which we can gaze at the universe more clearly and converse with it more meaningfully.

Henryk Skolimowski has announced specific concepts of participatory philosophy. These are: participatory reality, the co-creative Mind, the spiral of understanding, the repertoire of sensitivities, the Evolutionary Telos, the methodology of participation, participatory research programmes, participatory truth, participatory space of grace, participatory sense of experience, courage to be and courage to become.

Henryk makes it clear that participatory philosophy is a store of ready-made concepts, formulated once and for all. "Participatory philosophy is first and foremost a *process* philosophy," Henryk says making it clearer further. "It outlines a framework and a strategy. It liberates the Mind to fly high and to explore deep – without constraining this Mind by determining what it ought to find."

5. Participatory Ethics

The world, Shakespeare said, is a stage on which we are all in a play. But the play that we enact on the world's stage is a divine play.[5] – The Speaking Tree, *The Times of India*

Participation itself is a creative term, creative notion, creative state of being. Participation itself illumines the Mind. Human ethics and human behaviour are rooted firmly into participation. Participation itself serves as a fertile ground for the philosophy to flower. Participation, according to Henryk Skolimowski, spells out our obligations as well as our behavioural strategies, on at least three levels:

(1) on the interpersonal level (person to person relationships);
(2) on the interspecies level (person to other species relationships);
(3) on the cosmic level (person to God relationship).

(1) PARTICIPATORY ETHICS ON THE INTERPERSONAL LEVEL

Nothing in the world is single;
All things by a law divine
In one another's being mingle – Why not I with thyne?[6]
– Percy Bysshe Shelley

"To be a person in the participatory universe entails the recognition of the bond of participation," says Henryk emphasizing that we must recognize this bond, or we shall have relinquished our rights to live in the participatory universe. And if we recognize this bond, then 'we ipso facto recognize empathy for other persons, reverence for other persons, responsibility for other persons'. Henryk adds: "Genuinely to partake in the meaning of our humanness is to act out the bond of empathy with the other. To treat the other with reverence is to take the responsibility for the whole context in which the well-being of the other resides."

When we don't recognize the bond of participation, we fall into the abyss of selfishness. The kind of the ethics then developed is non-participatory ethics. "Non-participatory ethics satisfies the ego, but leaves the soul and the inner person deeply unsatisfied," Skolimowski says deploring the non-participatory philosophy. "Such ethics cannot be path to genuine happiness, let alone serve as a foundation for social justice. When selfish ethics prevails for a long time, social injustices build up and then explode with vengeance and violence." Participation thus evolves, rears and sustains an ethics that strengthens bond of one's own selflessness, one's own responsibility, and, consequently, strengthens the bonds of fraternity, peace and co-creativity amongst fellow human beings and within society. The bond of participation extends beyond individual beings. It has been discussed under next two heads.

(2) PARTICIPATORY ETHICS ON THE INTERSPECIES LEVEL

When participatory ethics develops, evolves and sustains on the interspecies level, Skolimowski calls it ecological ethics. "We participate in the glories and riches of nature, for nature is us and we are it," Skolimowski puts it in beauty-emanating words. "Nature is of intrinsic value, as much as we are." He quotes Chief Seattle (1814): "Whatever befalls the earth befalls the sons of earth. Man did not weave the web of life, he is merely a strand in it. Whatever he does to the web he does to himself." A splash of the beauty of ideas coming from Skolimowskian writing is felt in the following paragraph:

> Reverence for natural systems is a consequence of our participation in nature's project. To encourage and maintain diversity is a part of the ethical imperative of participating in the riches of creation. . . Thus reverence for all life, and for all creation, is part of the ethical imperative of participating in life at large, and of recognizing all creation as a part of our larger being. Let us remind ourselves: if we

recognize the nature of the participatory Mind, we thereby recognize our larger being, as co-extensive with the cosmic consciousness of the human species.

Ecological ethics is of great significance for the life on Earth and for the living planet itself to be intact. Skolimowskian Philosophy reverberates with ecological ethics. Let us hear some stupendous things about ecological ethics from Skolimowski himself:

> Ecological ethics based on reverence for life, conceived within the larger panorama of the participatory Mind, does not necessarily imply species egalitarianism. . . We need something much stronger, much deeper and more fundamental than the mere recognition of all other species. . . We need strong concepts, such as reverence and compassion, to safeguard the safety of the weak against the strong; and particularly against the fiendishly clever species *Homo sapiens.*

"Participatory ethics as ecological ethics is neither anthropocentric nor anti-anthropocentric," Skolimowski elaborates. "*It is evolution-centric.* . . Anti-anthropocentrism has been propounded as a part of a larger movement called Deep Ecology. . . Deep ecology is quite incoherent when it becomes virulently anti-anthropocentric." We cannot be anything but our own species, i.e., *Homo sapiens.* Every idea we perceive, every act we perform is enveloped in a kind of anthropocentrism. Therefore, Skolimowski does not condemn the anthropocentric nature of the things, for they all are the *products* of human Mind. "Through our acts of empathy, which stem from our deep participation in all there is, we can, because of the characteristics of the human consciousness, so identify with the well-being of other beings that this empathy becomes an act of reverence," Skolimowski enlightens with the ecological ethics. "This reverence stemming from the idea of participation becomes an assured ethical path of tolerance, of protection, of preservation, of care and of love."

(3) PARTICIPATORY ETHICS ON THE COSMIC LEVEL

Men create gods after their own image, not only with regard to their form but with regard to their mode of life.[7] – Aristotle

Participatory ethics on cosmic level, as Henryk Skolimowski elicits, connects us with things unseen; or one which relates us to God – if we allow ourselves to use the term. "How does participatory ethics spell out our relationship with God?" Henryk asks and explains. "If we remember what we have said about the power and the role of the participatory Mind, while it is acting in the participatory universe, then our relationship to God becomes immediately clear."

Live as if you were God – Henryk expresses it in the simplest possible terms. He considers it not an act of arrogance, but an act of human courage. "The principle clearly follows from the architecture of the participatory Mind," Henryk further reveals. "The participatory Mind enables the universe to articulate God which is latent in it. Even if God is conceived as the prime mover, we need the participatory Mind to discover God's nature." He is fascinated by the Hindu and the Buddhist cultures of the East and by the Christianity:

> The glory of man sung in the Upanishads is the glory of man who becomes God. . . Each of us has a Buddha hidden in us. To fulfill our destiny is to become a Buddha, is to release the Buddha from within us. To become a Buddha is to live like a God. . . We can indeed conceive of ourselves as God-in-the-process-of-becoming without feeling sacrilegious or unduly arrogant. For what can be our destiny if not to become God? . . . Christian religion teaches that we are the

children of God. One day the children of God will become
adults. And that means God!

Does participatory ethics claims to be entirely novel or unrelated to
other ethical systems? Henryk says that it does not. He summarizes its three
components:

❖ Its first component – reverence in interpersonal relationships – is
closely related to Kantian ethics, based on the moral imperative:
*'Act in such a way that you always treat humanity, whether in your
own person or in the person of any other, never simply as a means, but
always at the same time as an end.'*

❖ The second component of participatory ethics – reverence for
natural systems and for all beings – partly overlaps with Buddhist
ethics, and partly with a variety of ecological ethics proposed
in recent times (by Henryk Skolimowski); especially those that
attempt to elevate bio-centric communities to the level of ethical
entities.

❖ The third component of the participatory ethics – live as if you were
God – coincides with the teachings of Upanishads and with other
spiritual traditions. This has a distinctively religious connotation.

Summary

Henryk Skolimowski's participatory philosophy is full of promises. He has
presented to this world a new holistic philosophy which attempts to solve
all problems and establish meaningful relationships amongst individuals,
between human species and rest of the life, and between humans and the
universal being – God. It gives structure of support to our life. It is an
indomitable source of liberation.

Philosophy has reached many horizons. However, its coming down
from perennial philosophy to scientific philosophy is a matter of deep

concern. With Descartes, philosophy began to be fixated upon method. Philosophy dies when it is reduced to minute, specific, exact problems. Bertrand Russell's announcement of the idea of scientific philosophy injected pathogens of diseases in the *blood* of philosophy. Analytical philosophy has disappointed culture and it could not become a genuine part of culture. Novelty or originality offer a new interpretation of cosmos and of life. Power of sustenance of the culture and of succeeding cultures must be the indispensable ingredients of a creative philosophy.

Philosophy is an outcome of the continuous act of human courage. Philosophy will die the day human courage dies. Philosophy and courage are like two lovely sister-brother twins. Both are born together, both grow together, both love each other, both live for each other. Every new philosophy breaks down the cocoon of the established orthodoxy, and it is an act of stupendous courage. Philosophy can be distinguished into philosophy of creation and philosophy of justification. Early Greek philosophers, Socrates, Plato, Berkeley, Descartes, Galileo, Kant, Hegel and Marx belong to the first category, while Aristotle is a glaring example of the second category of philosophy.

Participatory philosophy is a potential powerhouse of ideas and energies. And it is first and foremost a process philosophy. It serves to outline a framework and strategy. It acts to liberate the Mind to let it fly high in joy and in search of new horizons of creativity. It attempts to search deepest layers of truth.

Participatory ethics can be interpreted on three levels, namely, i) interpersonal level, ii) interspecies level, and iii) cosmic level. Participatory ethics can neither be claimed to be novel nor unrelated to other ethical systems. On interpersonal level, the participatory ethics generates reverence in interpersonal relationships. Here it is closely related to Kantian ethics. On interspecies level, it generates reverence for natural systems and for all beings (ecological ethics). Here it partly overlaps Buddhists ethics, and partly exists with a variety of ecological ethics proposed in recent times. On cosmic level, the participatory ethics gives this message: *live as if you were God*. Here the ethics exists intensively as religious connotation.

Let us now be delighted by the summary of The Promise of Participatory Philosophy as presented by Henryk Skolimowski:

Philosophy is a quest for liberation. All philosophies seek to elevate man, release him from bondage, bring him closer to Nirvana, to heaven, to the inner god.

Some philosophies deliberately attempt to be a path joining man with God. In this quest, they become akin to religion. Eastern philosophies have never renounced the ambition of delivering man to heaven. They have tried to be liberators in the spiritual sense. In this role they are close to religion. In our language, these philosophies have not yet separated themselves from religion. Nor did they mean to. This is the source of their strength – they address themselves to the total person; and this is the source of their weakness – they are intellectually and rationally less rigorous than Western philosophies.

In the west, philosophy has become more and more instrumental. The business of philosophy is to liberate reason, which in turn will liberate man. In this process of the liberation of reason we have surely gone too far. Reason has now become an autonomous agency which has the power to control and often to oppress. Reason has alienated itself from the overall quest of the liberation of man. Instead of liberation and enlightenment our physical knowledge has brought us *power*, in terrifying degree. We are a power-hungry civilization which at the same time is scared of the power it has accumulated.

The time for a new liberating philosophy has arrived. Proposed in this volume (*The Participatory Mind: A New Theory of Knowledge and of the Universe*) is an outline of participatory philosophy which, by liberating the Mind, liberates our destiny, and in a sense the destiny of the cosmos.

Participatory philosophy is the ultimate courage of man to surprise himself by creating realities surrounding him/her; the ultimate courage to realize that all is a web of dreams, but dreams so tangible and lucid that we cannot distinguish them from reality because they are reality. Participatory philosophy is the realization that we create the universe in our own image – as we are in the image of the universe which, by creating us, wants to reflect itself in that which it has created.

Among the great spiritual traditions of the past, the Upanishads expressed the glory and mystery of the becoming of man through the Mind unfolding in the most luminous and persuasive manner. 'Mind is indeed the source of bondage, but also the source of liberation.' The Buddhist tradition is also supremely aware of the importance of the Mind. We read in the *Dhammapada*: 'What we are today is the result of our thoughts of yesterday. And our thoughts of today pave the way to what we shall become tomorrow.' Participatory philosophy is the courage of flying . . . flying in control. There is a sense of wonderful exhilaration when you ski down a demanding slope, almost flying, and yet in perfect control. Take another example: the sense of freedom and adventure when you let your Mind wander in front of an audience. You explore a new territory. You know that you may get stuck and perhaps make a fool of yourself. Yet you are inwardly assured that somehow your imagination will carry you through. This is flying in control. *Flying in control is living in freedom and in dignity.*

This mode of our being that we describe as flying in control is a psychological consequence of genuinely accepting the notion of the participatory universe and the participatory Mind. There is no co-creation without courage and without flying. Great artists have always known this simple and magnificent truth.

The process of flying in control is a precondition of following a spiritual path, a path of Enlightenment. Following such a path entails fearlessness resulting from the realization that when your inner essence is intact, then your life is in balance; then you can fly in control in whatever circumstances you find yourself. Flying in control is a central aspect of participatory philosophy: it is a description of the participatory Mind on its journey of fearless exploration, on its journey of perpetual becoming.

Participatory philosophy heralds hope as an inherent part of our being: as a part of our ontological structure; and also as a part of our psychological structure which sustains us daily. Hope is trans-rational. And yet hope is a precondition of all human rationality. To live in hope is to live in grace.

Participatory philosophy declares that to be a person in the participatory universe entails the recognition of the bond of participation. If we don't recognize this bond, we have relinquished our rights to live in the participatory universe. This simple insight, when spelled out, unveils the notion of participatory ethics – based on reverence and responsibility as aspects of participation in the deep sense.

Participatory ethics contains three levels: interpersonal, interspecies, God-man relationships. The three levels are all united by the notion of participation and its consequences. To participate is to be responsible. The larger the reach of our participation the larger the scope of our responsibility. Thus participatory ethics should be seen as an integral aspect of the participatory Mind; both its consequence and its articulation.

Participatory philosophy is an act of courage: to live as if you were God, for what else is left to man if he takes his destiny seriously? To live as if you were God is both a principle of participatory ethics and a principle of human understanding.

The universe has created many wonders. Among these wonders was the creation of the Mind – which was no less spectacular than the creation of any galaxy. Perhaps more spectacular. For the Mind has become the eye through which the universe can look at itself. This is one of those truths: *through the human Mind, the universe appreciates itself.* Without the Mind, all the glory of the universe would be mute. When there is no Mind to comprehend, there is no universe to behold. What a marvel it was when the universe created the Mind to celebrate itself?

What I have described in this book (*The Participatory Mind: A New Theory of Knowledge and of the Universe*) is one sublime journey. The question may be asked: is such a sublime journey possible in our times? Yes, it is; because it is the only journey worth travelling. Embarking on this journey is a creative and necessary response to the forces of disintegration and darkness. The light will prevail because we shall prevail.

Let us end with a prayer to the universe.

Be benevolent to us, o universe
So that we can worship your glory.
As you have made us
So we reflect your splendour.
Allow us to become more splendid

So that you become more splendid.
Allow us to become more compassionate
So that the whole universe breathes more compassionately.
Be generous to us, o universe
So that we can be generous to you.

Out of the void of darkness
The light of understanding appeared.
We thank you, o universe
For the light of the Mind
Which can illumine the immensities
Including your own nature.
We are aware that when we think of you
You are thinking about yourself through us.
We are an instrument of thy glory.
We are delighted and grateful that in creating us
You made us your seeing and thinking eye.
We have no doubt that you have created us
To celebrate yourself.
May we have enough wisdom and courage
To celebrate your depth and mystery
In the grandeur that it requires.

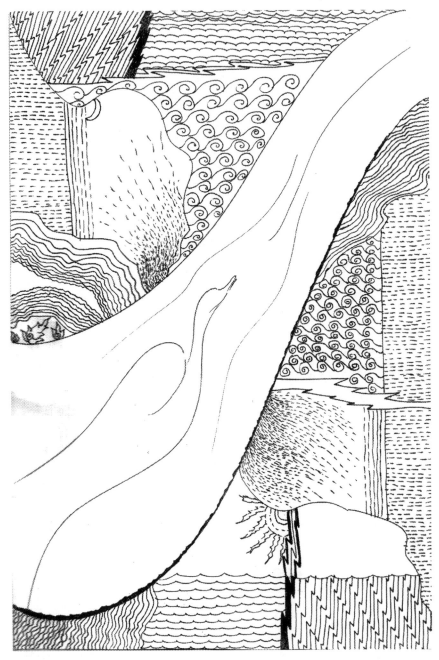

Drawing by Rajny Krishnan

EPILOGUE

Mahatama Gandhi believed in purity of soul, purity of heart, purity of actions. He said, "I will not let any one walk through my Mind with their dirty feet." Ultimately, what is most sacred? It is Mind. Ralph Waldo Emerson would support this: Nothing is at last sacred but the integrity of your own Mind. Henryk Skolimowski's discourses on Mind cultivate sacredness in human Mind. This sacredness is the real value of all existence.

Truth is something humanity has always sung. Truth is an inevitable phenomenon human species cannot live without. Living with truth is a quest of human soul. With truth we blossom, without truth we wither away. Truth flowers in heart like a lotus. Truth nourishes soul. Truth gives us courage to resurge, and to revolutionize everything. Truth gives us courage to change the world. With the participatory Mind, we firmly and courageously stand on the ground of truth, for truth is a consequence of participatory context, as the participatory Mind reveals. The philosophy of the participatory Mind unequivocally serves as an illuminating source of truth.

Participatory philosophy phenomenally helps us to be in the pursuit of life-style of grace. It is an eternal spring of courage. Participatory ethics sprouting on the fertile land of participatory thinking and participatory philosophy is a great promise for evolving a world of responsible and empowered humans: i) working synergistically in and with perfect peace, tranquility, and sustainable joy; ii) living in and with symbiosis and perfect harmony with all living species infusing enhancement into life and living planet; and iii) living with and in godliness by transcendental ascent from a spiritual human to divine being.

As everything else in this universe and the universe itself is evolutionary, we need to pursue a philosophy which nourishes our evolutionary quests. The philosophy of the participatory Mind transcends all the previous theories of evolution, and works riding on the ever moving *chariot* of cosmic evolution, and attempting to pervade all levels—individual to species to cosmos. Having passed through four great cycles, the Western Mind is now reverberating with evolutionary 'telos' emerging as new logos of the Western civilization. Logos, Henryk says, is the lucid Mind of the cosmos. New logos are the creative forms of light. The Skolimowskian Philosophy of the Participatory Mind is especially curious to sparkle new logos, to sparkle new creativities. Creativities of the participatory Mind are co-creativities of the cosmos.

Empiricists theory of the Mind is now outdated. Objective Mind is not evolutionary one. It is cool, inert and stays in bondage. For an empiricist Mind knowledge is a source of power; for a participatory Mind, knowledge is a source of liberation. The Participatory Mind philosophy of Skolimowski is evolutionary and all-creative and it complements the purpose of evolution. Participatory methodologies, participatory research programmes, participatory strategies and participatory thinking proposed by Skolimowski are vital for the new civilization, are vital to nourish co-creation—creation by the cosmic evolution complemented by the participatory Mind.

Structures symbolize ascent of evolution and symbols that of humankind. We need to owe reverential attitude towards structures and symbols. Mind is a wonderful creator of symbols, and it creates symbols for a great cause. Symbols the participatory Mind creates are life-enhancing, creativity-spelling and continually lead us to our ascent, to our glory. Philosophy of the Participatory Mind unfolds some of the most stupendous structures of evolution and offers life-enhancing and creativity-inducing symbols for human civilization.

Experiences are a treasure of individual life. Significant experiences are gems of this treasure. Experiences encountered through creativity by one are experiences sparkling creativity by others. The philosophy of the participatory Mind teaches to articulate significant experiences and thus offers to enrich the human life with the gems of experiences. Aldous Huxley says: Experience is not what happens to a man; it is what a man does with what happens to him.

Every thing pure, everything great, every evolutionary phenomenon, the whole world, the entire cosmos and all what is becoming is, indeed, measured by the yardstick of Mind. All mysteries of the cosmic light are revealed by Mind. No Mind, no unfolding. No Mind, no magic. No Mind, no wonder. No Mind, and everything would be reduced to nothingness.

Of all the wonders the universe has created, Mind is the most outstanding – as spectacular as the creation of the galaxies. Mind is the greatest glory the universe achieved through its evolutionary journey of creativity. And the universe realizes this glory through the Mind it has created through its evolutionary journey. The essence of the Participatory Mind is that *All is Mind*. The glory of individuals, of human species, of the world and of the cosmos, is eventually the glory of the Mind, because, after all, Mind is all and ALL IS MIND.

Notes

INRODUCTION: Mind of the Universe and Universe of the Mind

[1] This sentence is said to be the first sentence of the only book Anaxagoras wrote – title unknown (http://www.egs.edu/library/anaxagoras/quotes/). Anaxagoras (500 BC–428 BC) is the pre-Socratic Greek philosopher.

[2] Henryk Skolimowski coined the term 'Eco-Philosophy' in 1974, which has been mentioned in many works, e.g., *Eco-philosophy: Designing New Tactics for Living* by Henryk Skolimowski (1981), Ideas in Progress Series, Marion Boyers, Salem, NH., pp.117.

[3] Skolimowski, H. (1994). *The Participatory Mind: A New Theory of Knowledge and of the Universe.* London: Penguin Arkana, pp. 395.

CHAPTER 1: Structure of the Participatory Mind

[1] Quotations by Anaxagoras. Anaxagoras quoted in Simplicius, *Commentary on Aristotle's Physics.* (http://www-history.mcs.st-and.ac.uk./Quotations/Anaxagoras.html)

[2] The Quotes Tree – Aristotle Quotes. (http://www.quotestree.com/aristotle-quotes.html)

CHAPTER 2: Mind in Retrospect

[1] Aristotle's quote about Anaxagoras (http://www.egs.edu/library/anaxagoras/quotes/)

[2] It is a famous and oft-quoted quote of Frederick Douglass. According to Wikipedia, Frederick Douglass (1818–1895) was an African-American social reformer, orator, writer and statesman. After escaping from slavery, he became a leader of the abolitionist movement, gaining note of his

dazzling oratory and incisive antislavery writing (http://en.wikipedia.org/wiki/Frederick_Douglass)

[3] Skrbina, D. (2005). *Panpsychism in the West*. Bradford Books, pp. 314. (David Skrbina's views about the Western culture in the book are based on the review of his book)

CHAPTER 3: Understanding the Spiral of Understanding

[1] Confucius (551 B.C.–479 B.C.), a Chinese social philosopher, whose teachings deeply influenced East Asian people, quoted in goodreads (https://www.goodreads.com/quotes/23540-to-know-that-we-know-what-we-know-and-that)

[2] "Nothing happens until something moves" is a famous quote from Albert Einstein (1879–1955), well-known Western physicist, Nobel Laureate and philosopher. Perceive everything to be in a dynamic state and the universe becomes a dynamic entity for you.

[3] Oft-quoted quote of Albert Einstein (http://pandawhale.com/post/1321/if-you-cant-explain-it-simply-you-dont-understand-it-well-enough-albert-einstein)

CHAPTER 4: Complexity and Beauty of the Teilhard's Story

[1] Pierre Teilhard de Chardin (1881–1955) quote (http://www.brainyquote.com/quotes/quotes/p/pierreteil381892.html)

[2] Wikiquote of Pierre Teilhard de Chardin

CHAPTER 5: The Western Mind and its Four Great Cycles

[1] S. Radhakrishnan (1948). Indian Philosophy, Vol I. London: Allen and Unwin, p. 22-3 (Quoted in Swami Tathagatananda, 2005. *Light from the Orient: Essays on the Impact of India's Sacred Literature in the West*, Kolkata: AdvaitaAshrama, p. 7.)

[2] Socrates in *Great Dialogues of Plato: Complete Texts of The Republic, Apology, Crito, Phaedo, Ion, Meno, Symposium*. A Mentor Book, New American Library, New York (1956), p. 27.

[3] *The Urantia Book*; Paper 75, Section 8, quoted in the essay "The So-Called Fall of Man" under *The Urantia Book Fellowship: Cultivating the Spirit of Religion*.

CHAPTER 6: The Participation Methodology and its Consequences

[1] Skolimowski, H. (1994). *The Participatory Mind: A New Theory of Knowledge and of the Universe*. Penguin Arkana, London, p.158-159.

[2] The Quotes Tree – Plato Quotes. (http://www.quotestree.com/plato-quotes.html)

CHAPTER 7: The Structure-Symbol-Evolution Axis

[1] Longfellow's poem quoted by Har Dayal in his *Hints for Self Culture*. Dehradun: Current Events, p. 84

[2] C.F. Holland quoted by Har Dayal, 1974. *Hints for Self Culture*. Current Events, p. 150

CHAPTER 8: Understanding the Individual Spiral of Understanding

[1] Excerpted from *Great Dialogues of Plato: Complete Texts of the Republic, Apology, Crito, Phaedo, Ion, Meno, Symposium*, published by the New American Library of World Literature, Inc., New York (1956), p. 54.

[2] Pierre Teilhard de Chardin quote extracted from http://www.brainyquote.com/quotes/authors/pierre_teilhard_de_chardin

[3] Quote from the *Amrita-Bindu-Upanishad*, a Medieval Sanskrit text. When Mind is in bondage, it means it is bound by fear, anger, lust, jealousy, competitiveness and all sorts of desires of mundane life. Liberation of Mind means the attainment of spiritual knowledge, wisdom, joy and freedom, and quest for right, integrative, life-enhancing actions.

[4] *A Commentary of the Upanishads* by Swami Nirmalananda Giri, Atma Jyoti Ashrama, India, p. 305.

CHAPTER 9: Understanding the Universal Spiral of Understanding

[1] Odysseus quoted by Har Dayal (1974). *Hints for Self Culture*. Dehradun: Current Events, p. 2.

[2] Har Dayal (1974). *Hints for Self Culture*. Dehradun: Dehradun: Current Events, p. 1.

CHAPTER 10: Prevalence of Participatory Truth

[1] The verse from the *Isha Upanishad* 15 has been quoted by J.C. Kapur in his article "Visions and Actions for a New Order" published in *Towards a Sustainable Society: Perceptions,* edited by M.L. Dewan, 1995, published by Clarion Books, p. 39.

[2] The Quotes Tree – Chanakya Quotes. (http://www.quotestree.com/chanakya-quotes.html).

CHAPTER 11: Revisiting the Grand Theory on the Participatory Ground

[1] Statement of Barnes and Gregory has been extracted from *Grand Theory – Ask.com Encyclopaedia.* The term Grand Theory was invented by the American sociologist C. Wright Mills in the *Sociological Imagination* to refer to the form of highly abstract theorizing in which the formal organization and arrangement of concepts takes priority over understanding the social world. In his view, Grand Theory was more or less separated from the concrete concerns of everyday life and its variety in time and space. . . In Parsons view the Grand Theory integrated not only sociological concepts, but also psychological, economic, political, and religious or philosophical components. He tried to integrate all the social sciences within an overarching theoretical framework. By the 1980s the Grand Theory was reformulated and included theories such as critical theory, structuralism, structural Marxism, and Structuration Theory, all influenced human geography (Source: Gregory, D., Johnston, R., Pratt, G., Watts, M., Whatmore, S. (2009). *The Dictionary of Human Geography*, 5th edition. London: Wiley-Blackwell Publishing.; http://www.ask.com/wiki/Grand_theory).

[2] Aldous Huxley (1894 – 1963), an English critic and novelist writes, "Experience is not what happens to a man; it is what a man does with what happens to him" in *Texts and Pretexts*, 1932.

CHAPTER 12: Participatory Philosophy for the New World

[1] *The Urantia Book: Revealing the Mysteries of God, the Universe, World History, Jesus and Ourselves*, (1874.4) 171:7.1. Urantia Foundation

[2] Friedrich Nietzsche Quotes – Brainy Quote. (http://www.brainyquote. com/quotes/authors/f/friedrich_nietzsche.html)

[3] Ernest Hemingway Brainy Quotes (http://www.brainyquote.com/quotes/ quotes/e/ernesthemi131094.html)

[4] Skolimowski, H. (1981). *Eco-philosophy: Designing New Tactics for Living.* Ideas in Progress Series, Marion Boyers, Salem, NH., pp.117.

[5] In William Shakespeare's *As You like It*, Act II, sc. Vii, Jaques says: "All the world's a stage, and all the men and women are merely players. They have their exits and their entrances, and one man in his time plays many parts." However, Vijay M. Sethi makes it more meaningful by modifying it as *"The world is a stage on which we are all in a play. But the play that we enact on the world's stage is a divine play.* Please see "The Speaking Tree", *The Times of India*, New Delhi, October 25, 2012.

[6] Shelley quoted by Har Dayal, 1974. *Hints for Self Culture.* Dehradun: Current Events, p. 202. Percy Bysshe Shelley (1792 – 1822) wrote a poem "Love's Philosophy" from which Hard Dayal has quoted these lines. Shelley's complete poem goes like this:

The fountains mingle with the river,
And the rivers with the ocean;
The winds of heaven mix forever,
With a sweet emotion;
Nothing in the world is single;
All things by a law divine
In one another's being mingle;

Why not I with thine?

See the mountain kiss high heaven,
And the waves clasp one another;
No sister flower would be forgiven,
If it disdained it's brother;
And the sunlight clasps the earth,
And the moonbeams kiss the sea;
What are these kissings worth,
If thou kiss not me?

Har Dayal writes: True love rather resembles hard anthracite, which takes fire very slowly, but lasts a long time, when it has begun to burn. At a certain point in the friendly intercourse of a man and a woman, a deeper personal interest manifests itself, and the nerves also feel the thrill of the sex impulse. Then both ask as Shelley asked (quoted above). Thus is true love born, and a couple is formed. To such happy and virtuous lovers, one may say with Freiligrath (Ferdinand Freiligrath, 1810–1876):

O love as long as you can
O love as long as you may.

[7] Aristotle Quotes – The Quotes Tree. (http://www.quotestree.com/aristotle-quotes.html)